Skull-face Bookseller Honda-san

HONDA

CHAPTER 15

The New Releases Rundown

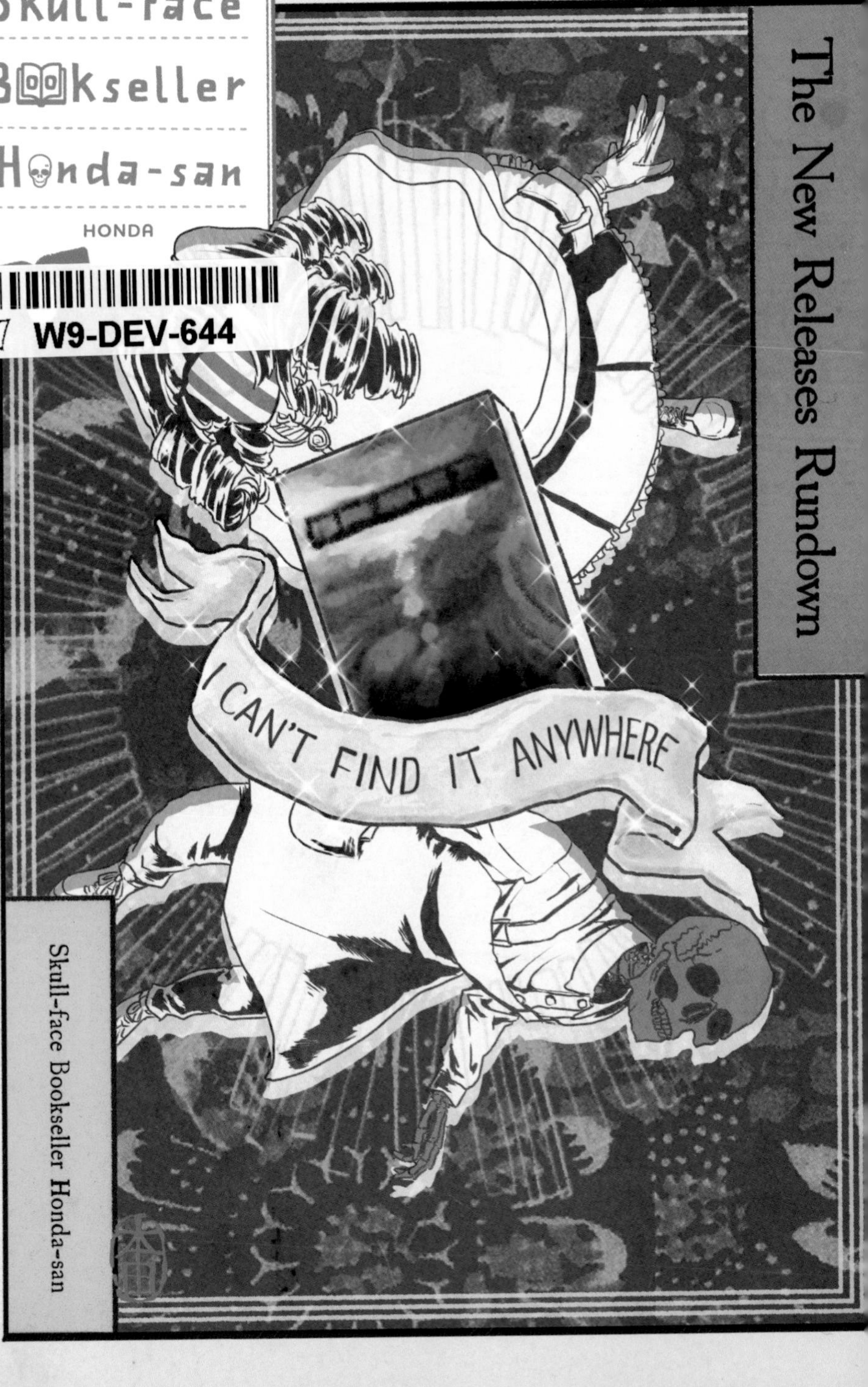
I CAN'T FIND IT ANYWHERE

Skull-face Bookseller Honda-san

Skull-face Bookseller Honda-san

CONTENTS

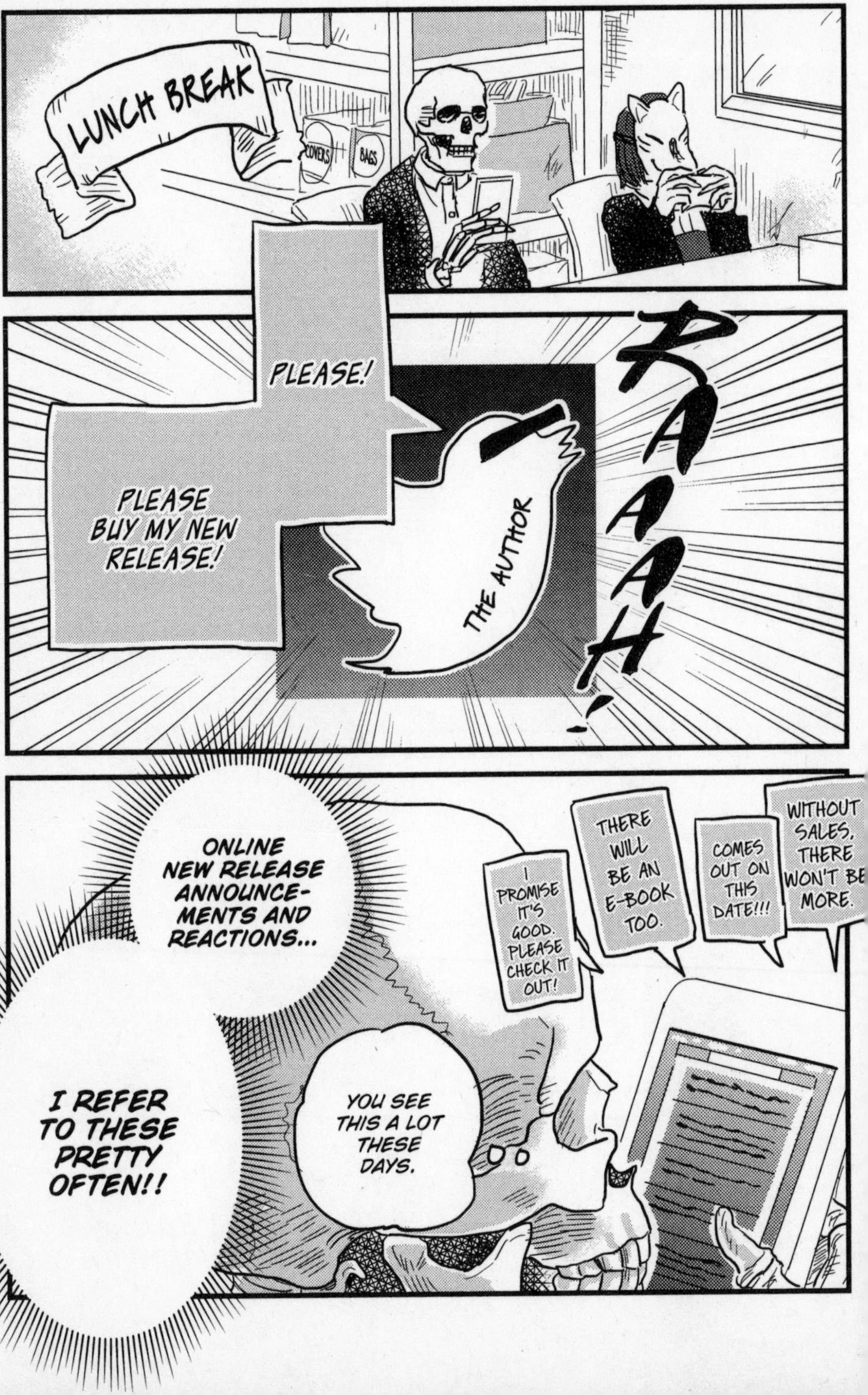
LUNCH BREAK
COVERS
BAGS
RAAAH!
PLEASE!
PLEASE BUY MY NEW RELEASE!
THE AUTHOR
WITHOUT SALES, THERE WON'T BE MORE.
COMES OUT ON THIS DATE!!!
THERE WILL BE AN E-BOOK TOO.
I PROMISE IT'S GOOD. PLEASE CHECK IT OUT!
ONLINE NEW RELEASE ANNOUNCE-MENTS AND REACTIONS...
YOU SEE THIS A LOT THESE DAYS.
I REFER TO THESE PRETTY OFTEN!!

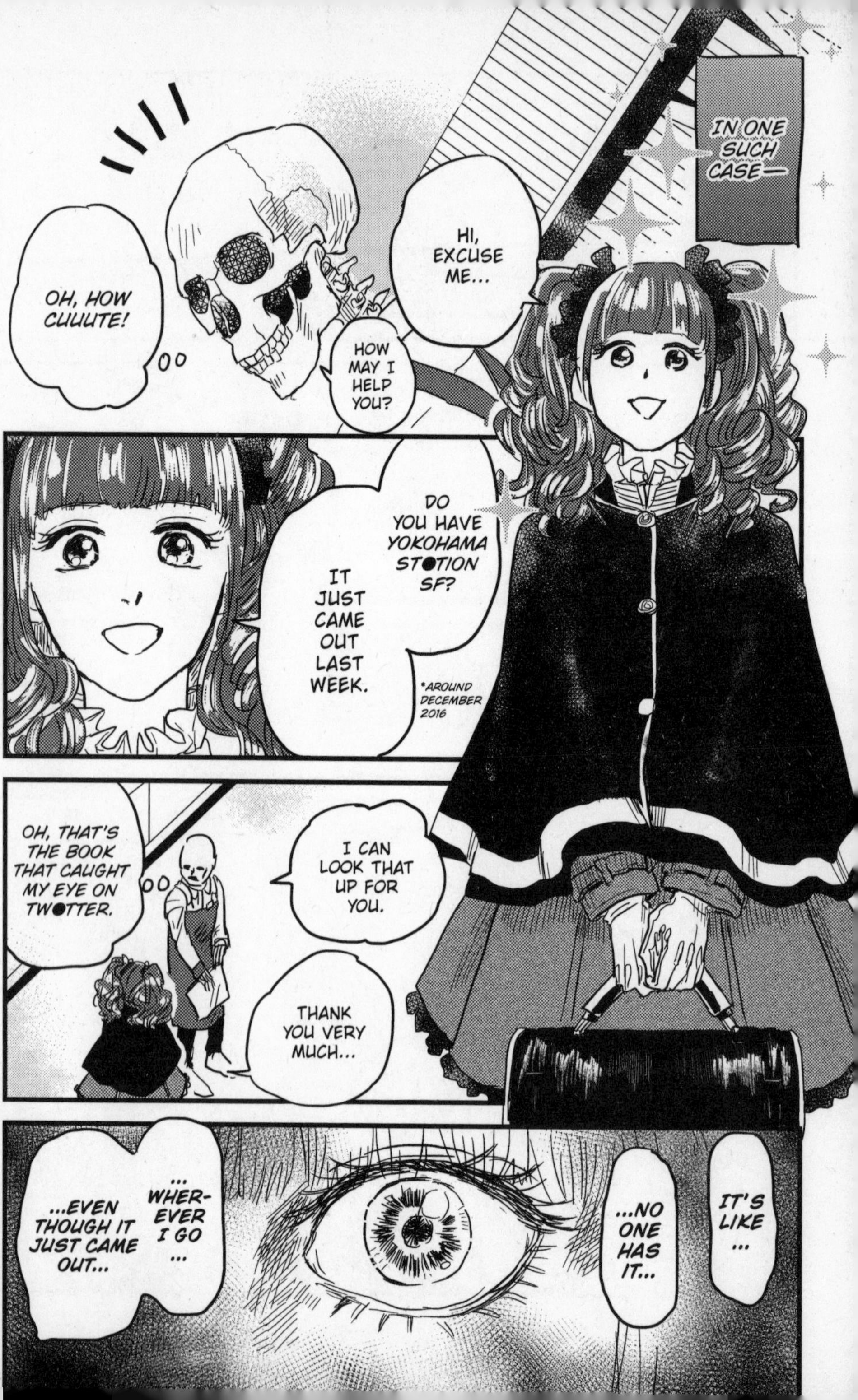
IN ONE SUCH CASE—
HI, EXCUSE ME...
HOW MAY I HELP YOU?
OH, HOW CUUUTE!
DO YOU HAVE YOKOHAMA ST●TION SF?
IT JUST CAME OUT LAST WEEK.
*AROUND DECEMBER 2016
I CAN LOOK THAT UP FOR YOU.
OH, THAT'S THE BOOK THAT CAUGHT MY EYE ON TW●TTER.
THANK YOU VERY MUCH...
IT'S LIKE...
...NO ONE HAS IT...
...WHER-EVER I GO...
...EVEN THOUGH IT JUST CAME OUT...

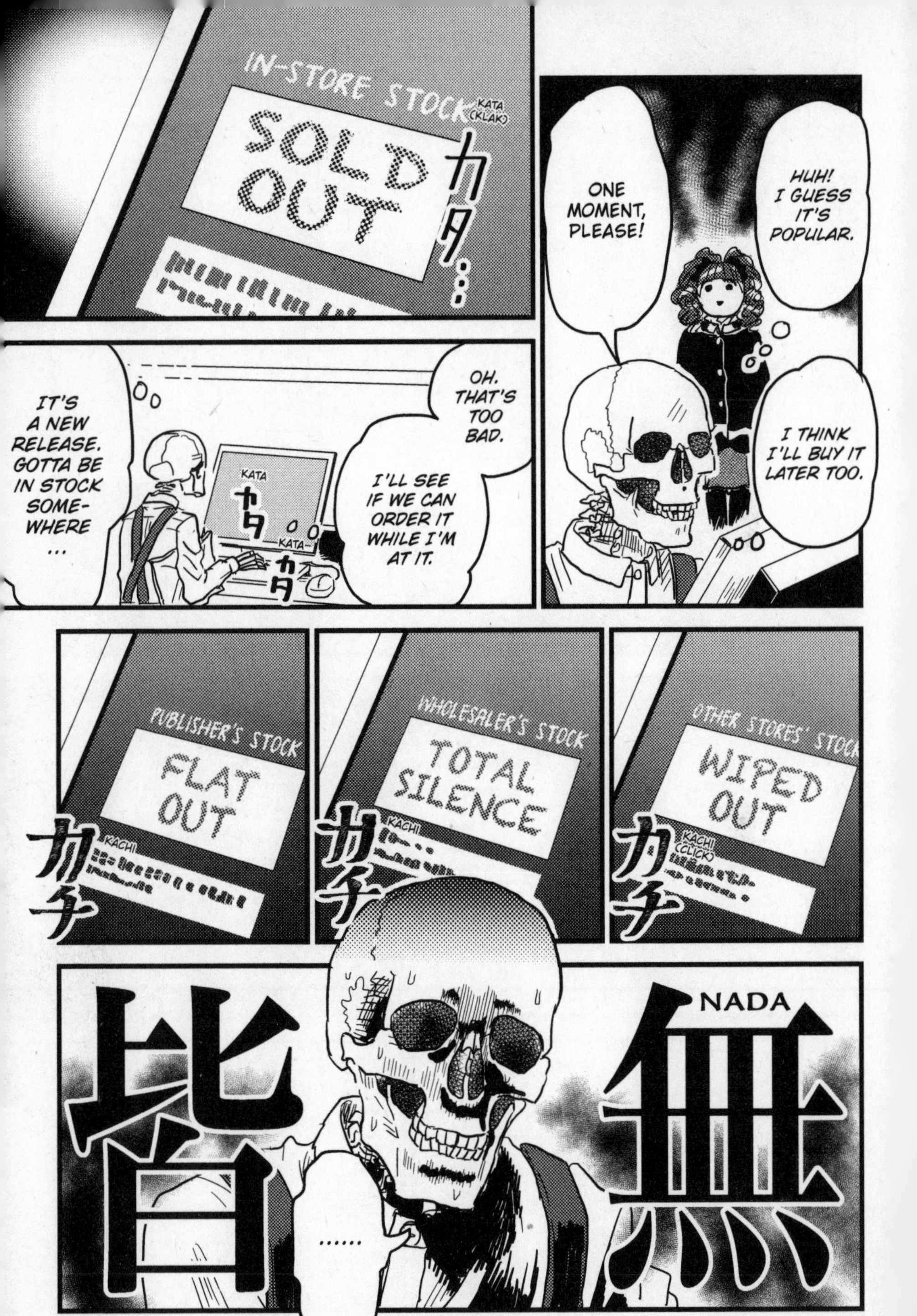
HUH! I GUESS IT'S POPULAR.
ONE MOMENT, PLEASE!
I THINK I'LL BUY IT LATER TOO.
IN-STORE STOCK
SOLD OUT
KATA (KLAK)
カタ…
OH. THAT'S TOO BAD.
I'LL SEE IF WE CAN ORDER IT WHILE I'M AT IT.
KATA
カタ
KATA-
カタ
IT'S A NEW RELEASE. GOTTA BE IN STOCK SOME-WHERE...
OTHER STORES' STOCK
WIPED OUT
KACHI (CLICK)
カチ
WHOLESALER'S STOCK
TOTAL SILENCE
KACHI
カチ
PUBLISHER'S STOCK
FLAT OUT
KACHI
カチ
NADA
皆無
......

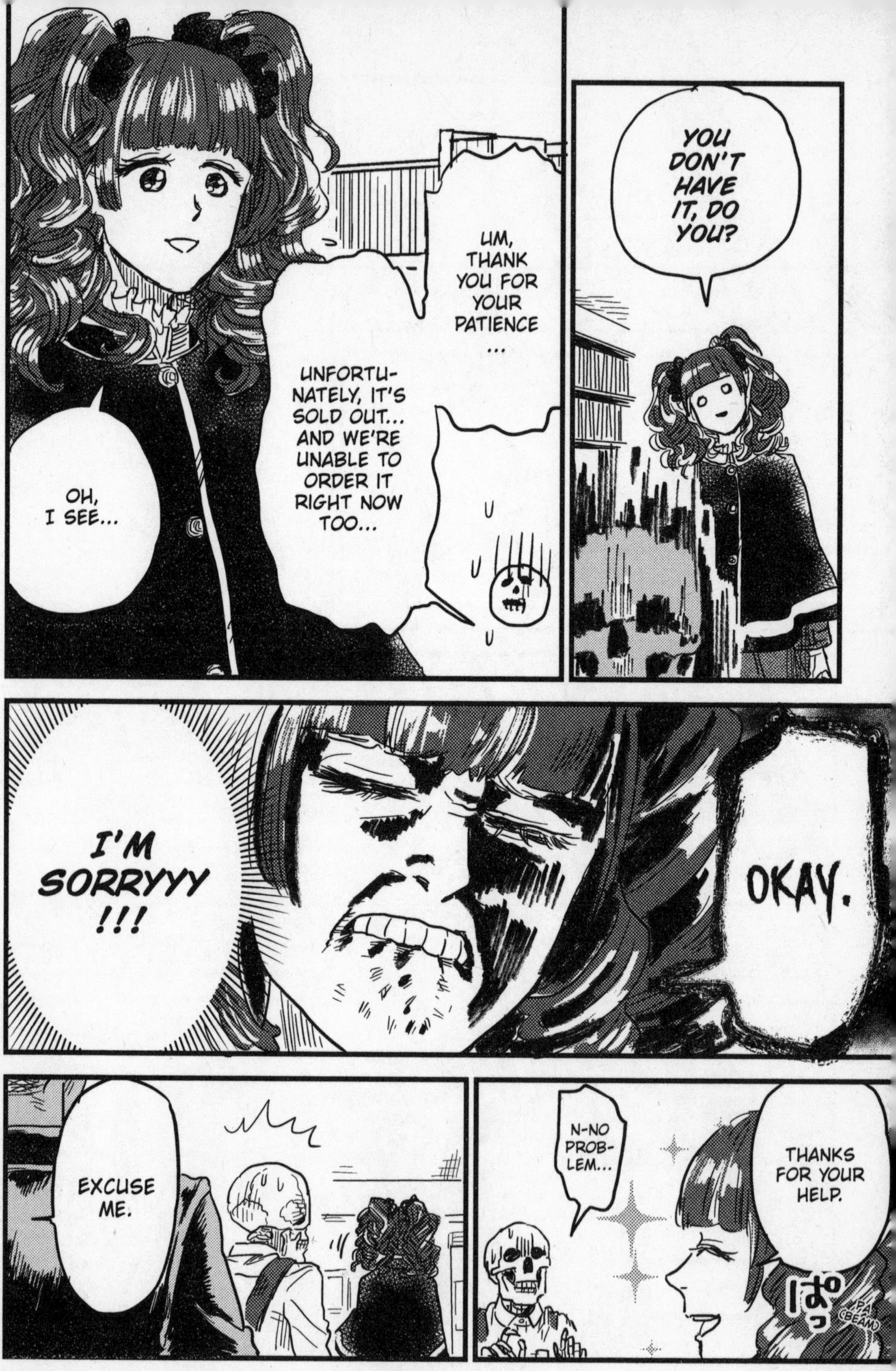
YOU DON'T HAVE IT, DO YOU?
UM, THANK YOU FOR YOUR PATIENCE...
UNFORTUNATELY, IT'S SOLD OUT... AND WE'RE UNABLE TO ORDER IT RIGHT NOW TOO...
OH, I SEE...
OKAY.
I'M SORRYYY!!!
THANKS FOR YOUR HELP.
ぱっ
PA (BEAM)
N-NO PROBLEM...
EXCUSE ME.

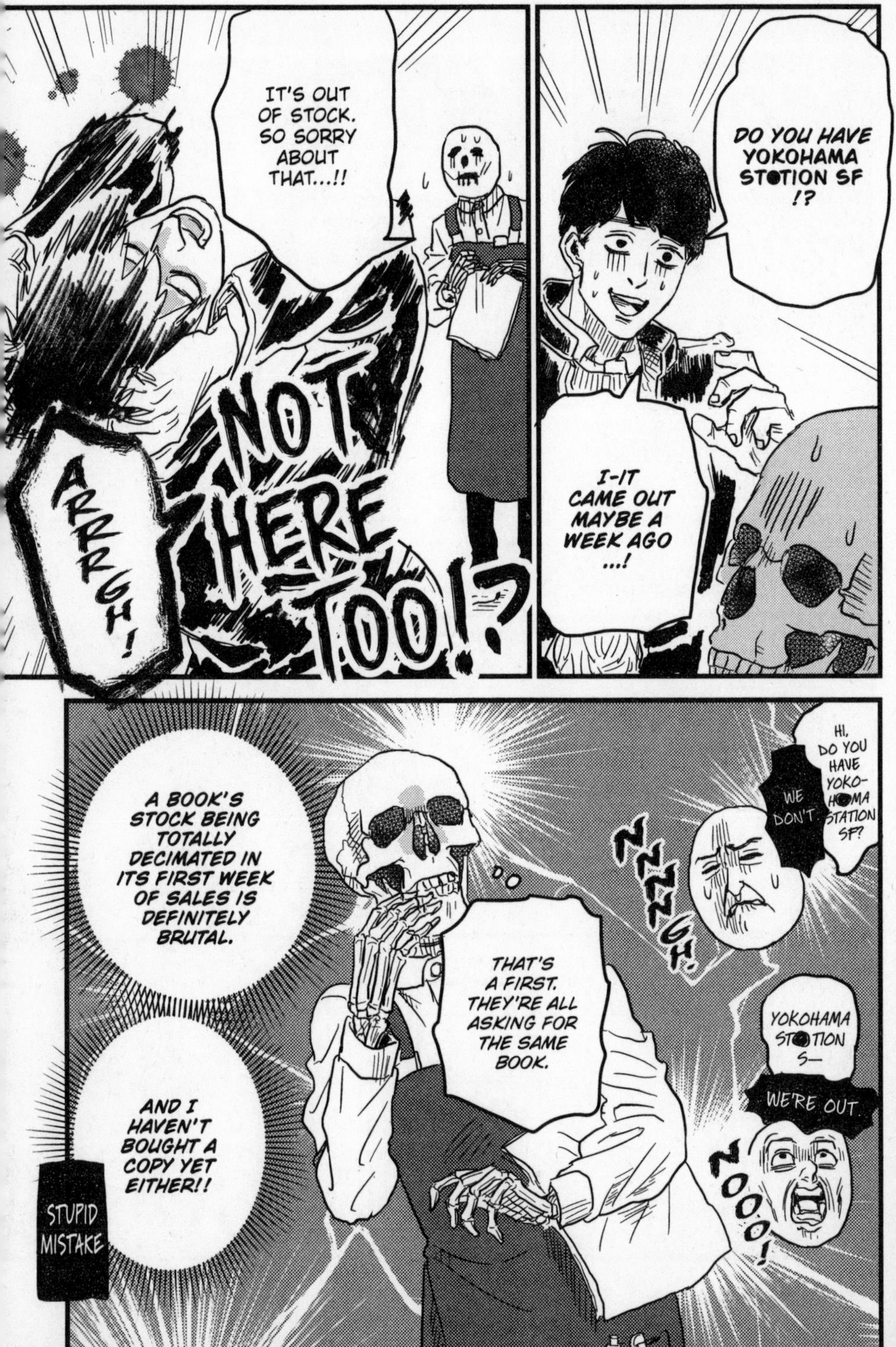
DO YOU HAVE YOKOHAMA STATION SF !?
I-IT CAME OUT MAYBE A WEEK AGO ...!
IT'S OUT OF STOCK. SO SORRY ABOUT THAT...!!
NOT HERE TOO!?
ARRRGH!
HI, DO YOU HAVE YOKO-HOMA STATION SF?
WE DON'T.
NNNGH!
YOKOHAMA STATION S—
WE'RE OUT.
NOOO!
THAT'S A FIRST. THEY'RE ALL ASKING FOR THE SAME BOOK.
A BOOK'S STOCK BEING TOTALLY DECIMATED IN ITS FIRST WEEK OF SALES IS DEFINITELY BRUTAL.
AND I HAVEN'T BOUGHT A COPY YET EITHER!!
STUPID MISTAKE

BUT KADOKAWA IS RELATIVELY SLOW ABOUT REPRINTS. WHO KNOWS WHEN WE'LL GET THEM...

SINCE IT'S A HOT SELLER, I'M PRETTY SURE THEY'LL PRINT MORE.

OF COURSE!

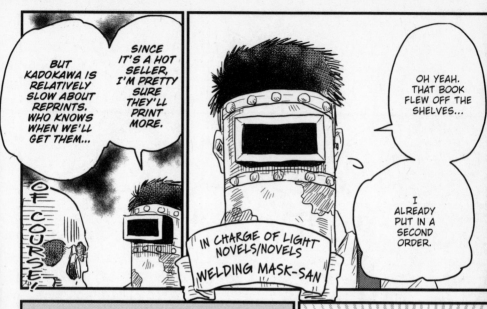

IN CHARGE OF LIGHT NOVELS/NOVELS
WELDING MASK-SAN

OH YEAH. THAT BOOK FLEW OFF THE SHELVES...

I ALREADY PUT IN A SECOND ORDER.

...THE RATE OF SALES IN THE **FIRST WEEK** AFTER A BOOK'S RELEASE IS CALLED "INITIAL SALES."

AS HONDA LEARNED IT...

SUN	M	T	W	TH	F	SAT
1	2	3	4	5	6	7
8	9	10	11	12	13	14
15	16	17	18	19	20	21
22	23	24	25	26	27	28
29	30	31				

AS A GENERAL GUIDE FOR ORDER QUANTITIES, INITIAL SALES SHOULD EQUAL HALF YOUR STOCK.

IT'S OUT!

INITIAL SALES!!

AUTHORS ARE USING THIS KEY PHRASE A LOT LATELY.

NEW RELEASE

NEW RELEASE

WOOOO!

8

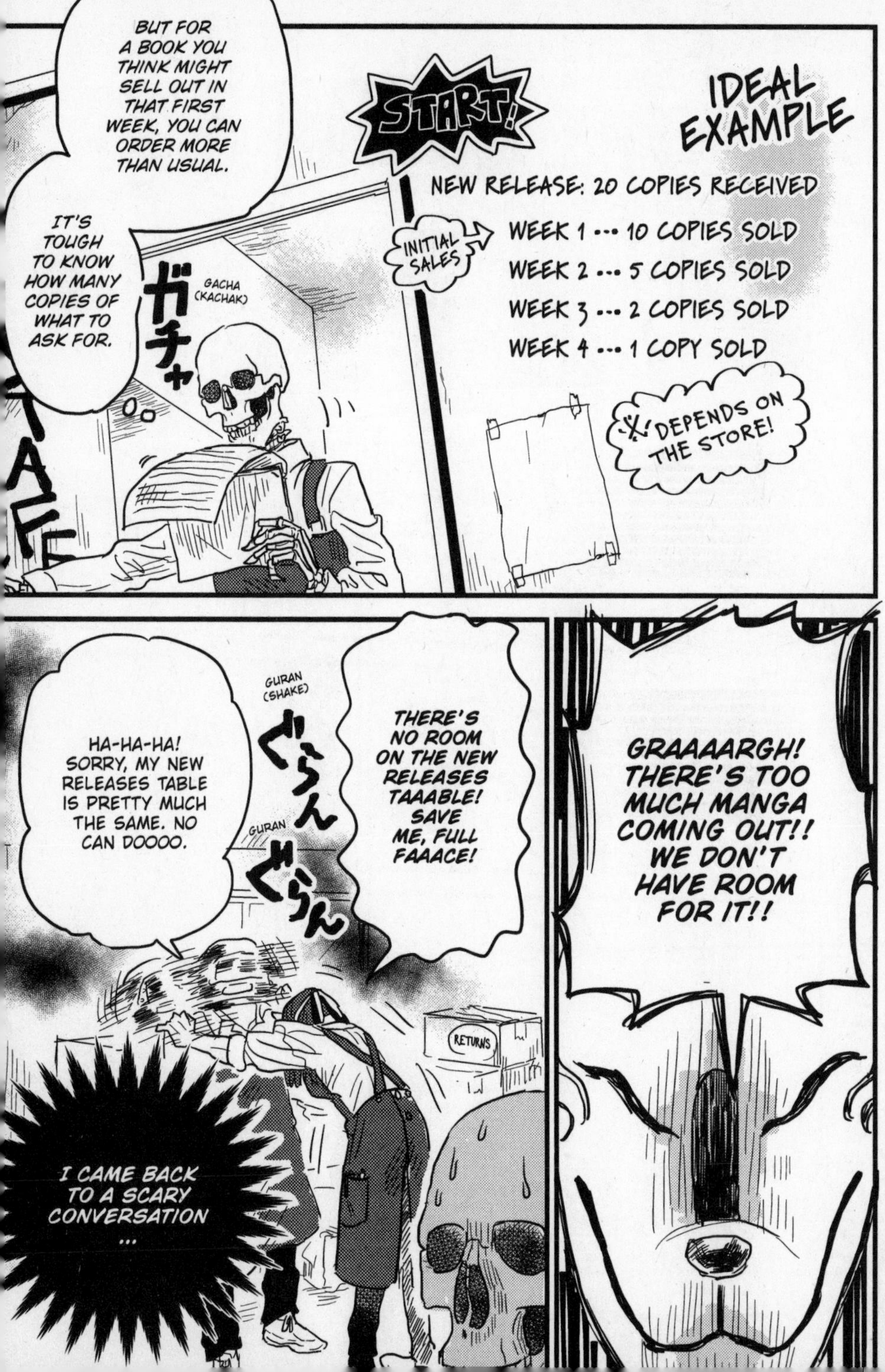
IDEAL EXAMPLE
START!
NEW RELEASE: 20 COPIES RECEIVED
INITIAL SALES
WEEK 1 ··· 10 COPIES SOLD
WEEK 2 ··· 5 COPIES SOLD
WEEK 3 ··· 2 COPIES SOLD
WEEK 4 ··· 1 COPY SOLD
※! DEPENDS ON THE STORE!
BUT FOR A BOOK YOU THINK MIGHT SELL OUT IN THAT FIRST WEEK, YOU CAN ORDER MORE THAN USUAL.
ガチャ
GACHA (KACHAK)
IT'S TOUGH TO KNOW HOW MANY COPIES OF WHAT TO ASK FOR.
GRAAAARGH! THERE'S TOO MUCH MANGA COMING OUT!! WE DON'T HAVE ROOM FOR IT!!
THERE'S NO ROOM ON THE NEW RELEASES TAAABLE! SAVE ME, FULL FAAACE!
ぐらん
GURAN (SHAKE)
ぐらん
GURAN
HA-HA-HA! SORRY, MY NEW RELEASES TABLE IS PRETTY MUCH THE SAME. NO CAN DOOOO.
RETURNS
I CAME BACK TO A SCARY CONVERSATION ...

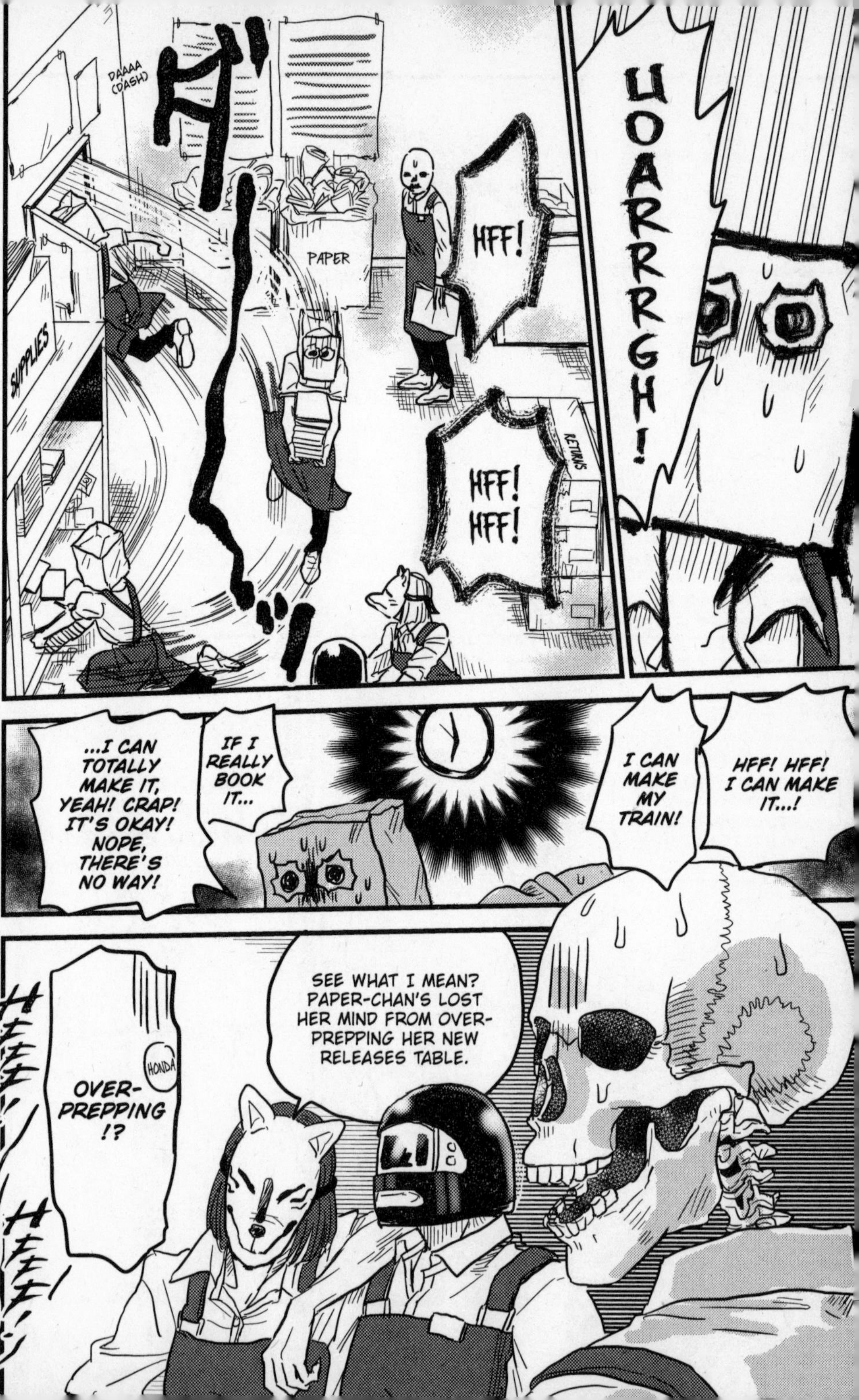
UOARRRGH!
DAAAA (DASH)
PAPER
SUPPLIES
HFF!
RETURNS
HFF! HFF!
HFF! HFF! I CAN MAKE IT...!
I CAN MAKE MY TRAIN!
IF I REALLY BOOK IT...
...I CAN TOTALLY MAKE IT, YEAH! CRAP! IT'S OKAY! NOPE, THERE'S NO WAY!
SEE WHAT I MEAN? PAPER-CHAN'S LOST HER MIND FROM OVER-PREPPING HER NEW RELEASES TABLE.
HONDA
OVER-PREPPING!?

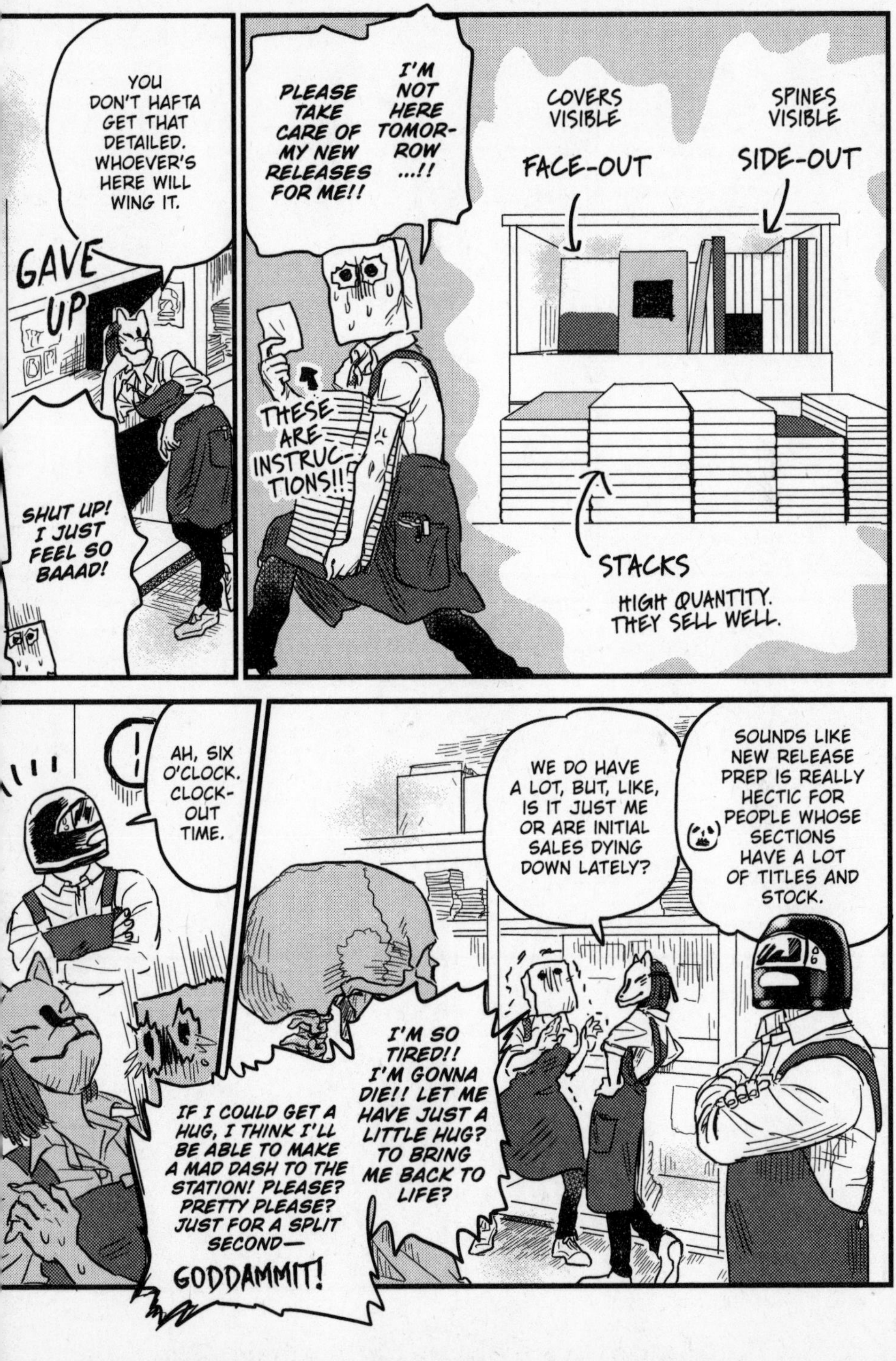
SPINES VISIBLE
SIDE-OUT
COVERS VISIBLE
FACE-OUT
STACKS
HIGH QUANTITY. THEY SELL WELL.
I'M NOT HERE TOMORROW ...!!
PLEASE TAKE CARE OF MY NEW RELEASES FOR ME!!
THESE ARE INSTRUCTIONS!!!
YOU DON'T HAFTA GET THAT DETAILED. WHOEVER'S HERE WILL WING IT.
GAVE UP
SHUT UP! I JUST FEEL SO BAAAD!
SOUNDS LIKE NEW RELEASE PREP IS REALLY HECTIC FOR PEOPLE WHOSE SECTIONS HAVE A LOT OF TITLES AND STOCK.
WE DO HAVE A LOT, BUT, LIKE, IS IT JUST ME OR ARE INITIAL SALES DYING DOWN LATELY?
!
AH, SIX O'CLOCK. CLOCK-OUT TIME.
I'M SO TIRED!! I'M GONNA DIE!! LET ME HAVE JUST A LITTLE HUG? TO BRING ME BACK TO LIFE?
IF I COULD GET A HUG, I THINK I'LL BE ABLE TO MAKE A MAD DASH TO THE STATION! PLEASE? PRETTY PLEASE? JUST FOR A SPLIT SECOND—
GODDAMMIT!

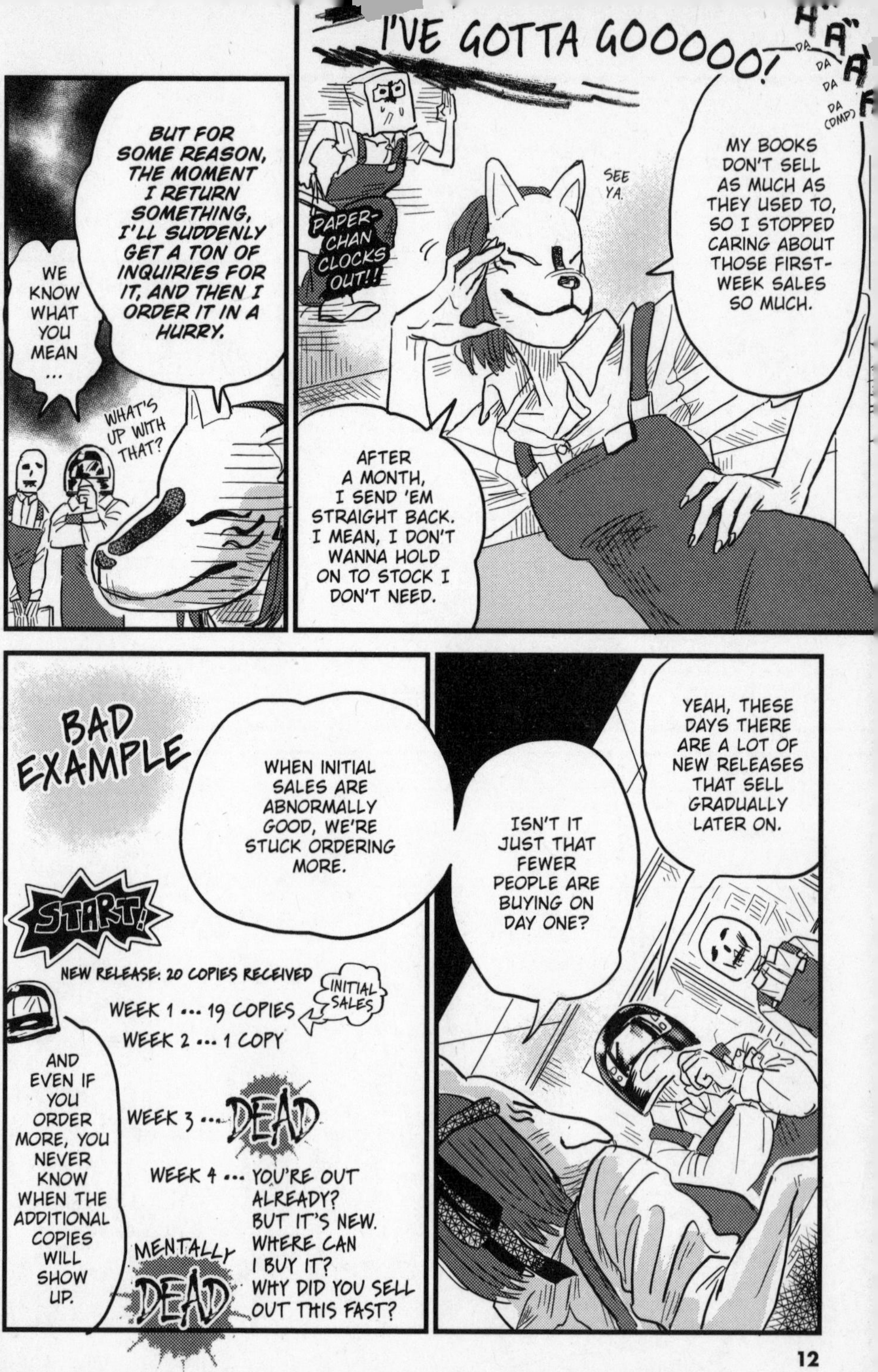
I'VE GOTTA GOOOOOO!
DA DA DA DA (DMP)
MY BOOKS DON'T SELL AS MUCH AS THEY USED TO, SO I STOPPED CARING ABOUT THOSE FIRST-WEEK SALES SO MUCH.
SEE YA.
PAPER-CHAN CLOCKS OUT!!
AFTER A MONTH, I SEND 'EM STRAIGHT BACK. I MEAN, I DON'T WANNA HOLD ON TO STOCK I DON'T NEED.
BUT FOR SOME REASON, THE MOMENT I RETURN SOMETHING, I'LL SUDDENLY GET A TON OF INQUIRIES FOR IT, AND THEN I ORDER IT IN A HURRY.
WE KNOW WHAT YOU MEAN...
WHAT'S UP WITH THAT?
YEAH, THESE DAYS THERE ARE A LOT OF NEW RELEASES THAT SELL GRADUALLY LATER ON.
ISN'T IT JUST THAT FEWER PEOPLE ARE BUYING ON DAY ONE?
WHEN INITIAL SALES ARE ABNORMALLY GOOD, WE'RE STUCK ORDERING MORE.
BAD EXAMPLE
START!
NEW RELEASE: 20 COPIES RECEIVED
WEEK 1 ... 19 COPIES
INITIAL SALES
WEEK 2 ... 1 COPY
WEEK 3 ... DEAD
WEEK 4 ... YOU'RE OUT ALREADY? BUT IT'S NEW. WHERE CAN I BUY IT? WHY DID YOU SELL OUT THIS FAST?
AND EVEN IF YOU ORDER MORE, YOU NEVER KNOW WHEN THE ADDITIONAL COPIES WILL SHOW UP.
MENTALLY DEAD

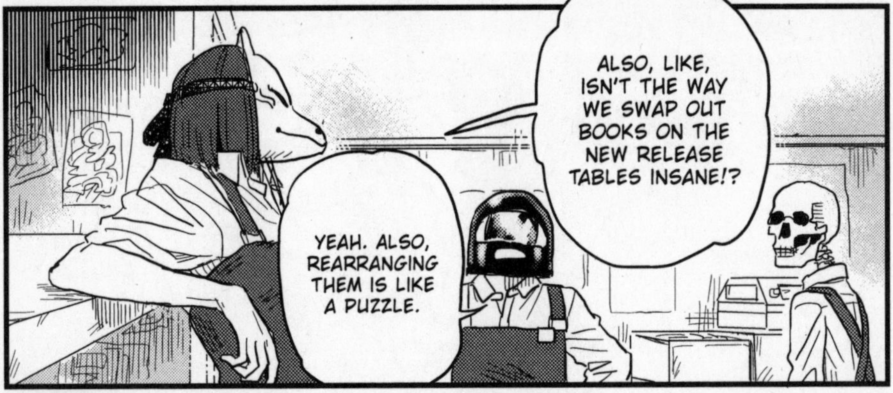
ALSO, LIKE, ISN'T THE WAY WE SWAP OUT BOOKS ON THE NEW RELEASE TABLES INSANE!?
YEAH. ALSO, REARRANGING THEM IS LIKE A PUZZLE.

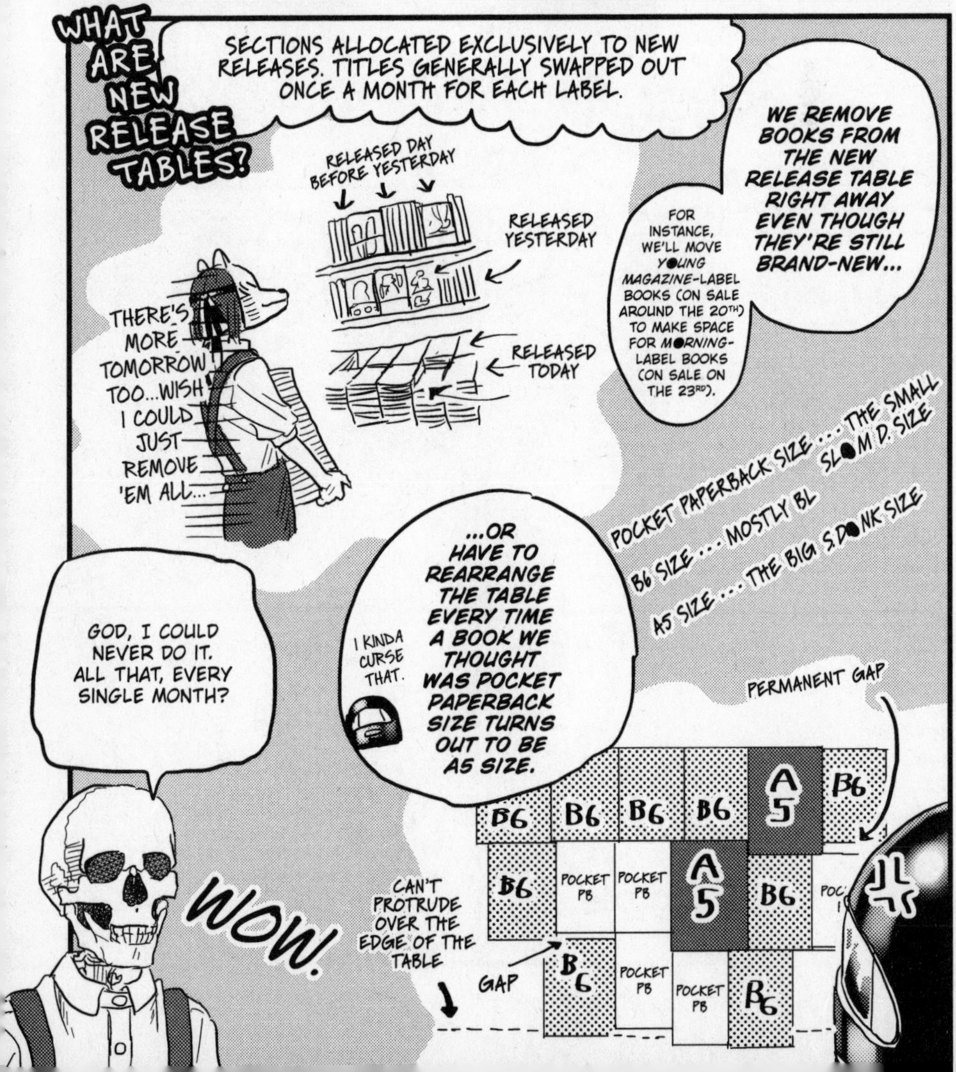
WHAT ARE NEW RELEASE TABLES?
SECTIONS ALLOCATED EXCLUSIVELY TO NEW RELEASES. TITLES GENERALLY SWAPPED OUT ONCE A MONTH FOR EACH LABEL.
WE REMOVE BOOKS FROM THE NEW RELEASE TABLE RIGHT AWAY EVEN THOUGH THEY'RE STILL BRAND-NEW...
FOR INSTANCE, WE'LL MOVE Y●UNG MAGAZINE-LABEL BOOKS (ON SALE AROUND THE 20TH) TO MAKE SPACE FOR M●RNING-LABEL BOOKS (ON SALE ON THE 23RD).
RELEASED DAY BEFORE YESTERDAY
RELEASED YESTERDAY
RELEASED TODAY
THERE'S MORE TOMORROW TOO...WISH I COULD JUST REMOVE 'EM ALL...
POCKET PAPERBACK SIZE ... THE SMALL SL●M D. SIZE
B6 SIZE ... MOSTLY BL
A5 SIZE ... THE BIG S.D●NK SIZE
...OR HAVE TO REARRANGE THE TABLE EVERY TIME A BOOK WE THOUGHT WAS POCKET PAPERBACK SIZE TURNS OUT TO BE A5 SIZE.
I KINDA CURSE THAT.
GOD, I COULD NEVER DO IT. ALL THAT, EVERY SINGLE MONTH?
WOW.
PERMANENT GAP
B6
B6
B6
B6
A5
B6
B6
POCKET PB
POCKET PB
A5
B6
CAN'T PROTRUDE OVER THE EDGE OF THE TABLE
GAP
B6
POCKET PB
POCKET PB
B6

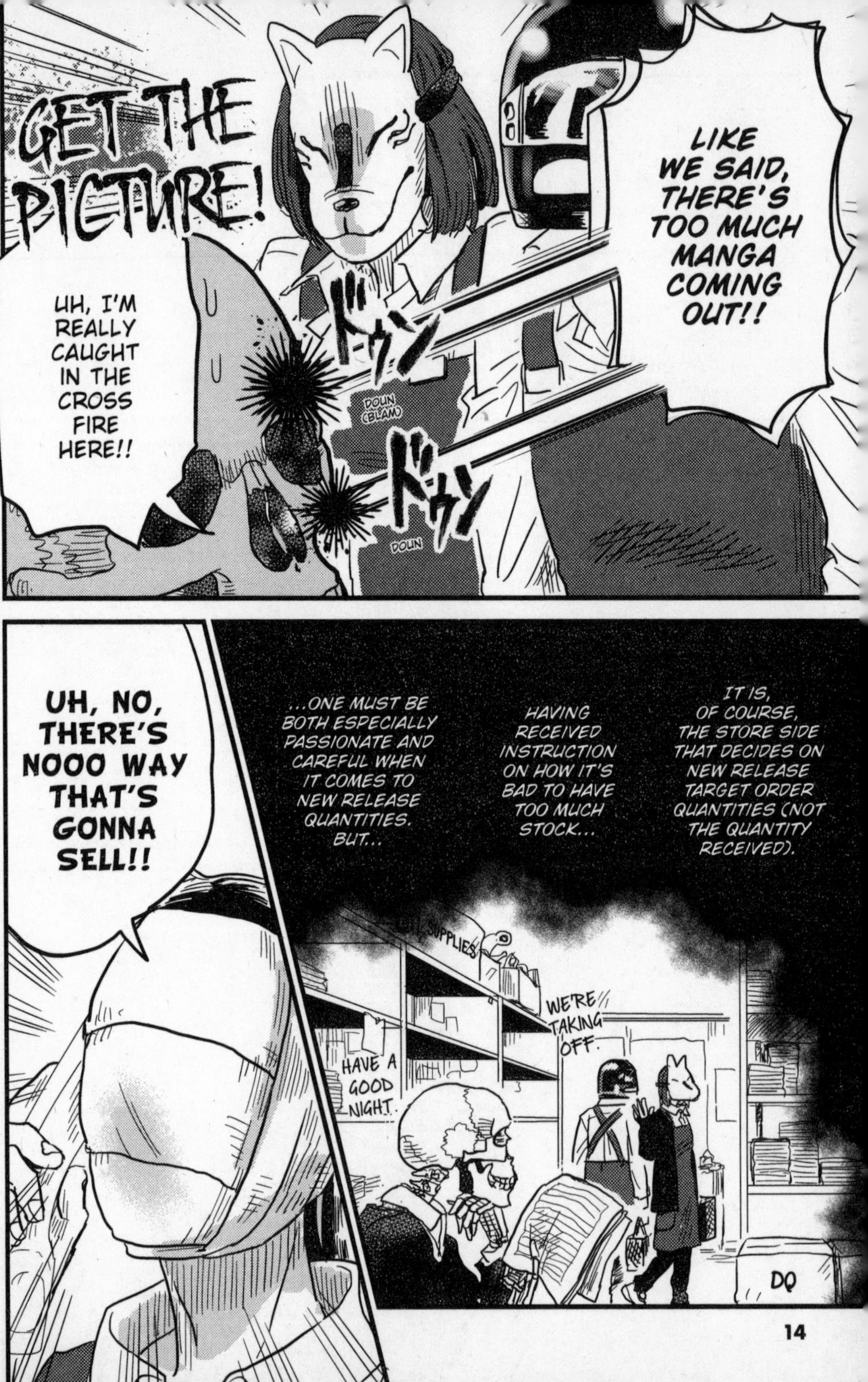
LIKE WE SAID, THERE'S TOO MUCH MANGA COMING OUT!!
GET THE PICTURE!
UH, I'M REALLY CAUGHT IN THE CROSS FIRE HERE!!
ドゥン
DOUN (BLAM)
ドゥン
DOUN
IT IS, OF COURSE, THE STORE SIDE THAT DECIDES ON NEW RELEASE TARGET ORDER QUANTITIES (NOT THE QUANTITY RECEIVED).
HAVING RECEIVED INSTRUCTION ON HOW IT'S BAD TO HAVE TOO MUCH STOCK...
...ONE MUST BE BOTH ESPECIALLY PASSIONATE AND CAREFUL WHEN IT COMES TO NEW RELEASE QUANTITIES. BUT...
SUPPLIES
WE'RE TAKING OFF.
HAVE A GOOD NIGHT.
DQ
UH, NO, THERE'S NOOO WAY THAT'S GONNA SELL!!

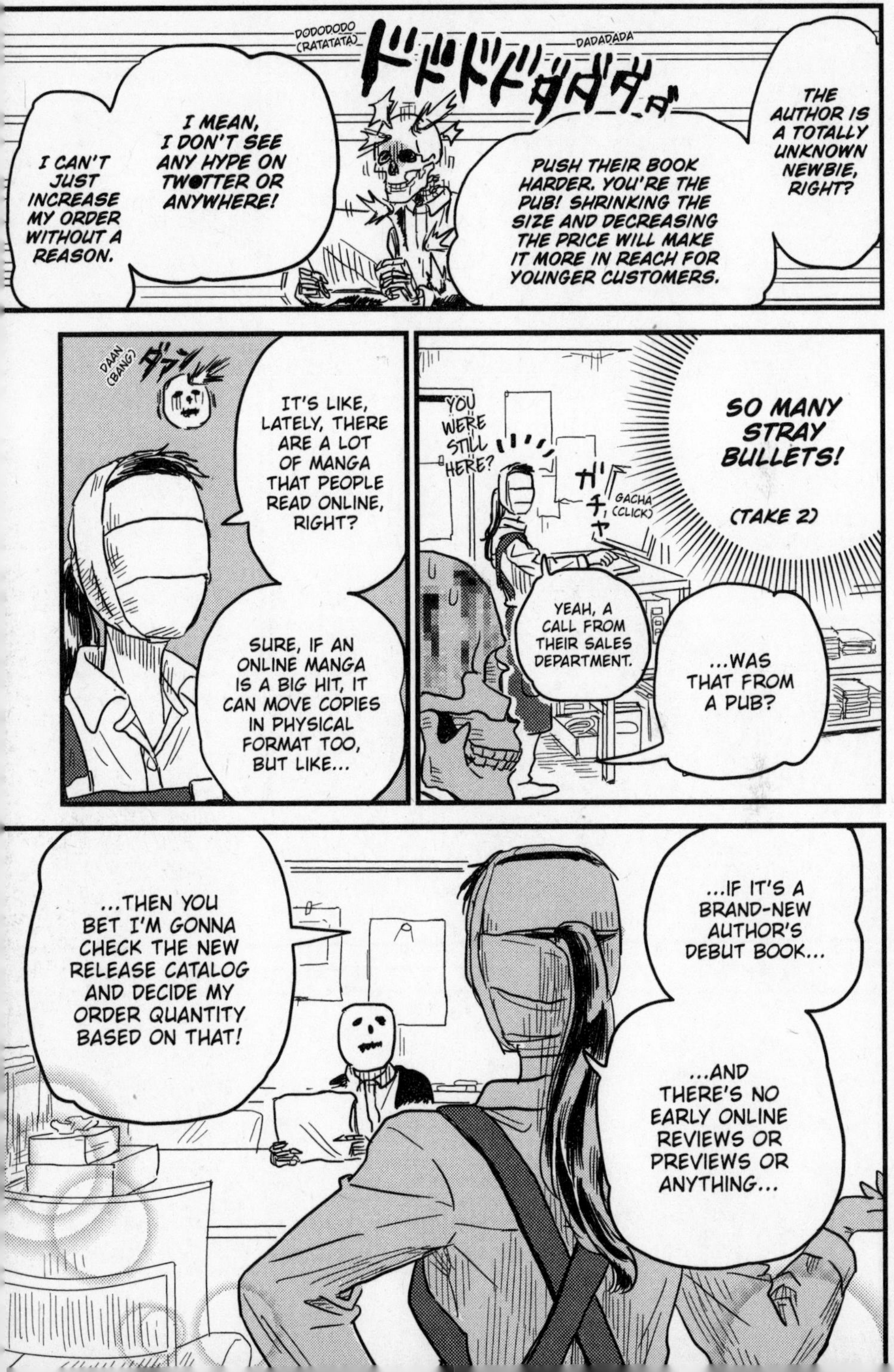
THE AUTHOR IS A TOTALLY UNKNOWN NEWBIE, RIGHT?
PUSH THEIR BOOK HARDER. YOU'RE THE PUB! SHRINKING THE SIZE AND DECREASING THE PRICE WILL MAKE IT MORE IN REACH FOR YOUNGER CUSTOMERS.
DADADADA
ドドドドダダダダ
DODODODO (RATATATA)
I MEAN, I DON'T SEE ANY HYPE ON TW●TTER OR ANYWHERE!
I CAN'T JUST INCREASE MY ORDER WITHOUT A REASON.
SO MANY STRAY BULLETS!
(TAKE 2)
ガチャ
GACHA (CLICK)
YOU WERE STILL HERE?
...WAS THAT FROM A PUB?
YEAH, A CALL FROM THEIR SALES DEPARTMENT.
ダァン
DAAN (BANG)
IT'S LIKE, LATELY, THERE ARE A LOT OF MANGA THAT PEOPLE READ ONLINE, RIGHT?
SURE, IF AN ONLINE MANGA IS A BIG HIT, IT CAN MOVE COPIES IN PHYSICAL FORMAT TOO, BUT LIKE...
...IF IT'S A BRAND-NEW AUTHOR'S DEBUT BOOK...
...AND THERE'S NO EARLY ONLINE REVIEWS OR PREVIEWS OR ANYTHING...
...THEN YOU BET I'M GONNA CHECK THE NEW RELEASE CATALOG AND DECIDE MY ORDER QUANTITY BASED ON THAT!

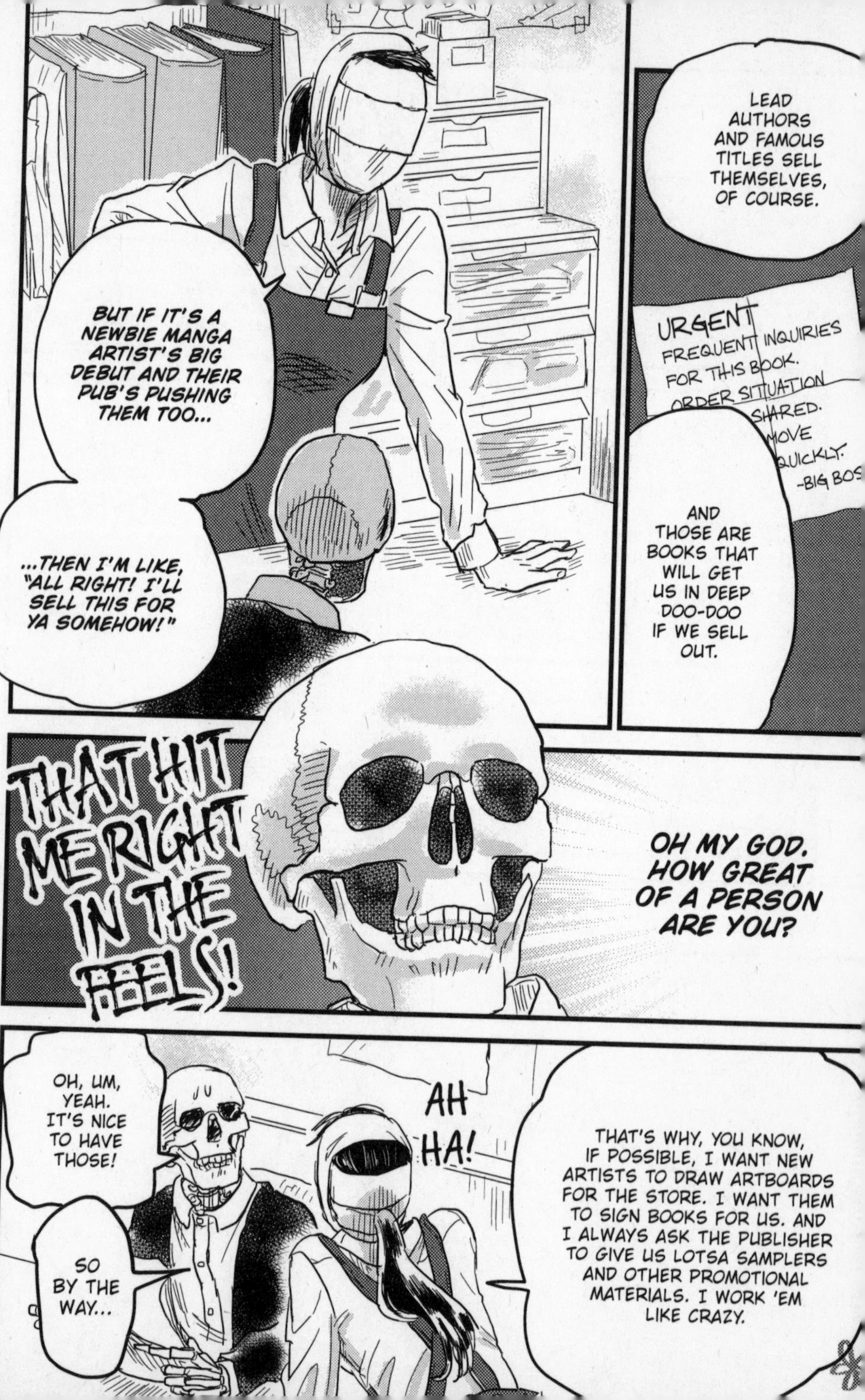
LEAD AUTHORS AND FAMOUS TITLES SELL THEMSELVES, OF COURSE.
URGENT
FREQUENT INQUIRIES FOR THIS BOOK. ORDER SITUATION SHARED. MOVE QUICKLY. -BIG BOS
AND THOSE ARE BOOKS THAT WILL GET US IN DEEP DOO-DOO IF WE SELL OUT.
BUT IF IT'S A NEWBIE MANGA ARTIST'S BIG DEBUT AND THEIR PUB'S PUSHING THEM TOO...
...THEN I'M LIKE, "ALL RIGHT! I'LL SELL THIS FOR YA SOMEHOW!"
OH MY GOD. HOW GREAT OF A PERSON ARE YOU?
THAT HIT ME RIGHT IN THE FEELS!
THAT'S WHY, YOU KNOW, IF POSSIBLE, I WANT NEW ARTISTS TO DRAW ARTBOARDS FOR THE STORE. I WANT THEM TO SIGN BOOKS FOR US. AND I ALWAYS ASK THE PUBLISHER TO GIVE US LOTSA SAMPLERS AND OTHER PROMOTIONAL MATERIALS. I WORK 'EM LIKE CRAZY.
AH HA!
OH, UM, YEAH. IT'S NICE TO HAVE THOSE!
SO BY THE WAY...

*AT DEATH'S DOOR: PRODUCTS WITH NO SALES IN A CERTAIN PERIOD OF TIME. THE OPPOSITE OF "HOT SELLERS."

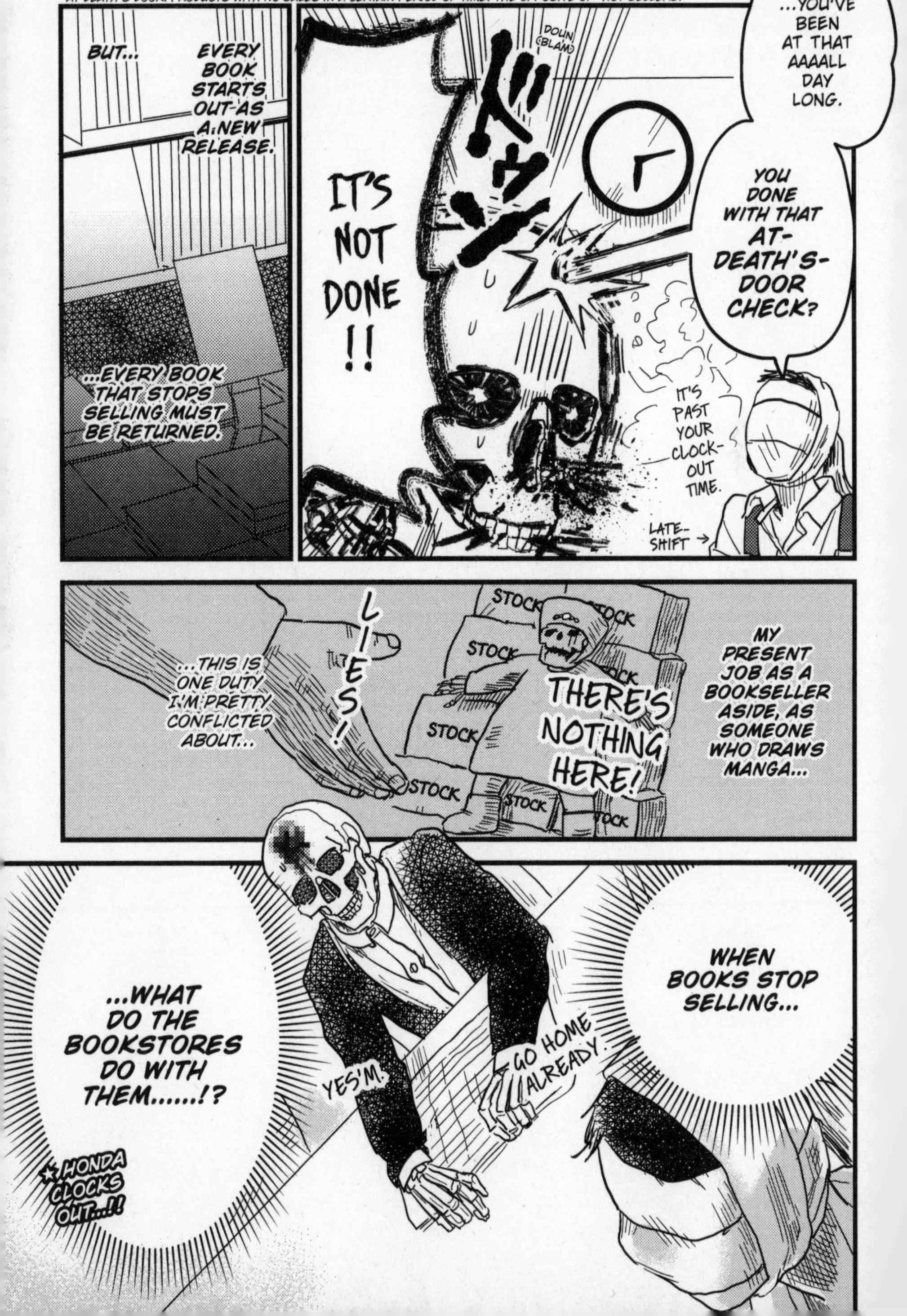
...YOU'VE BEEN AT THAT AAAALL DAY LONG.
YOU DONE WITH THAT AT-DEATH'S-DOOR CHECK?
DOUN (BLAM)
IT'S NOT DONE!!
IT'S PAST YOUR CLOCK-OUT TIME.
LATE-SHIFT →
EVERY BOOK STARTS OUT AS A NEW RELEASE.
BUT...
...EVERY BOOK THAT STOPS SELLING MUST BE RETURNED.
MY PRESENT JOB AS A BOOKSELLER ASIDE, AS SOMEONE WHO DRAWS MANGA...
THERE'S NOTHING HERE!
LIES!
...THIS IS ONE DUTY I'M PRETTY CONFLICTED ABOUT...
WHEN BOOKS STOP SELLING...
GO HOME ALREADY.
YES'M.
...WHAT DO THE BOOKSTORES DO WITH THEM......!?
☆ HONDA CLOCKS OUT...!!

Skull-face Bookseller Honda-san

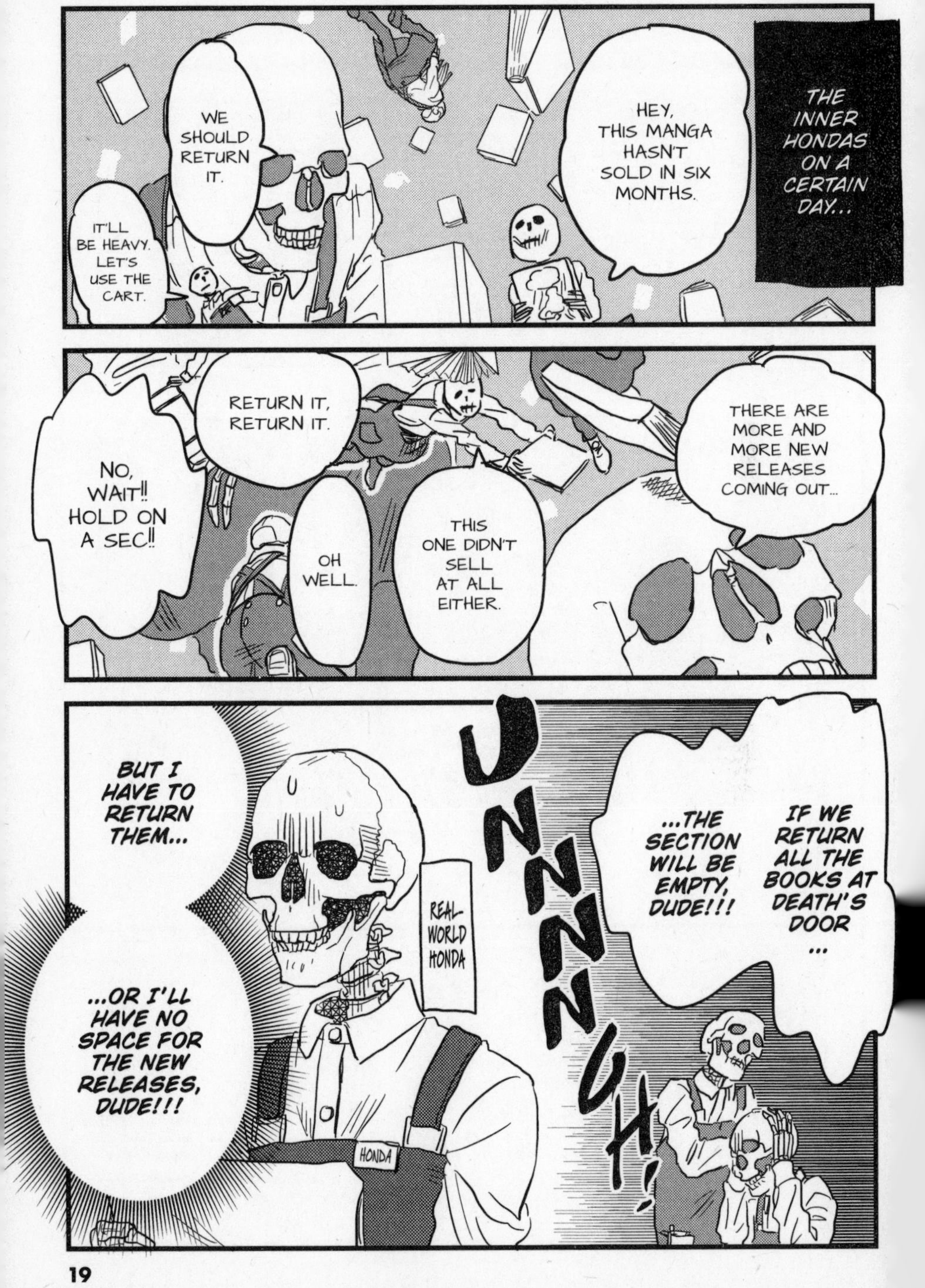
THE INNER HONDAS ON A CERTAIN DAY...
HEY, THIS MANGA HASN'T SOLD IN SIX MONTHS.
WE SHOULD RETURN IT.
IT'LL BE HEAVY. LET'S USE THE CART.
THERE ARE MORE AND MORE NEW RELEASES COMING OUT...
RETURN IT, RETURN IT.
THIS ONE DIDN'T SELL AT ALL EITHER.
OH WELL.
NO, WAIT!! HOLD ON A SEC!!
IF WE RETURN ALL THE BOOKS AT DEATH'S DOOR...
...THE SECTION WILL BE EMPTY, DUDE!!!
UNNNNUH!
REAL-WORLD HONDA
BUT I HAVE TO RETURN THEM...
...OR I'LL HAVE NO SPACE FOR THE NEW RELEASES, DUDE!!!
HONDA

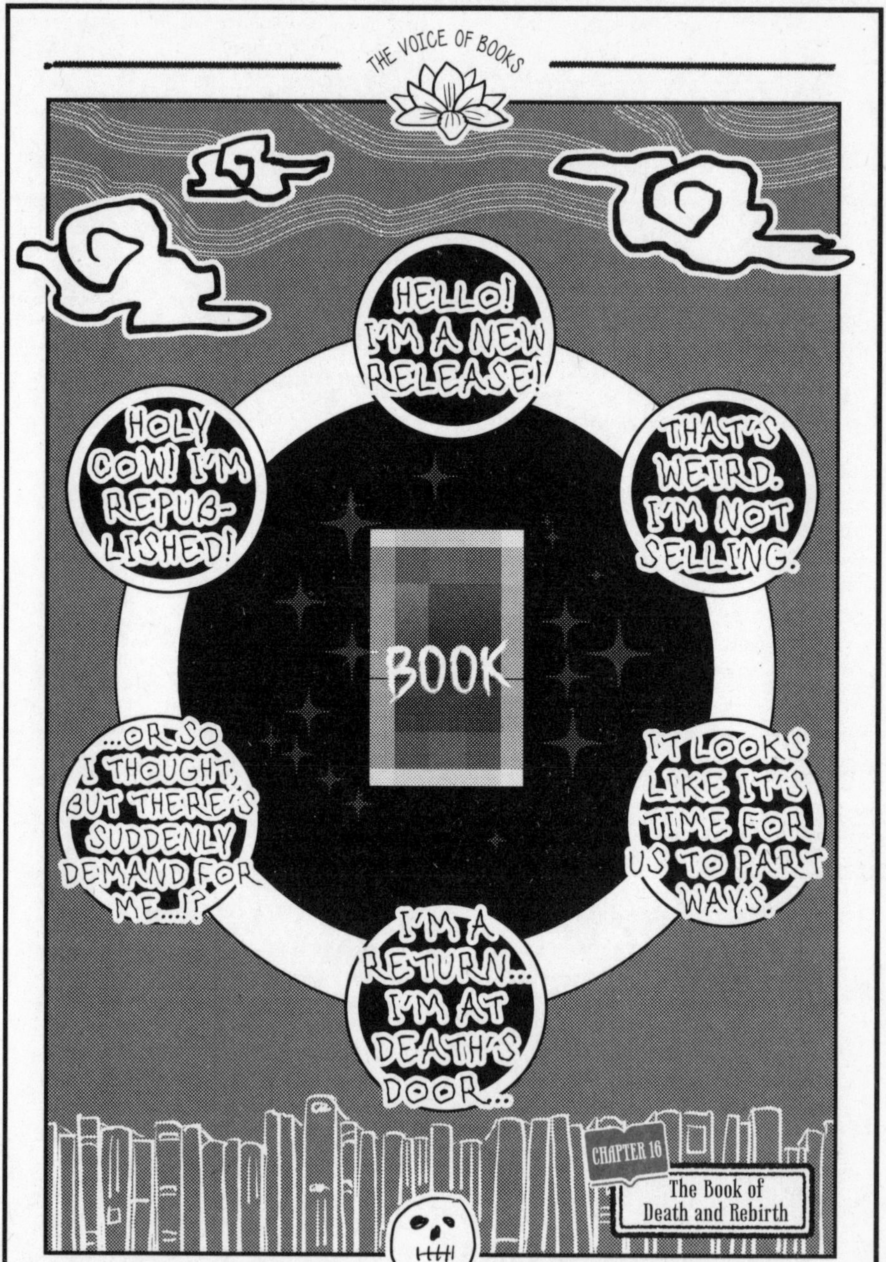
THE VOICE OF BOOKS
HELLO! I'M A NEW RELEASE!
THAT'S WEIRD. I'M NOT SELLING.
IT LOOKS LIKE IT'S TIME FOR US TO PART WAYS.
I'M A RETURN... I'M AT DEATH'S DOOR...
...OR SO I THOUGHT, BUT THERE'S SUDDENLY DEMAND FOR ME...!?
HOLY COW! I'M REPUBLISHED!
BOOK
CHAPTER 16
The Book of Death and Rebirth
DAYDREAMS

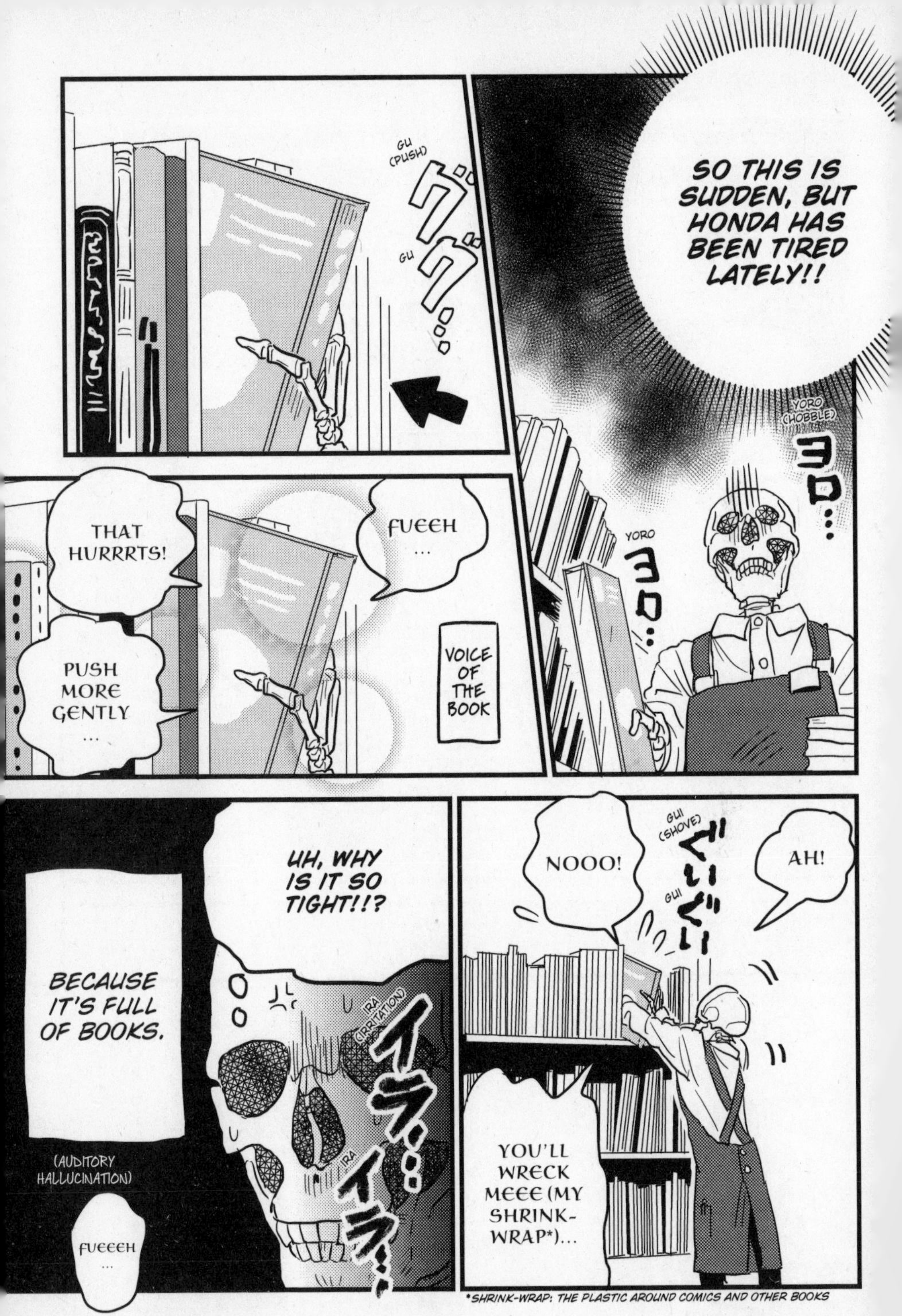
SO THIS IS SUDDEN, BUT HONDA HAS BEEN TIRED LATELY!!
YORO (HOBBLE)
ヨロ…
YORO
ヨロ…
GU (PUSH)
GU
グ グ…
THAT HURRRTS!
FUEEH …
PUSH MORE GENTLY …
VOICE OF THE BOOK
AH!
GUI (SHOVE)
GUI
NOOO!
YOU'LL WRECK MEEE (MY SHRINK-WRAP*)…
UH, WHY IS IT SO TIGHT!!?
IRA (IRRITATION)
IRA
イラ… イラ…
BECAUSE IT'S FULL OF BOOKS.
(AUDITORY HALLUCINATION)
FUEEEH …

*SHRINK-WRAP: THE PLASTIC AROUND COMICS AND OTHER BOOKS

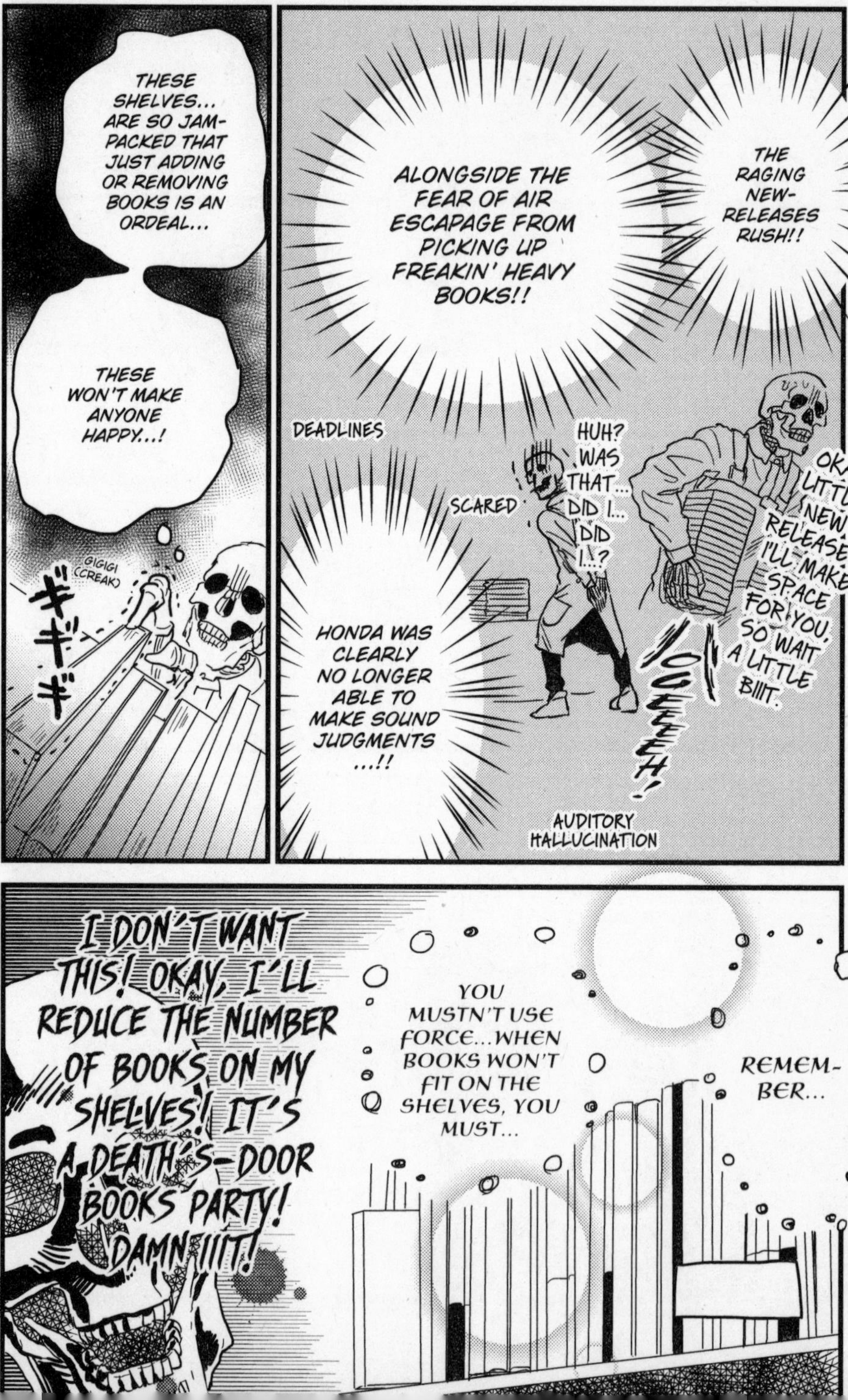
THE RAGING NEW-RELEASES RUSH!!
ALONGSIDE THE FEAR OF AIR ESCAPAGE FROM PICKING UP FREAKIN' HEAVY BOOKS!!
OKAY, LITTLE NEW RELEASES. I'LL MAKE SPACE FOR YOU, SO WAIT A LITTLE BIIIT.
OGEEEEH!
HUH? WAS THAT... DID I... DID I...?
SCARED
DEADLINES
HONDA WAS CLEARLY NO LONGER ABLE TO MAKE SOUND JUDGMENTS ...!!
AUDITORY HALLUCINATION
THESE SHELVES... ARE SO JAM-PACKED THAT JUST ADDING OR REMOVING BOOKS IS AN ORDEAL...
THESE WON'T MAKE ANYONE HAPPY...!
GIGIGI (CREAK)
ギギギ
REMEMBER...
YOU MUSTN'T USE FORCE...WHEN BOOKS WON'T FIT ON THE SHELVES, YOU MUST...
I DON'T WANT THIS! OKAY, I'LL REDUCE THE NUMBER OF BOOKS ON MY SHELVES! IT'S A DEATH'S-DOOR BOOKS PARTY! DAMNIIIIT!

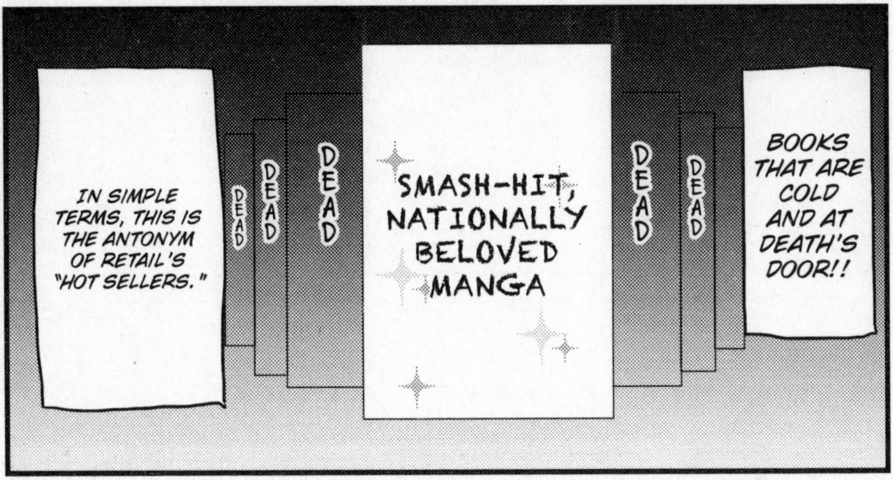
BOOKS THAT ARE COLD AND AT DEATH'S DOOR!!
DEAD
DEAD
SMASH-HIT, NATIONALLY BELOVED MANGA
DEAD
DEAD
DEAD
IN SIMPLE TERMS, THIS IS THE ANTONYM OF RETAIL'S "HOT SELLERS."

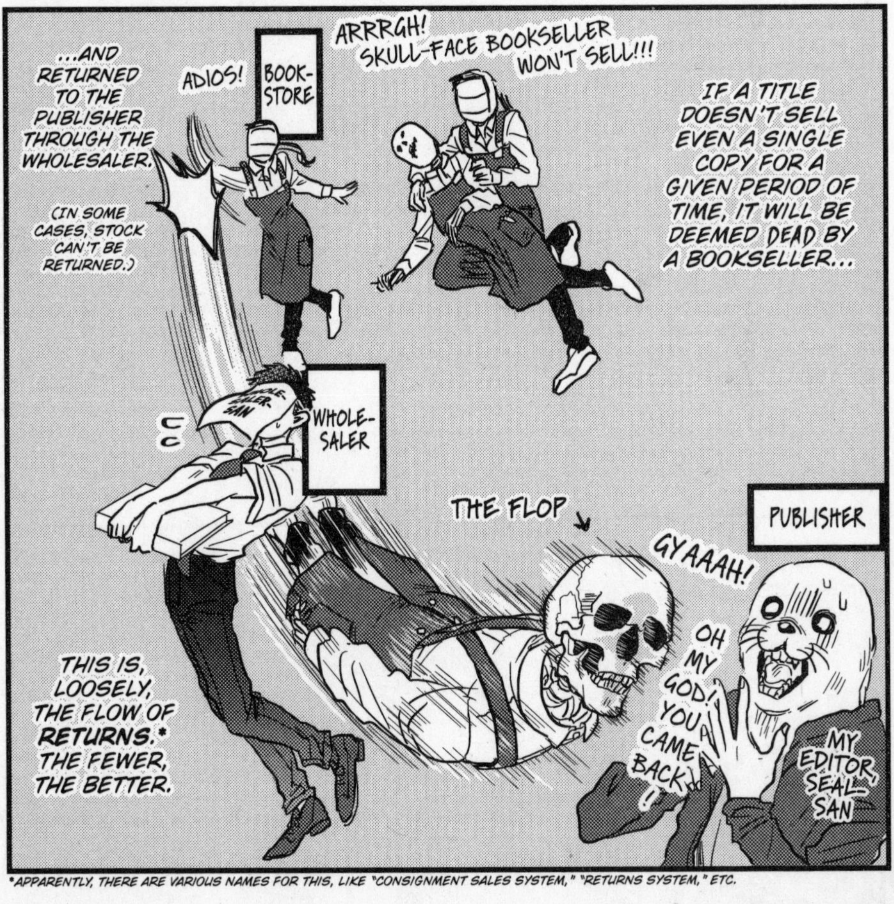
IF A TITLE DOESN'T SELL EVEN A SINGLE COPY FOR A GIVEN PERIOD OF TIME, IT WILL BE DEEMED DEAD BY A BOOKSELLER...
ARRRGH! SKULL-FACE BOOKSELLER WON'T SELL!!!
BOOK-STORE
ADIOS!
...AND RETURNED TO THE PUBLISHER THROUGH THE WHOLESALER.
(IN SOME CASES, STOCK CAN'T BE RETURNED.)
WHOLE-SALER
PUBLISHER
GYAAAH!
THE FLOP
MY EDITOR, SEAL SAN
OH MY GOD! YOU CAME BACK!
THIS IS, LOOSELY, THE FLOW OF **RETURNS.*** THE FEWER, THE BETTER.

*APPARENTLY, THERE ARE VARIOUS NAMES FOR THIS, LIKE "CONSIGNMENT SALES SYSTEM," "RETURNS SYSTEM," ETC.

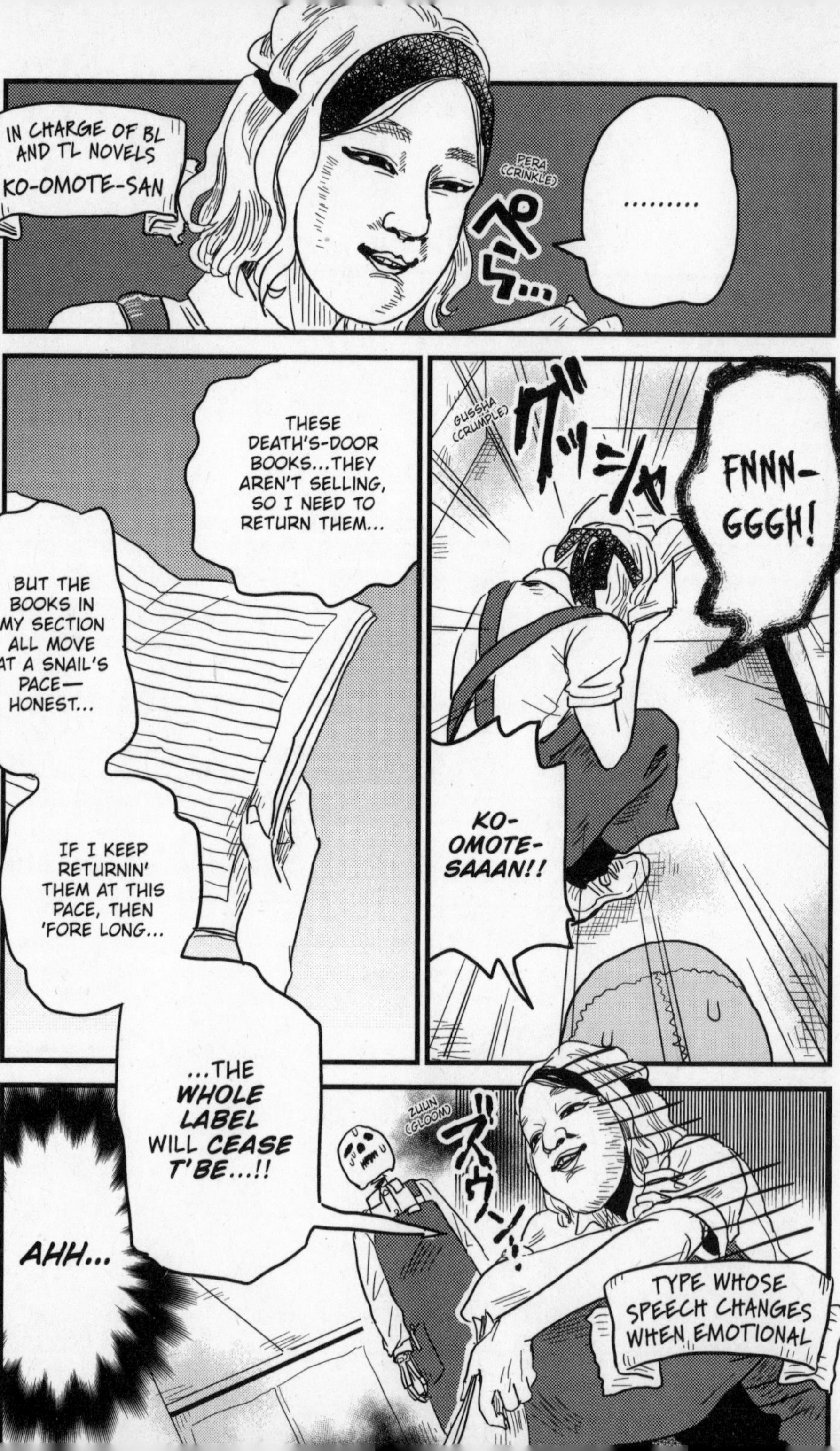
....
ぺら...
PERA (CRINKLE)
IN CHARGE OF BL AND TL NOVELS KO-OMOTE-SAN
FNNN-GGGH!
グッシャ
GUSSHA (CRUMPLE)
KO-OMOTE-SAAAN!!
THESE DEATH'S-DOOR BOOKS...THEY AREN'T SELLING, SO I NEED TO RETURN THEM...
BUT THE BOOKS IN MY SECTION ALL MOVE AT A SNAIL'S PACE—HONEST...
IF I KEEP RETURNIN' THEM AT THIS PACE, THEN 'FORE LONG...
...THE *WHOLE LABEL* WILL *CEASE T'BE*...!!
ズウーン
ZUUN (GLOOM)
TYPE WHOSE SPEECH CHANGES WHEN EMOTIONAL
AHH...

*WE CALL PRODUCTS SELLING AT A RELAXED PACE "SLOW MOVERS," ETC.

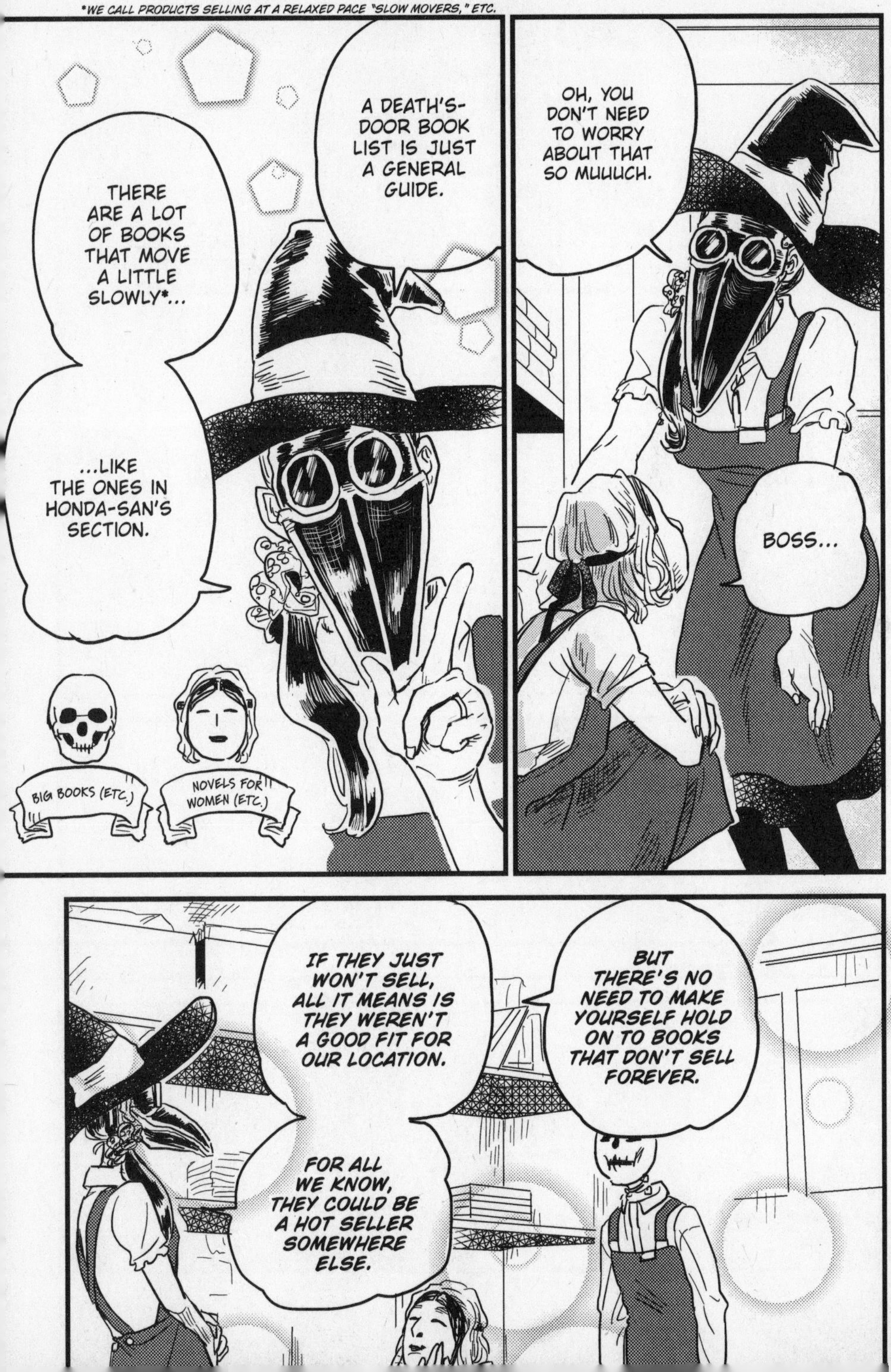
OH, YOU DON'T NEED TO WORRY ABOUT THAT SO MUUUCH.
BOSS...
A DEATH'S-DOOR BOOK LIST IS JUST A GENERAL GUIDE.
THERE ARE A LOT OF BOOKS THAT MOVE A LITTLE SLOWLY*...
...LIKE THE ONES IN HONDA-SAN'S SECTION.
BIG BOOKS (ETC.)
NOVELS FOR WOMEN (ETC.)
BUT THERE'S NO NEED TO MAKE YOURSELF HOLD ON TO BOOKS THAT DON'T SELL FOREVER.
IF THEY JUST WON'T SELL, ALL IT MEANS IS THEY WEREN'T A GOOD FIT FOR OUR LOCATION.
FOR ALL WE KNOW, THEY COULD BE A HOT SELLER SOMEWHERE ELSE.

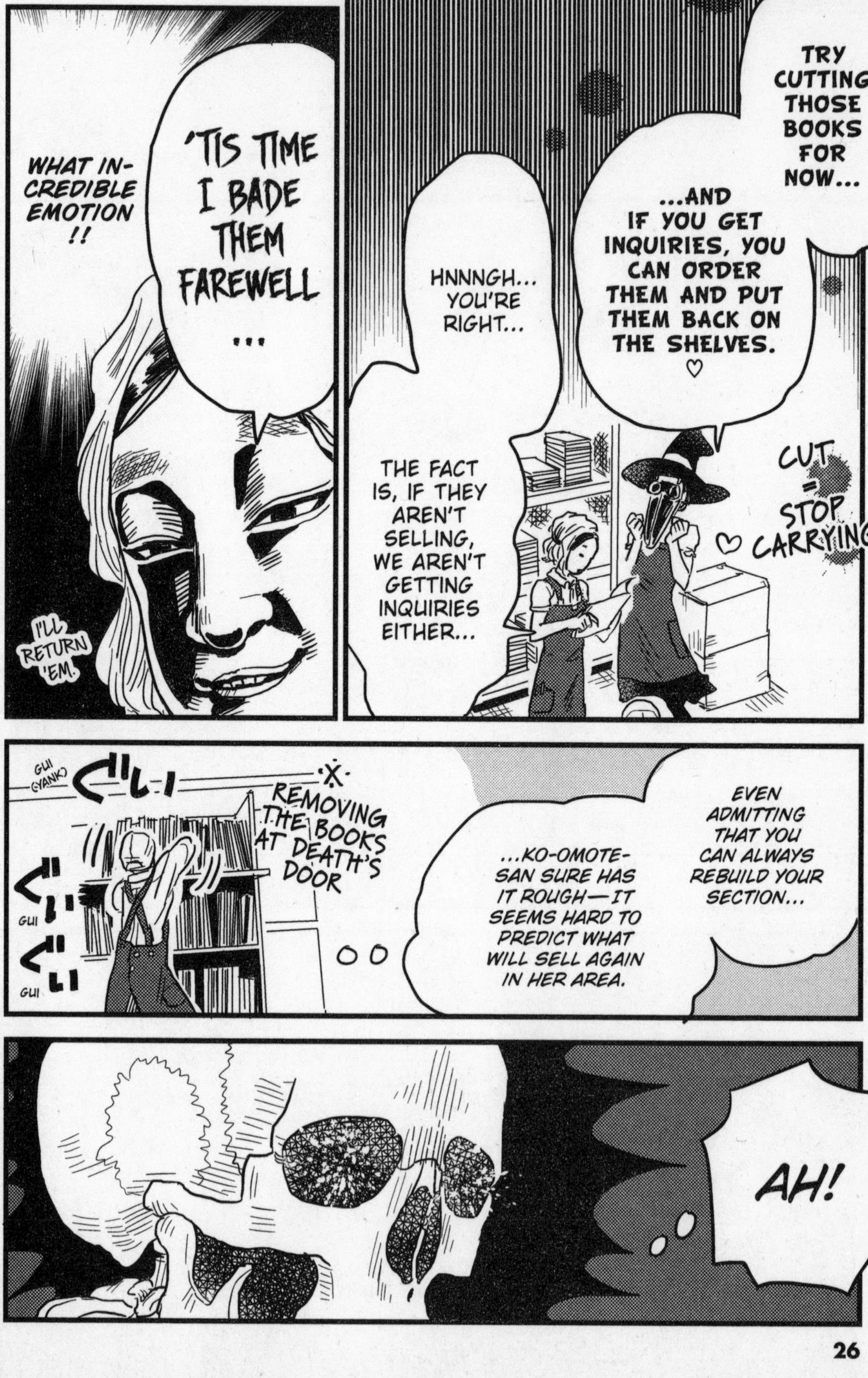
TRY CUTTING THOSE BOOKS FOR NOW...
...AND IF YOU GET INQUIRIES, YOU CAN ORDER THEM AND PUT THEM BACK ON THE SHELVES. ♡
HNNNGH... YOU'RE RIGHT...
THE FACT IS, IF THEY AREN'T SELLING, WE AREN'T GETTING INQUIRIES EITHER...
CUT = STOP CARRYING ♡
'TIS TIME I BADE THEM FAREWELL ...
WHAT IN-CREDIBLE EMOTION !!
I'LL RETURN 'EM.
EVEN ADMITTING THAT YOU CAN ALWAYS REBUILD YOUR SECTION...
...KO-OMOTE-SAN SURE HAS IT ROUGH—IT SEEMS HARD TO PREDICT WHAT WILL SELL AGAIN IN HER AREA.
※ REMOVING THE BOOKS AT DEATH'S DOOR
GUI (YANK)
GUI
GUI
AH!

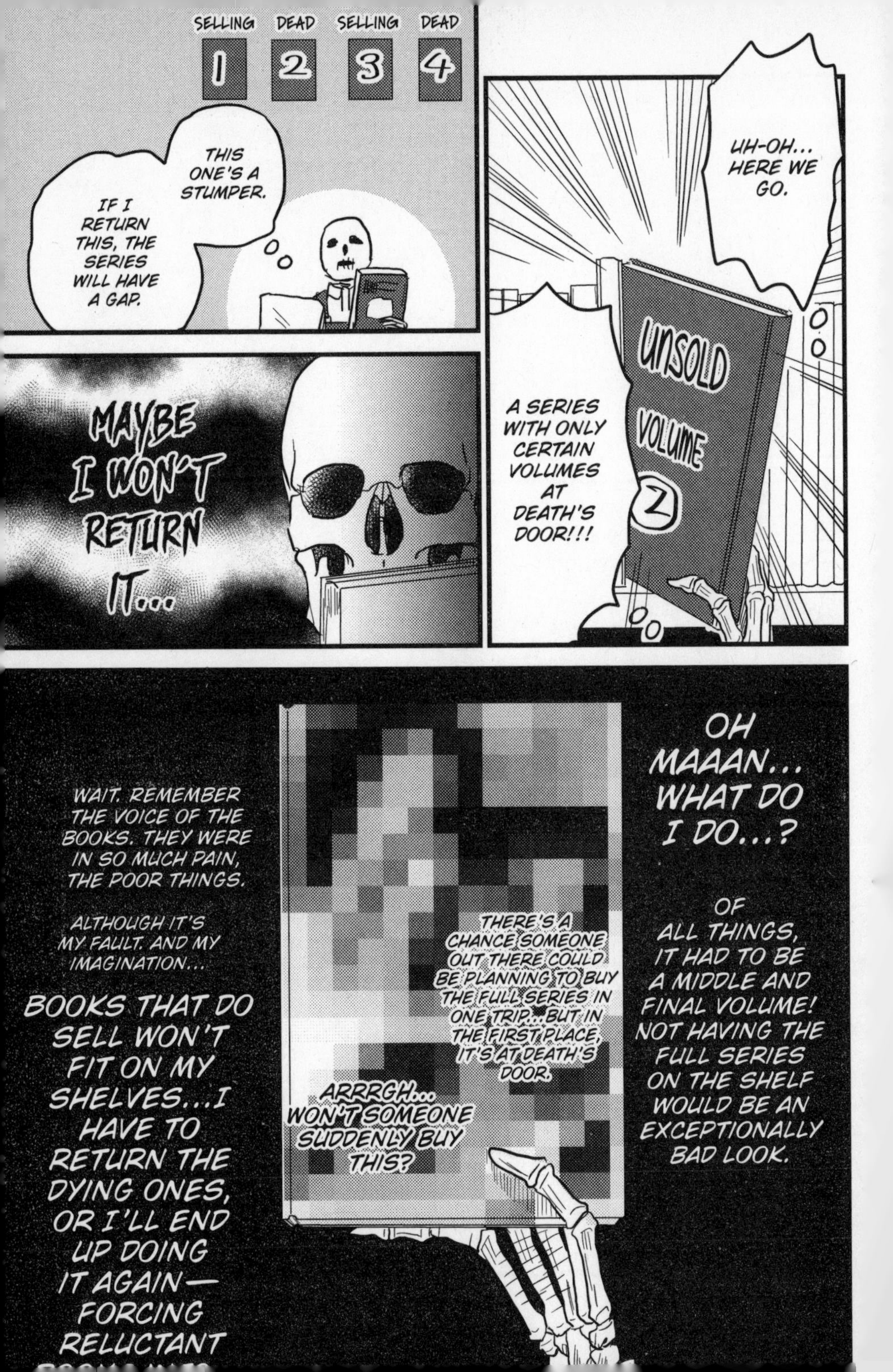
UH-OH... HERE WE GO.
UNSOLD VOLUME 2
A SERIES WITH ONLY CERTAIN VOLUMES AT DEATH'S DOOR!!!
SELLING DEAD SELLING DEAD
1 2 3 4
THIS ONE'S A STUMPER.
IF I RETURN THIS, THE SERIES WILL HAVE A GAP.
MAYBE I WON'T RETURN IT...
OH MAAAN... WHAT DO I DO...?
OF ALL THINGS, IT HAD TO BE A MIDDLE AND FINAL VOLUME! NOT HAVING THE FULL SERIES ON THE SHELF WOULD BE AN EXCEPTIONALLY BAD LOOK.
THERE'S A CHANCE SOMEONE OUT THERE COULD BE PLANNING TO BUY THE FULL SERIES IN ONE TRIP... BUT IN THE FIRST PLACE, IT'S AT DEATH'S DOOR.
ARRRGH... WON'T SOMEONE SUDDENLY BUY THIS?
WAIT. REMEMBER THE VOICE OF THE BOOKS. THEY WERE IN SO MUCH PAIN, THE POOR THINGS.
ALTHOUGH IT'S MY FAULT. AND MY IMAGINATION...
BOOKS THAT DO SELL WON'T FIT ON MY SHELVES...I HAVE TO RETURN THE DYING ONES, OR I'LL END UP DOING IT AGAIN—FORCING RELUCTANT

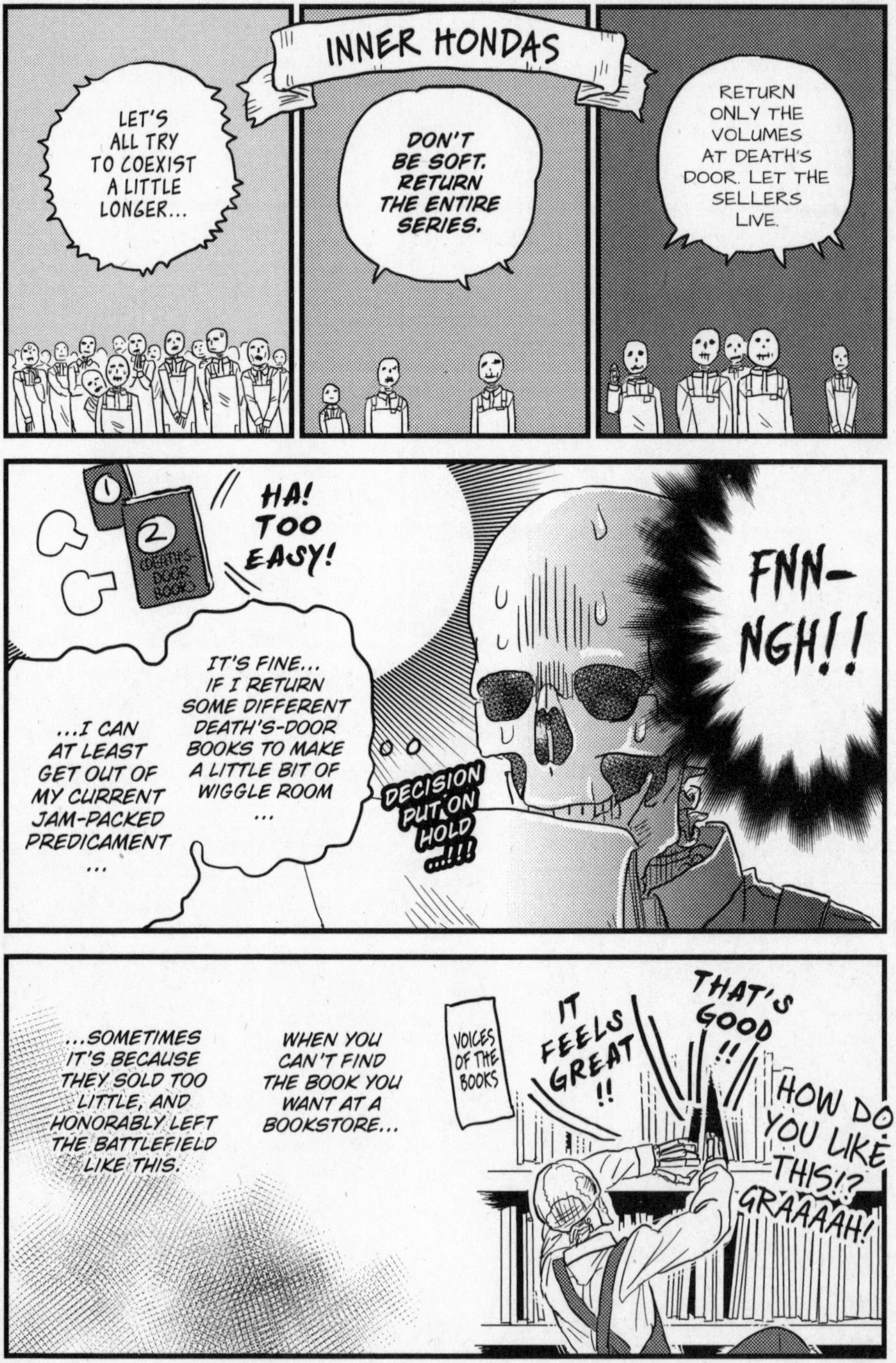
INNER HONDAS
RETURN ONLY THE VOLUMES AT DEATH'S DOOR. LET THE SELLERS LIVE.
DON'T BE SOFT. RETURN THE ENTIRE SERIES.
LET'S ALL TRY TO COEXIST A LITTLE LONGER...
FNN-NGH!!
DECISION PUT ON HOLD ...!!!
IT'S FINE... IF I RETURN SOME DIFFERENT DEATH'S-DOOR BOOKS TO MAKE A LITTLE BIT OF WIGGLE ROOM ...
...I CAN AT LEAST GET OUT OF MY CURRENT JAM-PACKED PREDICAMENT ...
HA! TOO EASY!
1
2 DEATH'S-DOOR BOOKS
HOW DO YOU LIKE THIS!? GRAAAAH!
THAT'S GOOD!!
IT FEELS GREAT!!
VOICES OF THE BOOKS
WHEN YOU CAN'T FIND THE BOOK YOU WANT AT A BOOKSTORE...
...SOMETIMES IT'S BECAUSE THEY SOLD TOO LITTLE, AND HONORABLY LEFT THE BATTLEFIELD LIKE THIS.

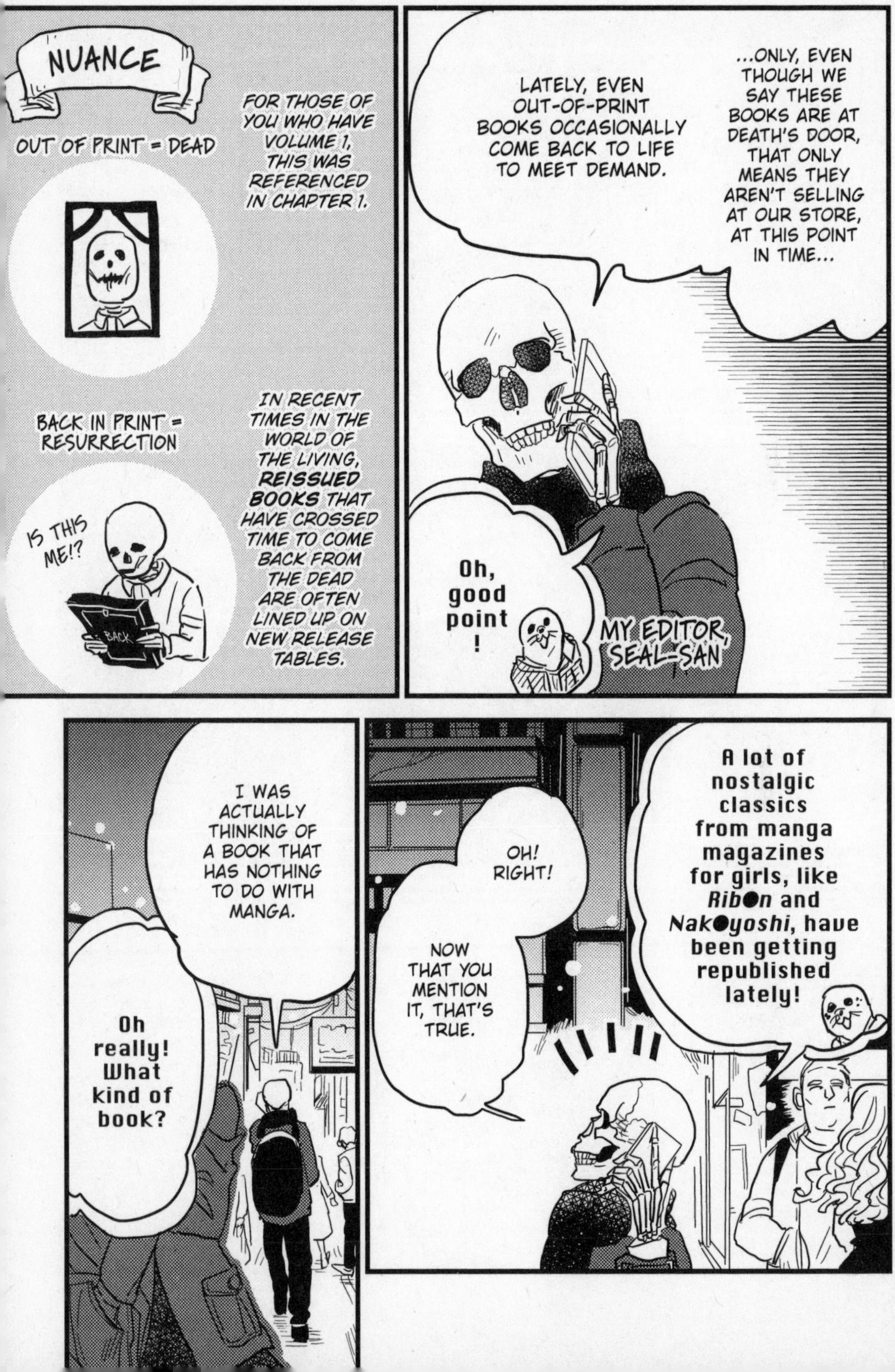
LATELY, EVEN OUT-OF-PRINT BOOKS OCCASIONALLY COME BACK TO LIFE TO MEET DEMAND.
...ONLY, EVEN THOUGH WE SAY THESE BOOKS ARE AT DEATH'S DOOR, THAT ONLY MEANS THEY AREN'T SELLING AT OUR STORE, AT THIS POINT IN TIME...
Oh, good point!
MY EDITOR, SEAL-SAN
NUANCE
OUT OF PRINT = DEAD
FOR THOSE OF YOU WHO HAVE VOLUME 1, THIS WAS REFERENCED IN CHAPTER 1.
BACK IN PRINT = RESURRECTION
IS THIS ME!?
BACK
IN RECENT TIMES IN THE WORLD OF THE LIVING, **REISSUED BOOKS** THAT HAVE CROSSED TIME TO COME BACK FROM THE DEAD ARE OFTEN LINED UP ON NEW RELEASE TABLES.
A lot of nostalgic classics from manga magazines for girls, like *Rib●n* and *Nak●yoshi*, have been getting republished lately!
OH! RIGHT!
NOW THAT YOU MENTION IT, THAT'S TRUE.
I WAS ACTUALLY THINKING OF A BOOK THAT HAS NOTHING TO DO WITH MANGA.
Oh really! What kind of book?

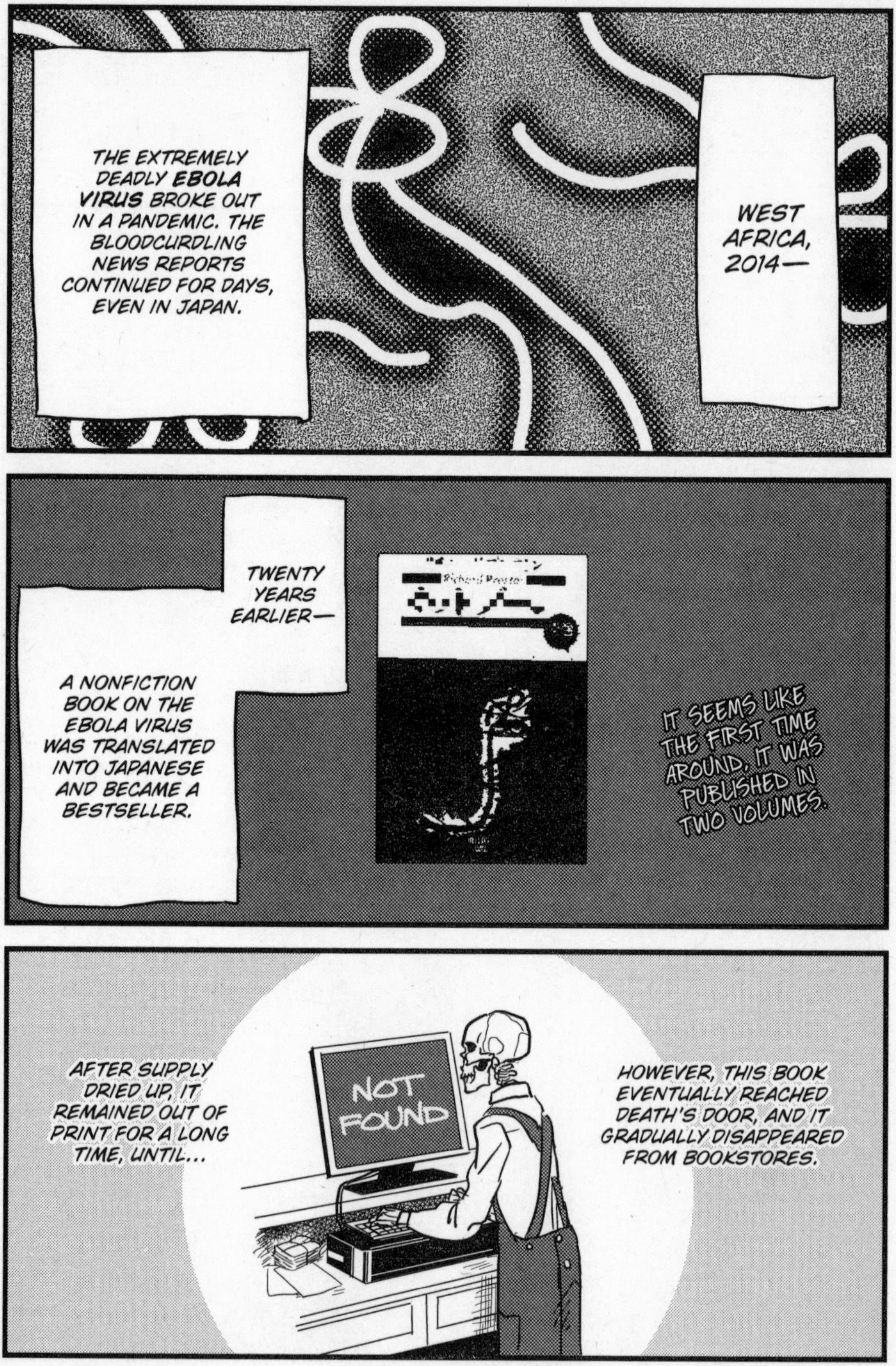
WEST AFRICA, 2014—
THE EXTREMELY DEADLY **EBOLA VIRUS** BROKE OUT IN A PANDEMIC. THE BLOODCURDLING NEWS REPORTS CONTINUED FOR DAYS, EVEN IN JAPAN.
TWENTY YEARS EARLIER—
A NONFICTION BOOK ON THE EBOLA VIRUS WAS TRANSLATED INTO JAPANESE AND BECAME A BESTSELLER.
IT SEEMS LIKE THE FIRST TIME AROUND, IT WAS PUBLISHED IN TWO VOLUMES.
HOWEVER, THIS BOOK EVENTUALLY REACHED DEATH'S DOOR, AND IT GRADUALLY DISAPPEARED FROM BOOKSTORES.
NOT FOUND
AFTER SUPPLY DRIED UP, IT REMAINED OUT OF PRINT FOR A LONG TIME, UNTIL...

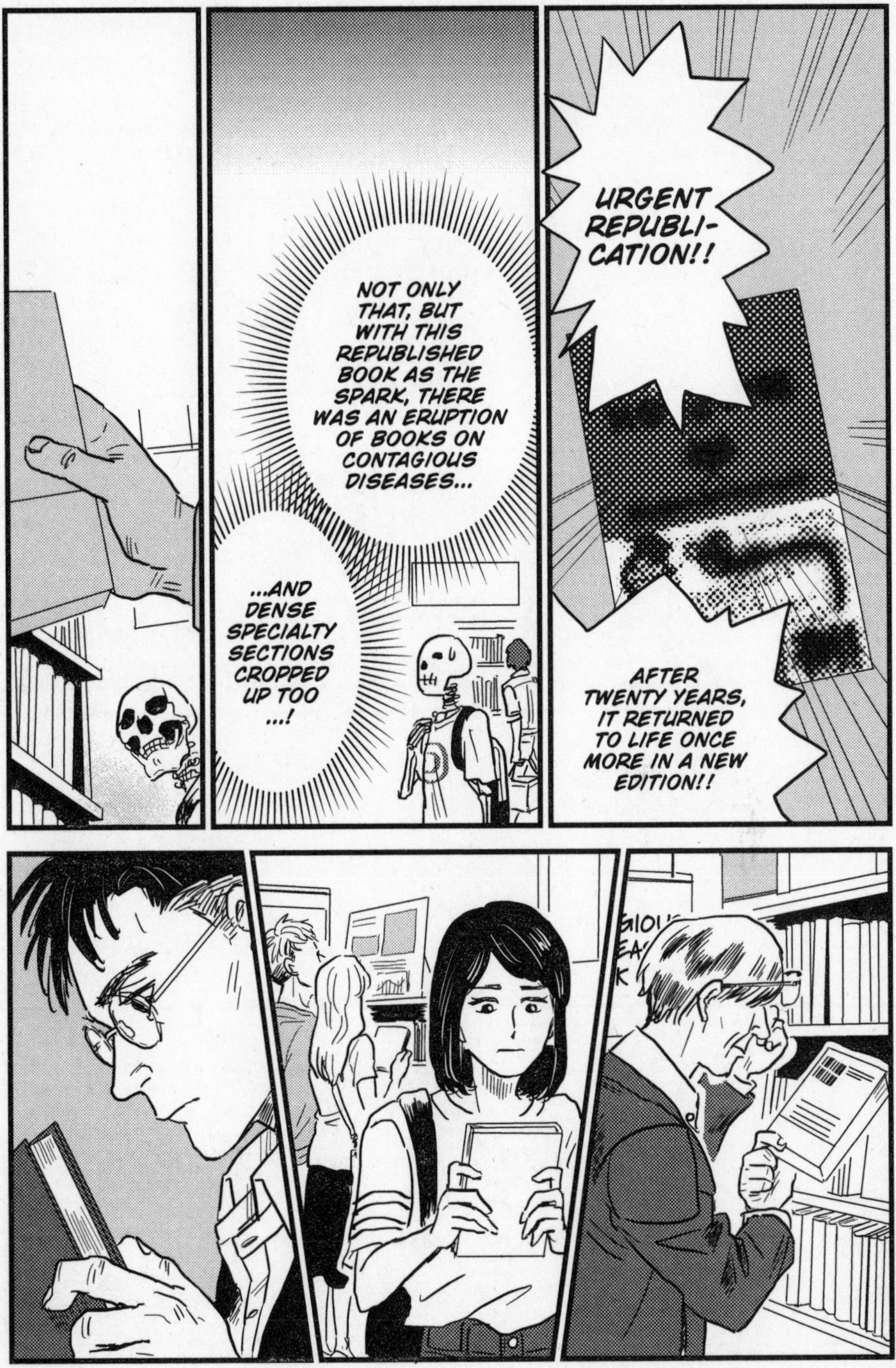
URGENT REPUBLI-CATION!!
AFTER TWENTY YEARS, IT RETURNED TO LIFE ONCE MORE IN A NEW EDITION!!
NOT ONLY THAT, BUT WITH THIS REPUBLISHED BOOK AS THE SPARK, THERE WAS AN ERUPTION OF BOOKS ON CONTAGIOUS DISEASES...
...AND DENSE SPECIALTY SECTIONS CROPPED UP TOO ...!

*According to the W.H.O. (World Health Organization) report dated June 10, 2016, the West Africa Ebola virus outbreak was basically eradicated.

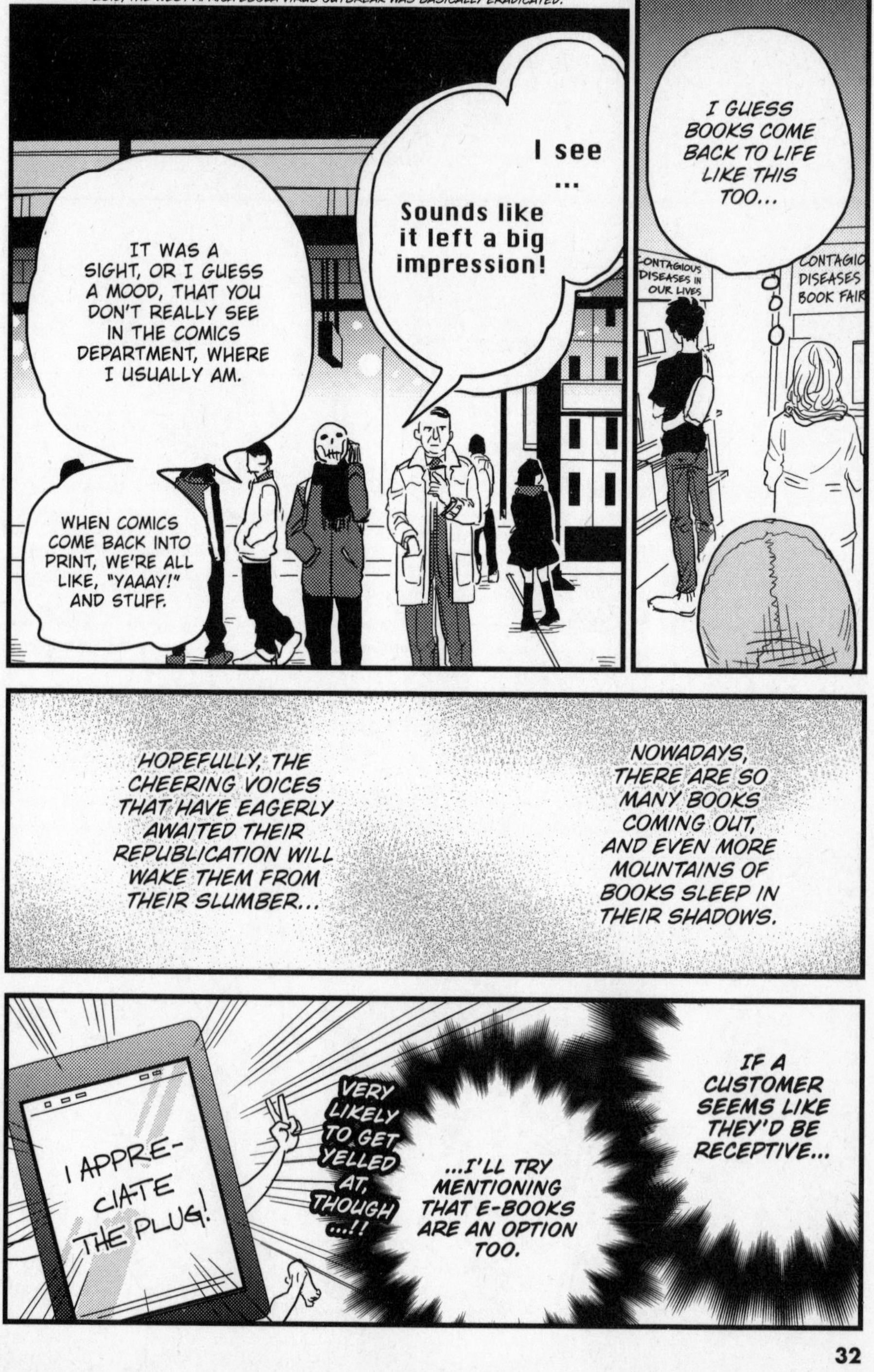
I GUESS BOOKS COME BACK TO LIFE LIKE THIS TOO...
CONTAGIOUS DISEASES IN OUR LIVES
CONTAGIO DISEASES BOOK FAIR
IT WAS A SIGHT, OR I GUESS A MOOD, THAT YOU DON'T REALLY SEE IN THE COMICS DEPARTMENT, WHERE I USUALLY AM.
WHEN COMICS COME BACK INTO PRINT, WE'RE ALL LIKE, "YAAAY!" AND STUFF.
I see ... Sounds like it left a big impression!
NOWADAYS, THERE ARE SO MANY BOOKS COMING OUT, AND EVEN MORE MOUNTAINS OF BOOKS SLEEP IN THEIR SHADOWS.
HOPEFULLY, THE CHEERING VOICES THAT HAVE EAGERLY AWAITED THEIR REPUBLICATION WILL WAKE THEM FROM THEIR SLUMBER...
IF A CUSTOMER SEEMS LIKE THEY'D BE RECEPTIVE...
...I'LL TRY MENTIONING THAT E-BOOKS ARE AN OPTION TOO.
VERY LIKELY TO GET YELLED AT, THOUGH ...!!
I APPRECIATE THE PLUG!

*THE NOVEL THAT BLEW UP IN CHAPTER 15.

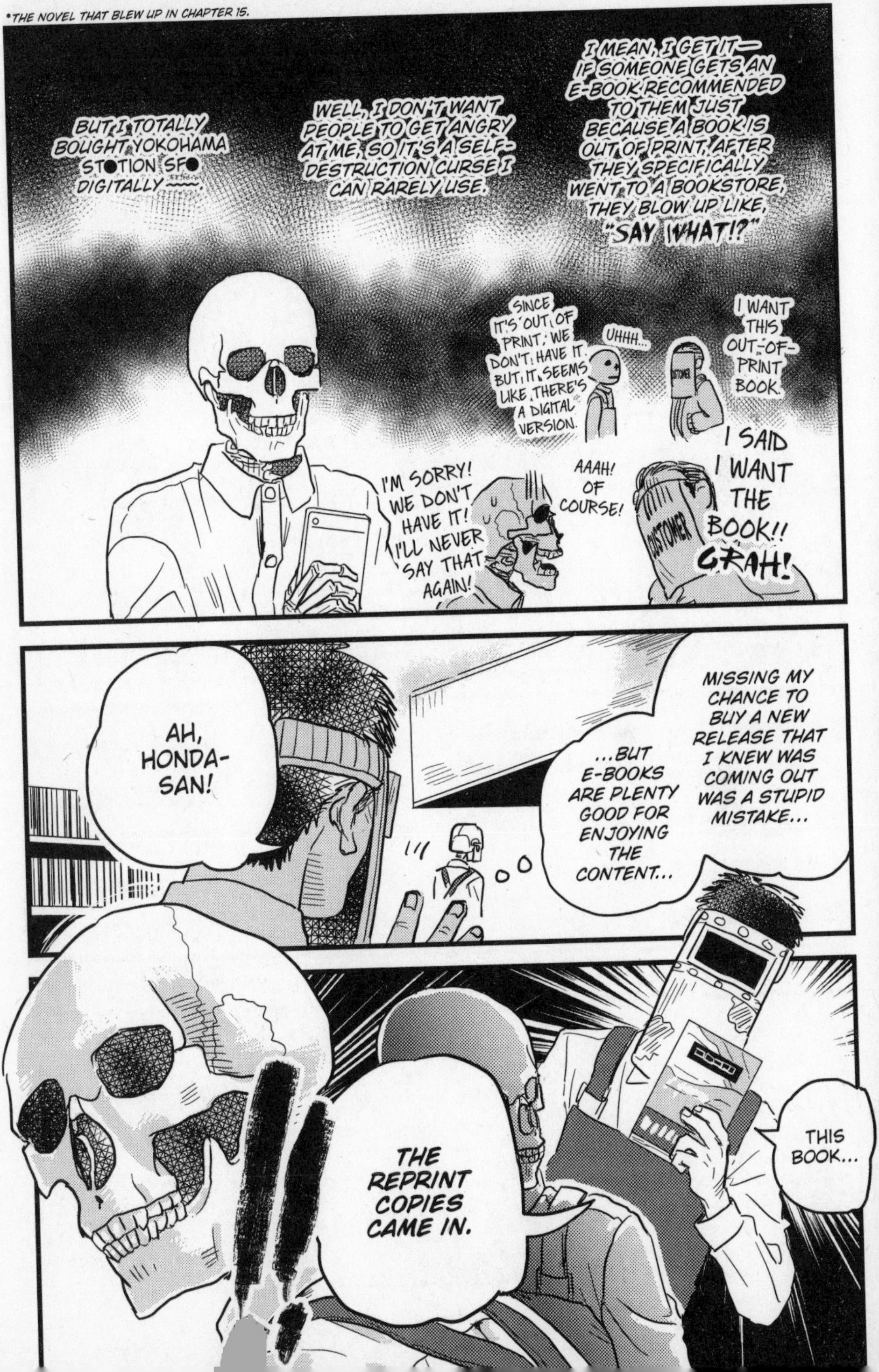
I MEAN, I GET IT— IF SOMEONE GETS AN E-BOOK RECOMMENDED TO THEM JUST BECAUSE A BOOK IS OUT OF PRINT, AFTER THEY SPECIFICALLY WENT TO A BOOKSTORE, THEY BLOW UP LIKE, "SAY WHAT!?"
WELL, I DON'T WANT PEOPLE TO GET ANGRY AT ME, SO IT'S A SELF-DESTRUCTION CURSE I CAN RARELY USE.
BUT I TOTALLY BOUGHT YOKOHAMA ST●TION SF● DIGITALLY~~.
I WANT THIS OUT-OF-PRINT BOOK.
CUSTOMER
UHHH...
SINCE IT'S OUT OF PRINT, WE DON'T HAVE IT. BUT IT SEEMS LIKE THERE'S A DIGITAL VERSION.
I SAID I WANT THE BOOK!! GRAH!
CUSTOMER
AAAH! OF COURSE!
I'M SORRY! WE DON'T HAVE IT! I'LL NEVER SAY THAT AGAIN!
MISSING MY CHANCE TO BUY A NEW RELEASE THAT I KNEW WAS COMING OUT WAS A STUPID MISTAKE...
...BUT E-BOOKS ARE PLENTY GOOD FOR ENJOYING THE CONTENT...
AH, HONDA-SAN!
THIS BOOK...
THE REPRINT COPIES CAME IN.

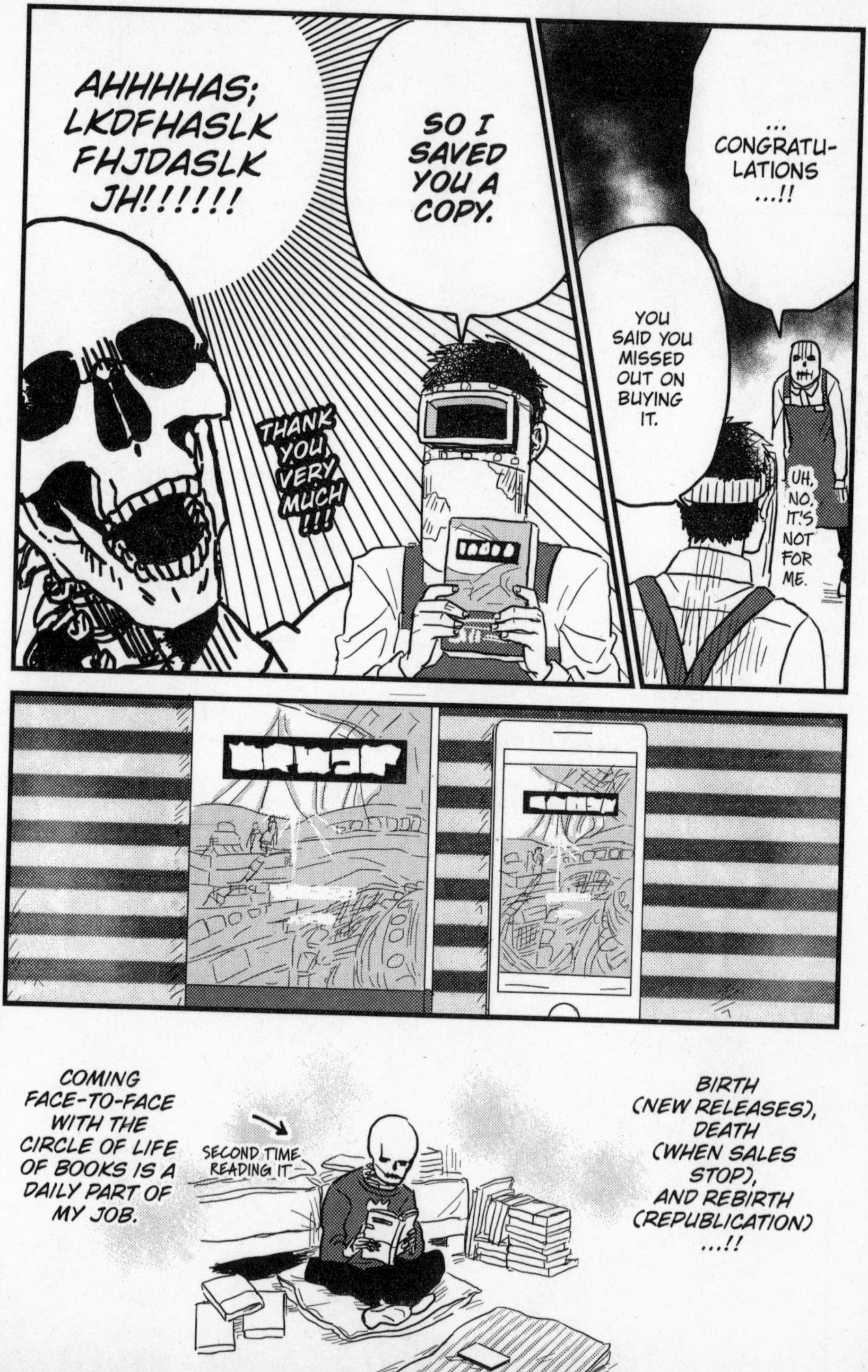
...CONGRATULATIONS...!!
YOU SAID YOU MISSED OUT ON BUYING IT.
UH, NO, IT'S NOT FOR ME.
SO I SAVED YOU A COPY.
AHHHHAS; LKDFHASLK FHJDASLK JH!!!!!!
THANK YOU VERY MUCH!!!
BIRTH (NEW RELEASES), DEATH (WHEN SALES STOP), AND REBIRTH (REPUBLICATION) ...!!
COMING FACE-TO-FACE WITH THE CIRCLE OF LIFE OF BOOKS IS A DAILY PART OF MY JOB.
SECOND TIME READING IT

Skull-face

Bookseller

Honda-san

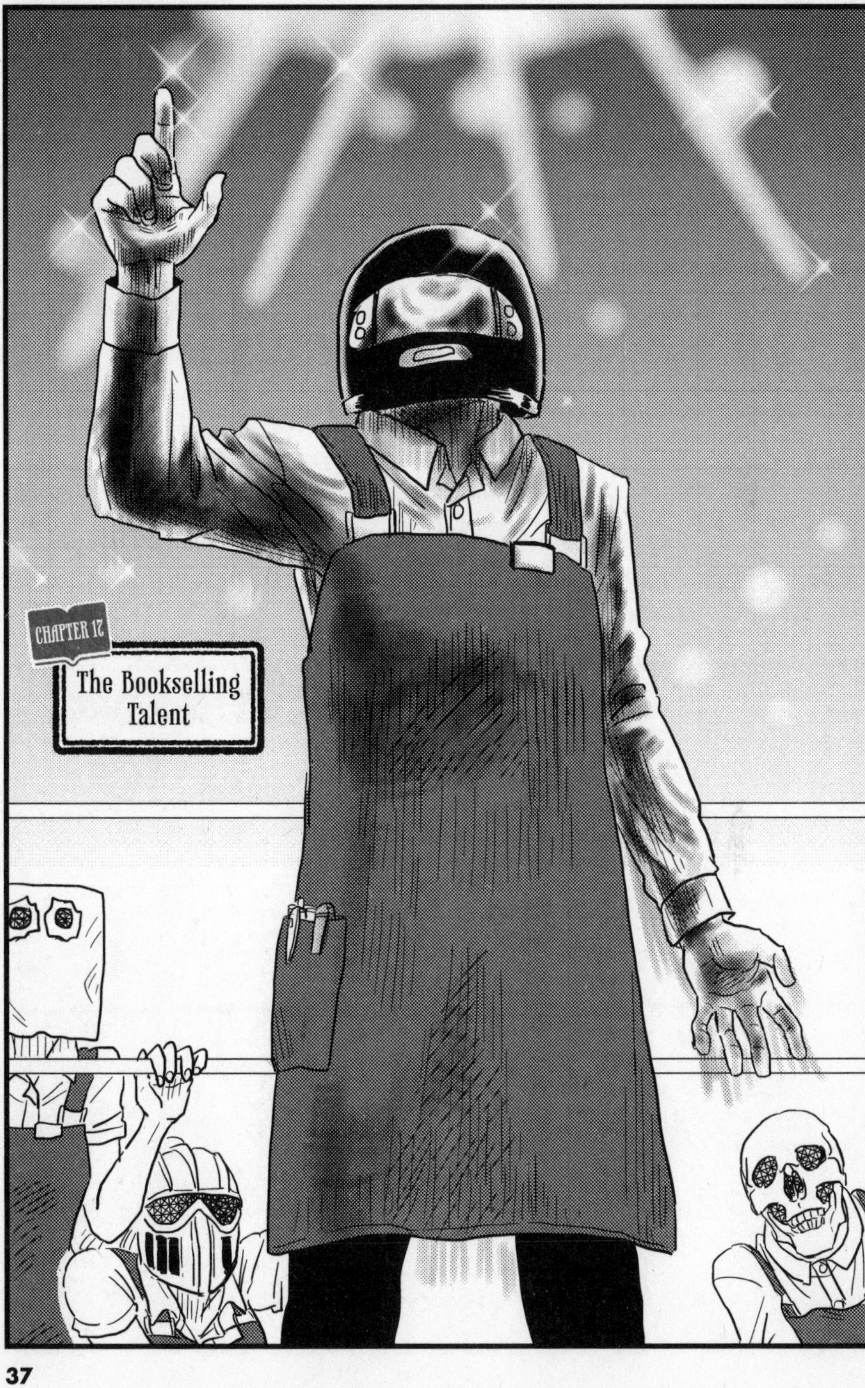
CHAPTER 17
The Bookselling Talent

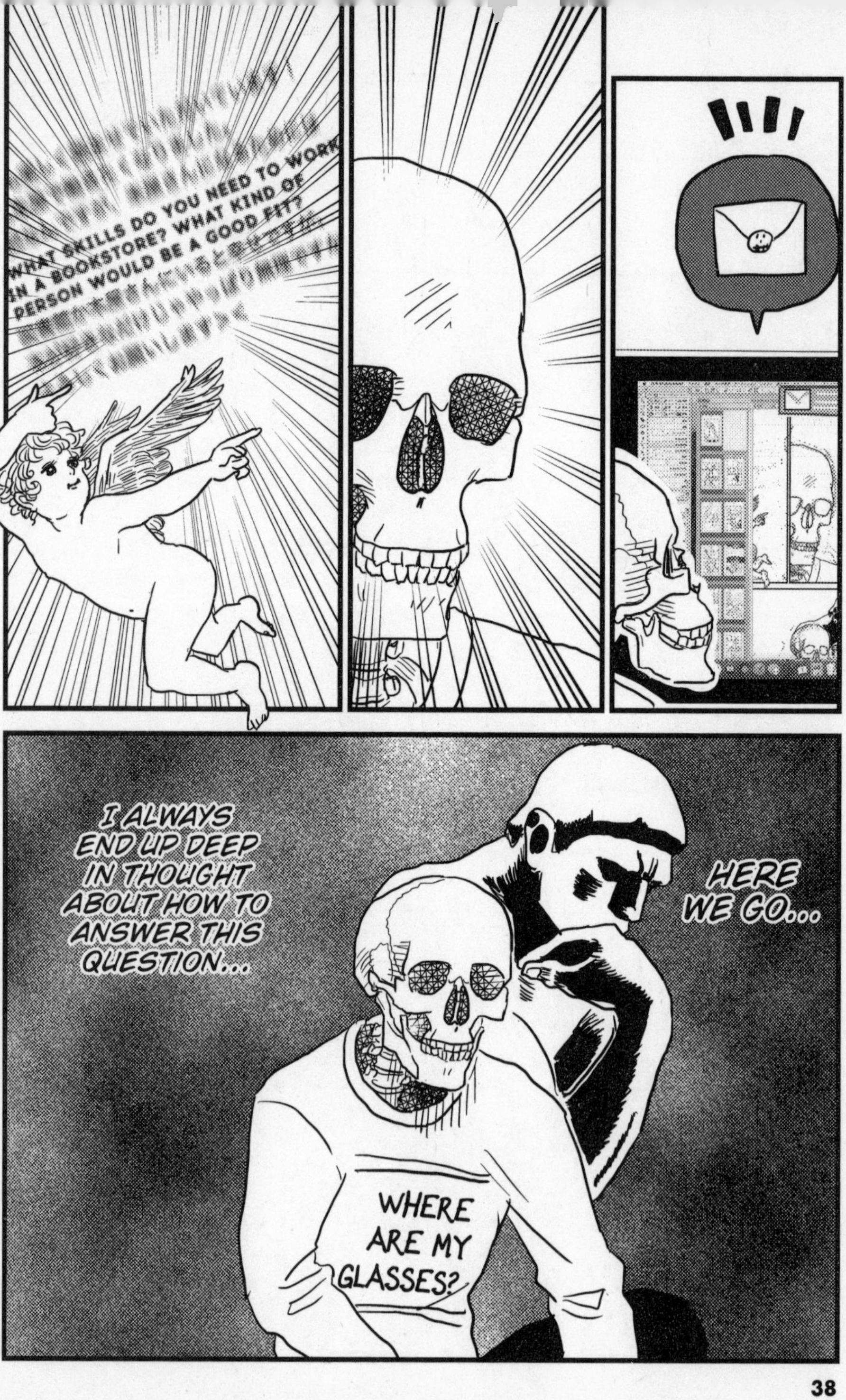
WHAT SKILLS DO YOU NEED TO WORK IN A BOOKSTORE? WHAT KIND OF PERSON WOULD BE A GOOD FIT?
HERE WE GO...
I ALWAYS END UP DEEP IN THOUGHT ABOUT HOW TO ANSWER THIS QUESTION...
WHERE ARE MY GLASSES?

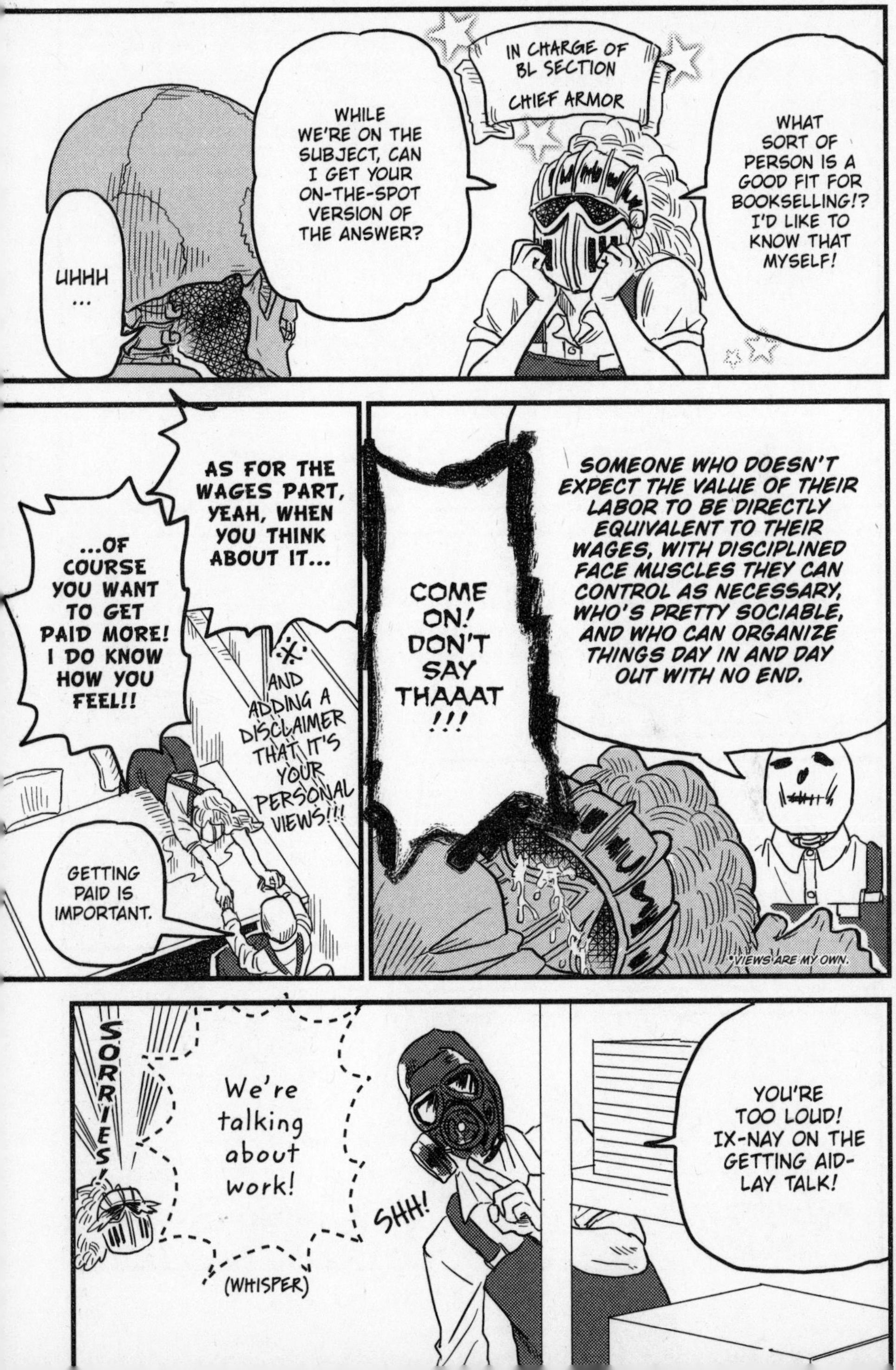
IN CHARGE OF BL SECTION
CHIEF ARMOR
WHILE WE'RE ON THE SUBJECT, CAN I GET YOUR ON-THE-SPOT VERSION OF THE ANSWER?
WHAT SORT OF PERSON IS A GOOD FIT FOR BOOKSELLING!? I'D LIKE TO KNOW THAT MYSELF!
UHHH ...
SOMEONE WHO DOESN'T EXPECT THE VALUE OF THEIR LABOR TO BE DIRECTLY EQUIVALENT TO THEIR WAGES, WITH DISCIPLINED FACE MUSCLES THEY CAN CONTROL AS NECESSARY, WHO'S PRETTY SOCIABLE, AND WHO CAN ORGANIZE THINGS DAY IN AND DAY OUT WITH NO END.
COME ON! DON'T SAY THAAAT !!!
*VIEWS ARE MY OWN.
AS FOR THE WAGES PART, YEAH, WHEN YOU THINK ABOUT IT...
AND ADDING A DISCLAIMER THAT IT'S YOUR PERSONAL VIEWS!!!
...OF COURSE YOU WANT TO GET PAID MORE! I DO KNOW HOW YOU FEEL!!
GETTING PAID IS IMPORTANT.
YOU'RE TOO LOUD! IX-NAY ON THE GETTING AID-LAY TALK!
SHH!
We're talking about work!
(WHISPER)
SORRIES!

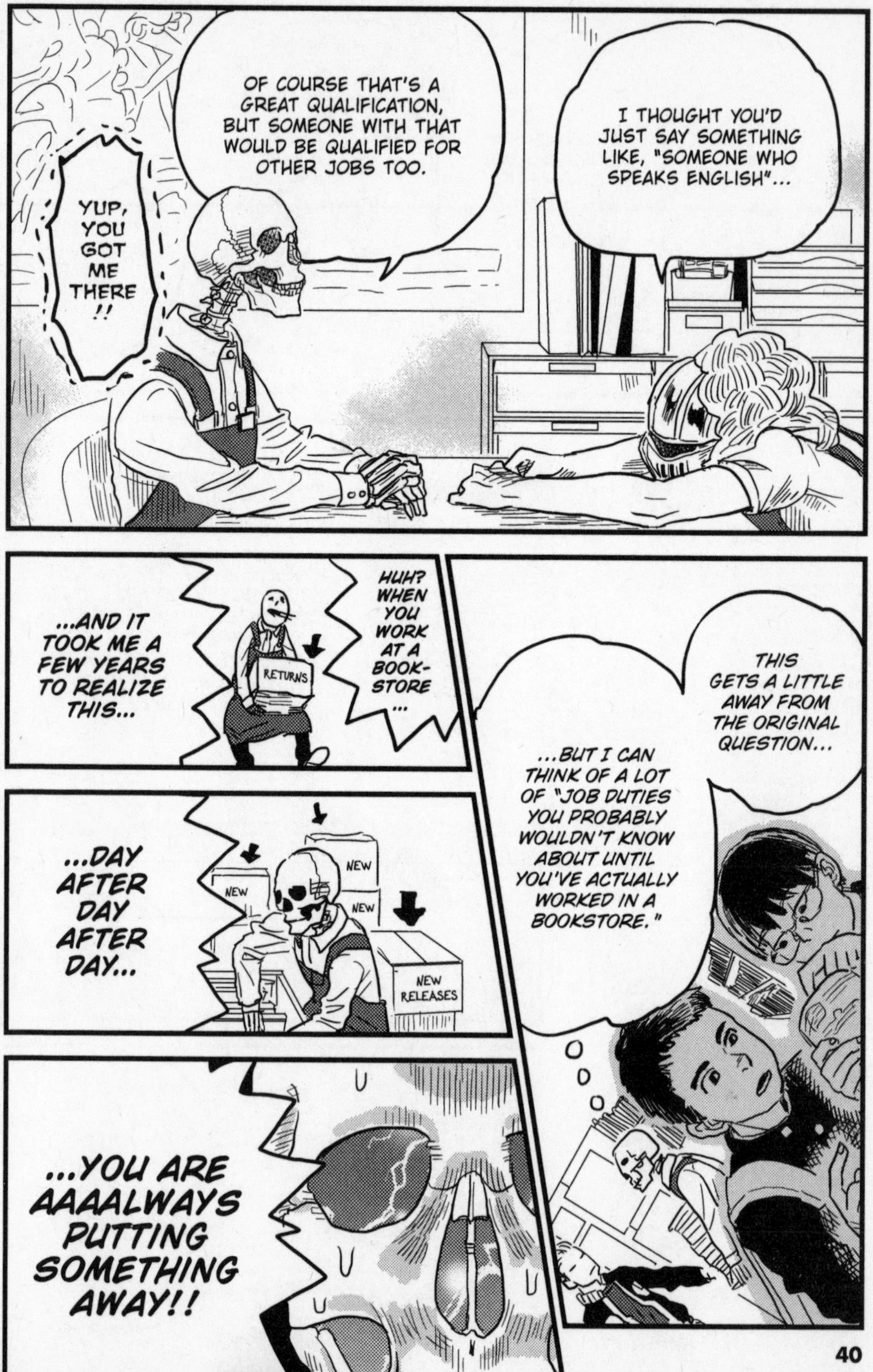
I THOUGHT YOU'D JUST SAY SOMETHING LIKE, "SOMEONE WHO SPEAKS ENGLISH"...
OF COURSE THAT'S A GREAT QUALIFICATION, BUT SOMEONE WITH THAT WOULD BE QUALIFIED FOR OTHER JOBS TOO.
YUP, YOU GOT ME THERE!!
THIS GETS A LITTLE AWAY FROM THE ORIGINAL QUESTION...
...BUT I CAN THINK OF A LOT OF "JOB DUTIES YOU PROBABLY WOULDN'T KNOW ABOUT UNTIL YOU'VE ACTUALLY WORKED IN A BOOKSTORE."
HUH? WHEN YOU WORK AT A BOOK-STORE...
...AND IT TOOK ME A FEW YEARS TO REALIZE THIS...
RETURNS
...DAY AFTER DAY AFTER DAY...
NEW
NEW
NEW
NEW RELEASES
...YOU ARE AAAALWAYS PUTTING SOMETHING AWAY!!
*VIEWS ARE MY OWN.

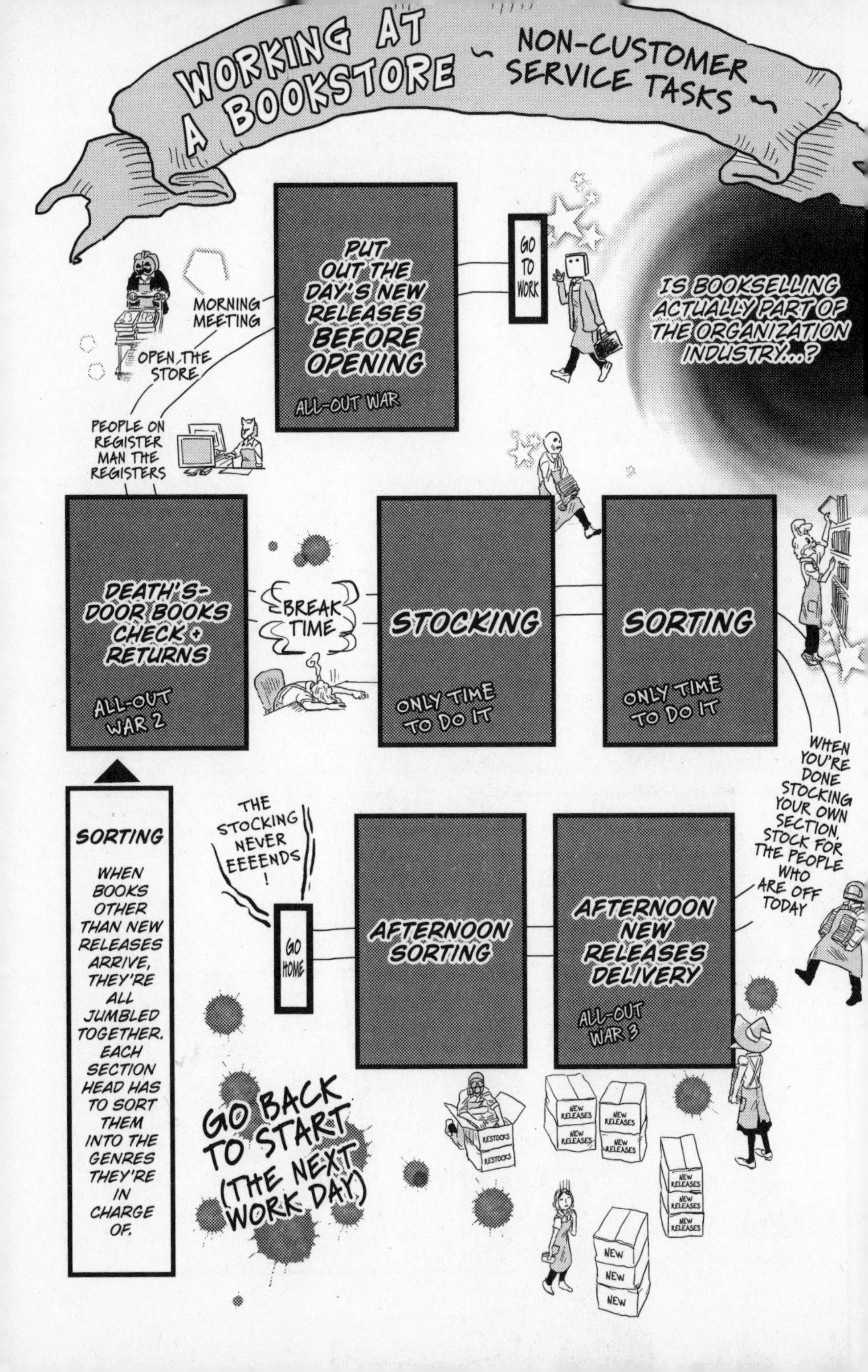
WORKING AT A BOOKSTORE ~ NON-CUSTOMER SERVICE TASKS ~
GO TO WORK
PUT OUT THE DAY'S NEW RELEASES BEFORE OPENING
ALL-OUT WAR
IS BOOKSELLING ACTUALLY PART OF THE ORGANIZATION INDUSTRY...?
MORNING MEETING
OPEN THE STORE
PEOPLE ON REGISTER MAN THE REGISTERS
DEATH'S-DOOR BOOKS CHECK + RETURNS
ALL-OUT WAR 2
BREAK TIME
STOCKING
ONLY TIME TO DO IT
SORTING
ONLY TIME TO DO IT
WHEN YOU'RE DONE STOCKING YOUR OWN SECTION, STOCK FOR THE PEOPLE WHO ARE OFF TODAY
AFTERNOON NEW RELEASES DELIVERY
ALL-OUT WAR 3
AFTERNOON SORTING
GO HOME
THE STOCKING NEVER EEEENDS!
SORTING
WHEN BOOKS OTHER THAN NEW RELEASES ARRIVE, THEY'RE ALL JUMBLED TOGETHER. EACH SECTION HEAD HAS TO SORT THEM INTO THE GENRES THEY'RE IN CHARGE OF.
GO BACK TO START (THE NEXT WORK DAY)
RESTOCKS
RESTOCKS
NEW RELEASES
NEW RELEASES
NEW RELEASES
NEW RELEASES
NEW RELEASES
NEW RELEASES
NEW RELEASES
NEW
NEW
NEW

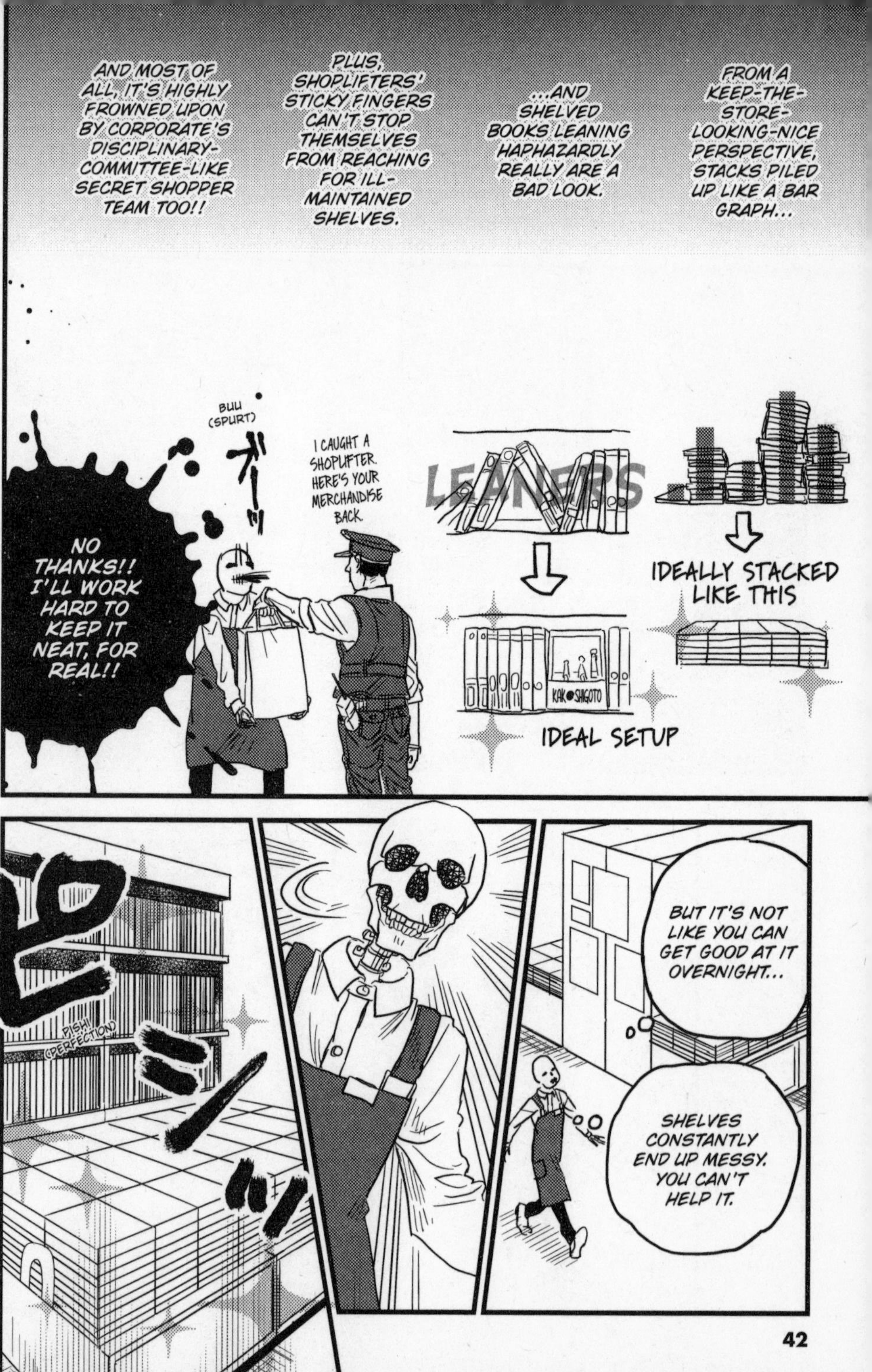
FROM A KEEP-THE-STORE-LOOKING-NICE PERSPECTIVE, STACKS PILED UP LIKE A BAR GRAPH...
...AND SHELVED BOOKS LEANING HAPHAZARDLY REALLY ARE A BAD LOOK.
PLUS, SHOPLIFTERS' STICKY FINGERS CAN'T STOP THEMSELVES FROM REACHING FOR ILL-MAINTAINED SHELVES.
AND MOST OF ALL, IT'S HIGHLY FROWNED UPON BY CORPORATE'S DISCIPLINARY-COMMITTEE-LIKE SECRET SHOPPER TEAM TOO!!
IDEALLY STACKED LIKE THIS
LEANERS
IDEAL SETUP
KAK●SHIGOTO
I CAUGHT A SHOPLIFTER. HERE'S YOUR MERCHANDISE BACK.
BUU (SPURT)
NO THANKS!! I'LL WORK HARD TO KEEP IT NEAT, FOR REAL!!
BUT IT'S NOT LIKE YOU CAN GET GOOD AT IT OVERNIGHT...
SHELVES CONSTANTLY END UP MESSY. YOU CAN'T HELP IT.
PISHI (PERFECTION)

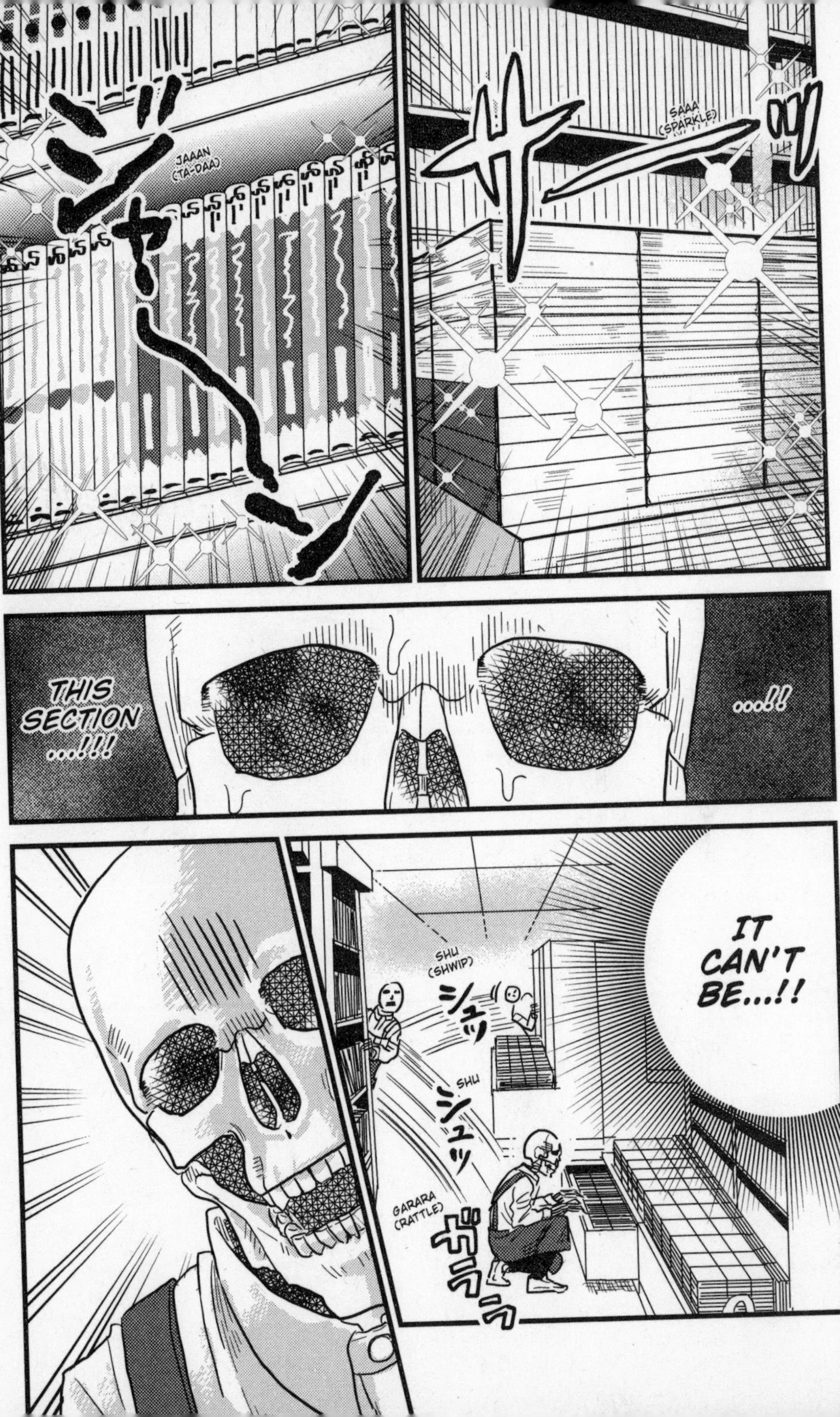
SAAA (SPARKLE)
JAAAN (TA-DAA)
...!!
THIS SECTION ...!!!
IT CAN'T BE...!!
SHU (SHWIP)
SHU
GARARA (RATTLE)

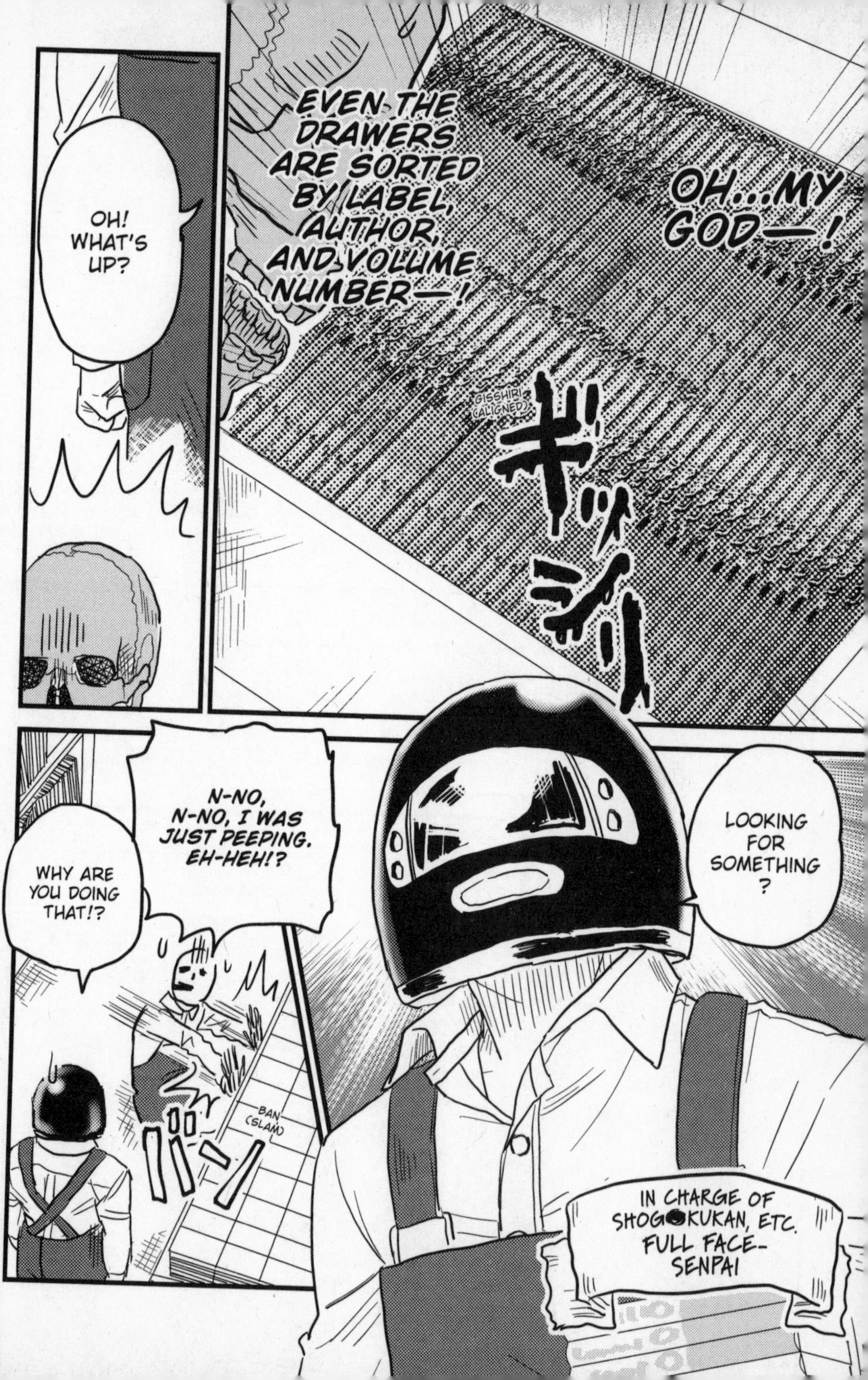
EVEN THE DRAWERS ARE SORTED BY LABEL, AUTHOR, AND VOLUME NUMBER—!
OH...MY GOD—!
GISSHIRI (ALIGNED)
ギッシリ
OH! WHAT'S UP?
LOOKING FOR SOMETHING?
IN CHARGE OF SHOGOKUKAN, ETC. FULL FACE-SENPAI
N-NO, N-NO, I WAS JUST PEEPING. EH-HEH!?
WHY ARE YOU DOING THAT!?
BAN (SLAM)

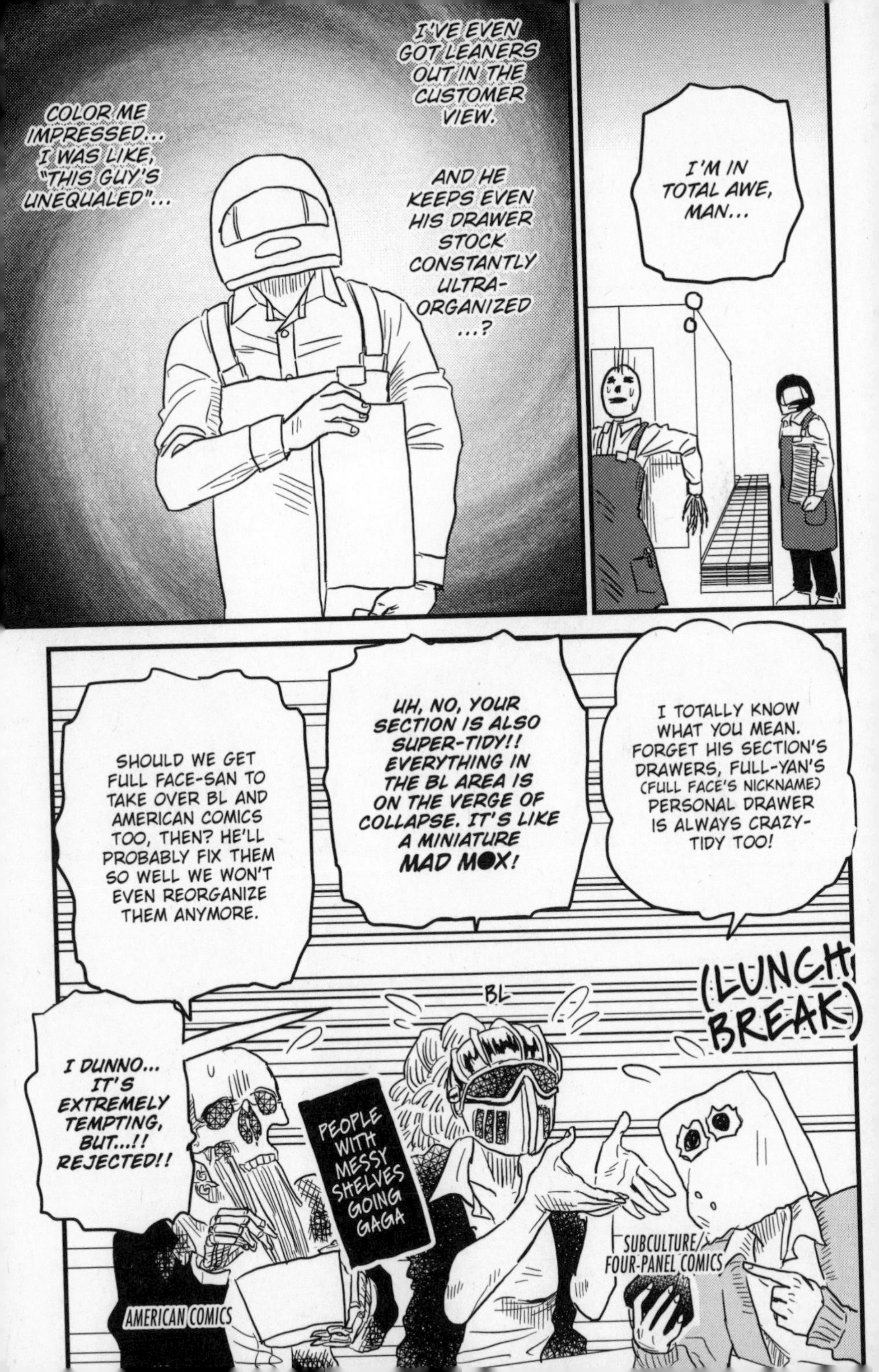
I'M IN TOTAL AWE, MAN...
I'VE EVEN GOT LEANERS OUT IN THE CUSTOMER VIEW.
AND HE KEEPS EVEN HIS DRAWER STOCK CONSTANTLY ULTRA-ORGANIZED ...?
COLOR ME IMPRESSED... I WAS LIKE, "THIS GUY'S UNEQUALED"...
I TOTALLY KNOW WHAT YOU MEAN. FORGET HIS SECTION'S DRAWERS, FULL-YAN'S (FULL FACE'S NICKNAME) PERSONAL DRAWER IS ALWAYS CRAZY-TIDY TOO!
UH, NO, YOUR SECTION IS ALSO SUPER-TIDY!! EVERYTHING IN THE BL AREA IS ON THE VERGE OF COLLAPSE. IT'S LIKE A MINIATURE MAD M●X!
SHOULD WE GET FULL FACE-SAN TO TAKE OVER BL AND AMERICAN COMICS TOO, THEN? HE'LL PROBABLY FIX THEM SO WELL WE WON'T EVEN REORGANIZE THEM ANYMORE.
(LUNCH BREAK)
BL
SUBCULTURE/FOUR-PANEL COMICS
I DUNNO... IT'S EXTREMELY TEMPTING, BUT...!! REJECTED!!
PEOPLE WITH MESSY SHELVES GOING GAGA
AMERICAN COMICS

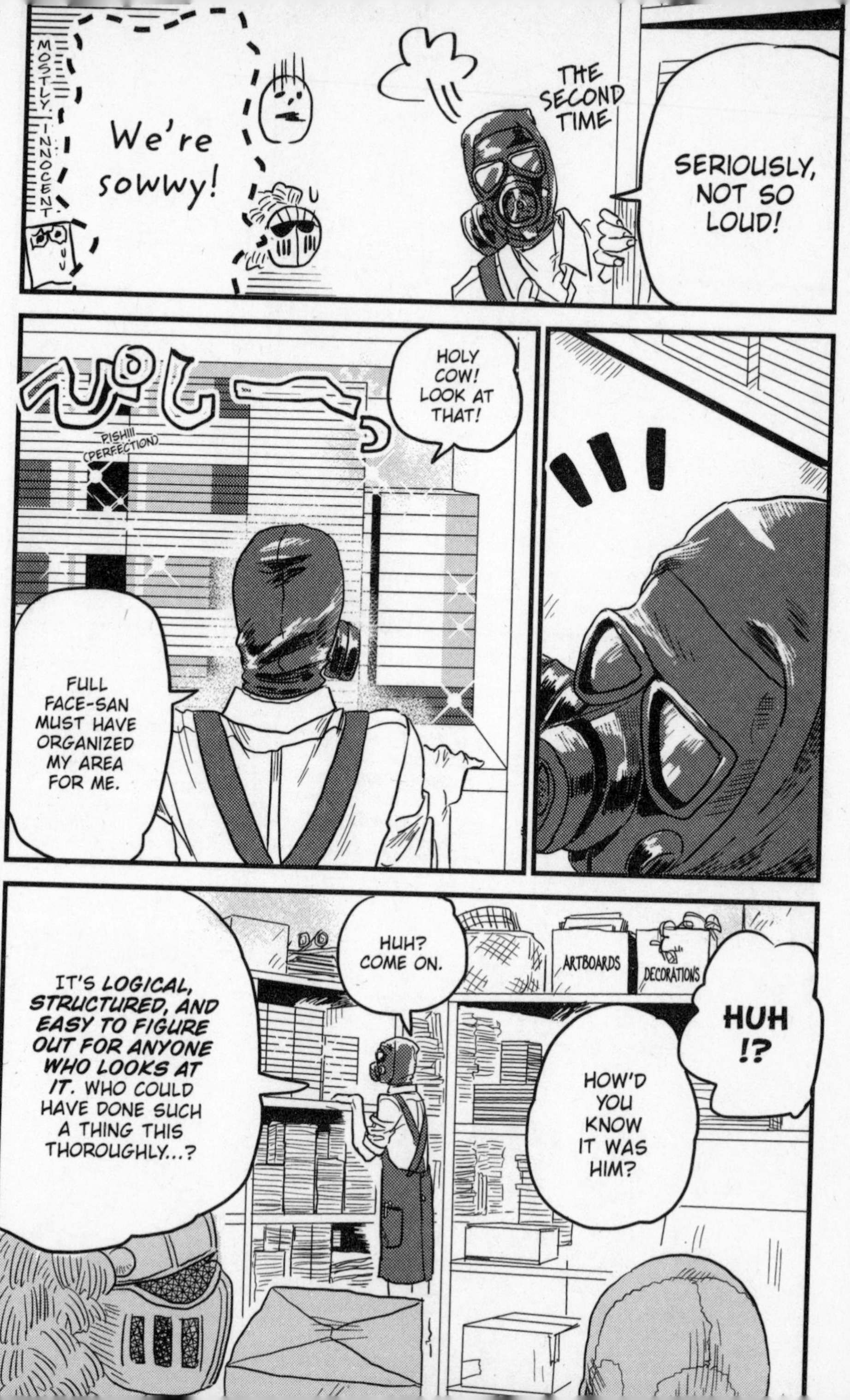
SERIOUSLY, NOT SO LOUD!
THE SECOND TIME
We're sowwy!
MOSTLY INNOCENT
HOLY COW! LOOK AT THAT!
PISHIII (PERFECTION)
FULL FACE-SAN MUST HAVE ORGANIZED MY AREA FOR ME.
ARTBOARDS
DECORATIONS
HUH!?
HOW'D YOU KNOW IT WAS HIM?
HUH? COME ON.
IT'S *LOGICAL, STRUCTURED, AND EASY TO FIGURE OUT FOR ANYONE WHO LOOKS AT IT*. WHO COULD HAVE DONE SUCH A THING THIS THOROUGHLY...?

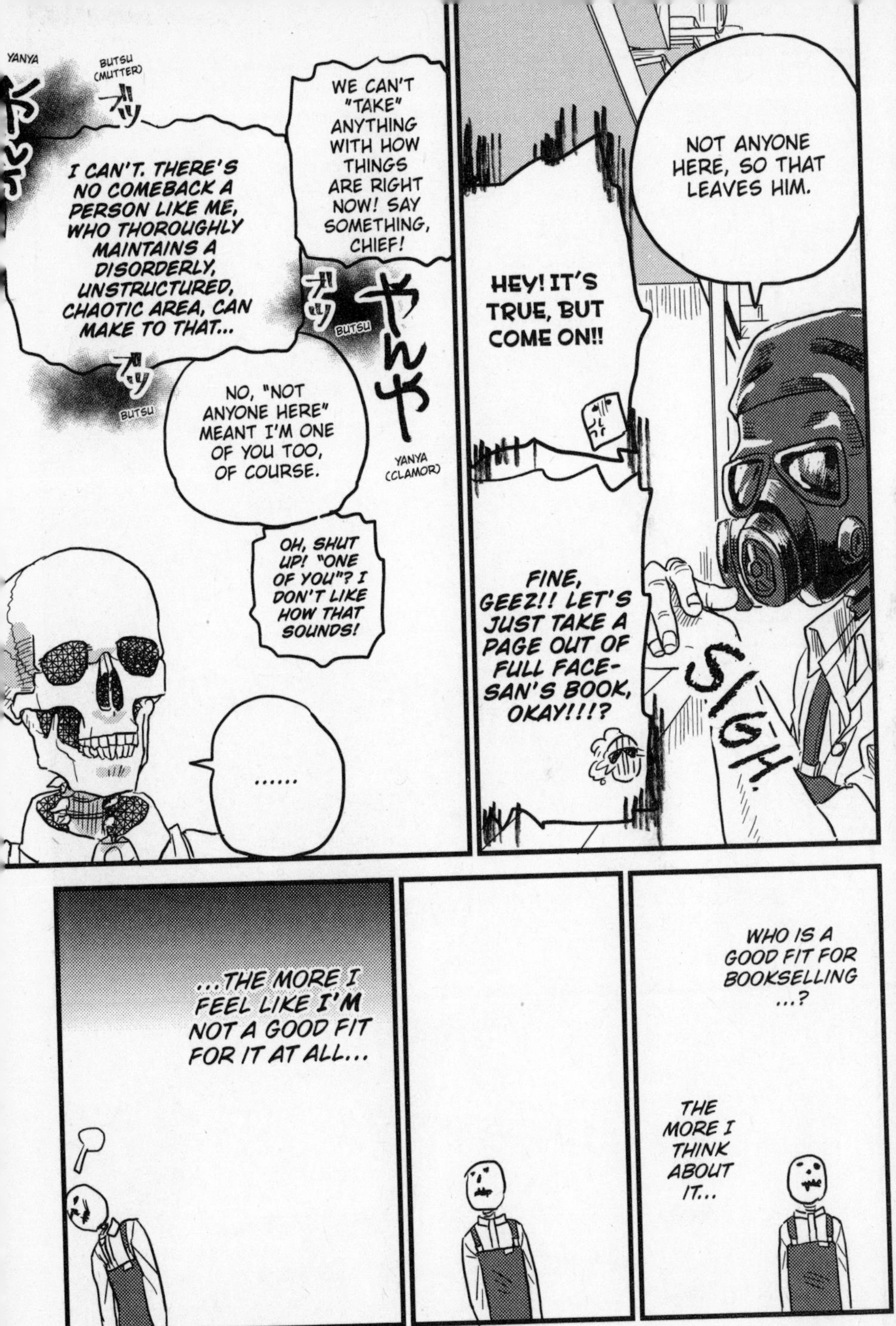
NOT ANYONE HERE, SO THAT LEAVES HIM.
HEY! IT'S TRUE, BUT COME ON!!
FINE, GEEZ!! LET'S JUST TAKE A PAGE OUT OF FULL FACE-SAN'S BOOK, OKAY!!!?
SIGH.
WE CAN'T "TAKE" ANYTHING WITH HOW THINGS ARE RIGHT NOW! SAY SOMETHING, CHIEF!
BUTSU (MUTTER)
YANYA
I CAN'T. THERE'S NO COMEBACK A PERSON LIKE ME, WHO THOROUGHLY MAINTAINS A DISORDERLY, UNSTRUCTURED, CHAOTIC AREA, CAN MAKE TO THAT...
BUTSU
YANYA (CLAMOR)
BUTSU
NO, "NOT ANYONE HERE" MEANT I'M ONE OF YOU TOO, OF COURSE.
OH, SHUT UP! "ONE OF YOU"? I DON'T LIKE HOW THAT SOUNDS!
......
WHO IS A GOOD FIT FOR BOOKSELLING ...?
THE MORE I THINK ABOUT IT...
...THE MORE I FEEL LIKE I'M NOT A GOOD FIT FOR IT AT ALL...

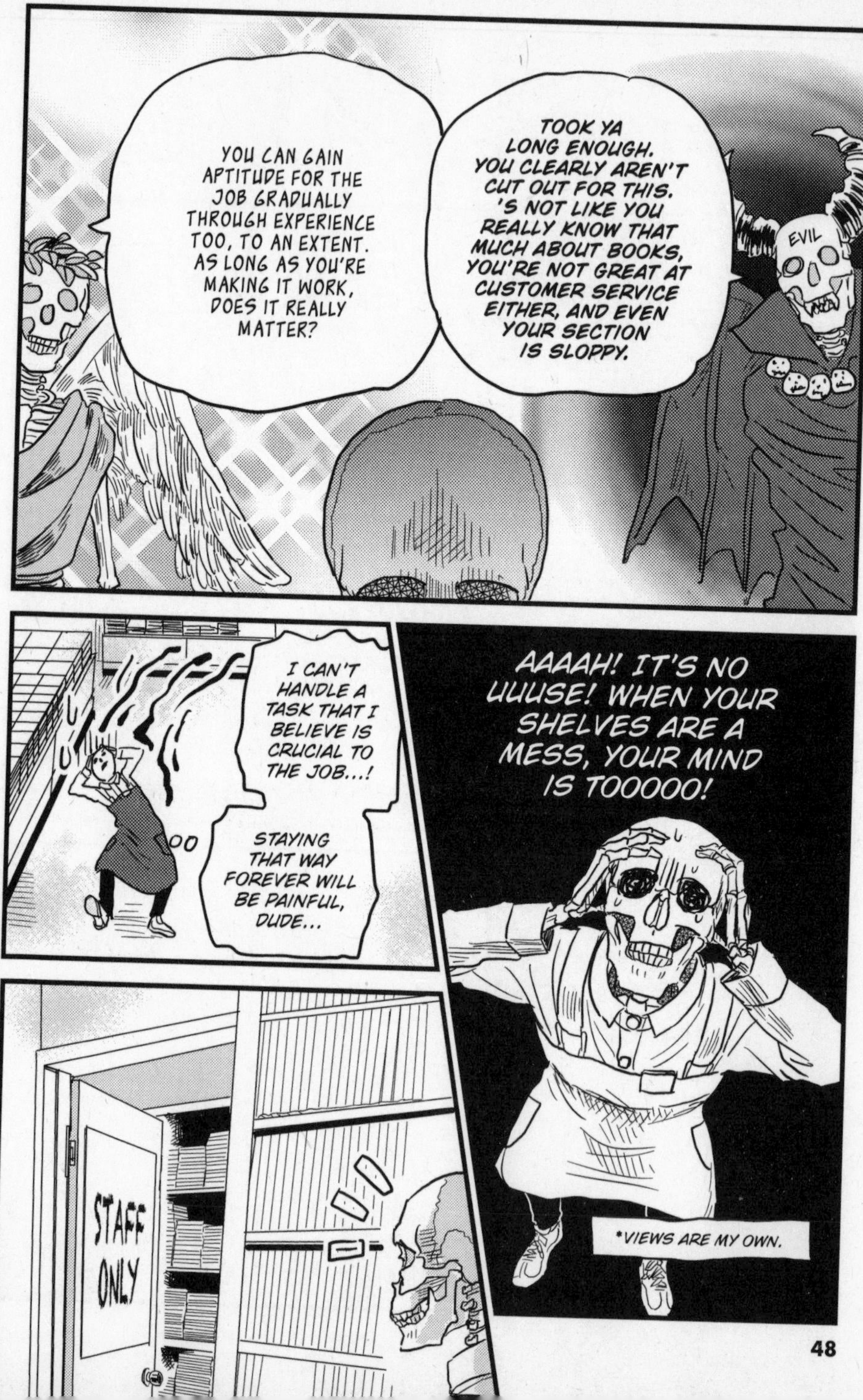
TOOK YA LONG ENOUGH. YOU CLEARLY AREN'T CUT OUT FOR THIS. 'S NOT LIKE YOU REALLY KNOW THAT MUCH ABOUT BOOKS, YOU'RE NOT GREAT AT CUSTOMER SERVICE EITHER, AND EVEN YOUR SECTION IS SLOPPY.
EVIL
YOU CAN GAIN APTITUDE FOR THE JOB GRADUALLY THROUGH EXPERIENCE TOO, TO AN EXTENT. AS LONG AS YOU'RE MAKING IT WORK, DOES IT REALLY MATTER?
AAAAH! IT'S NO UUUSE! WHEN YOUR SHELVES ARE A MESS, YOUR MIND IS TOOOOO!
*VIEWS ARE MY OWN.
I CAN'T HANDLE A TASK THAT I BELIEVE IS CRUCIAL TO THE JOB...!
STAYING THAT WAY FOREVER WILL BE PAINFUL, DUDE...
STAFF ONLY

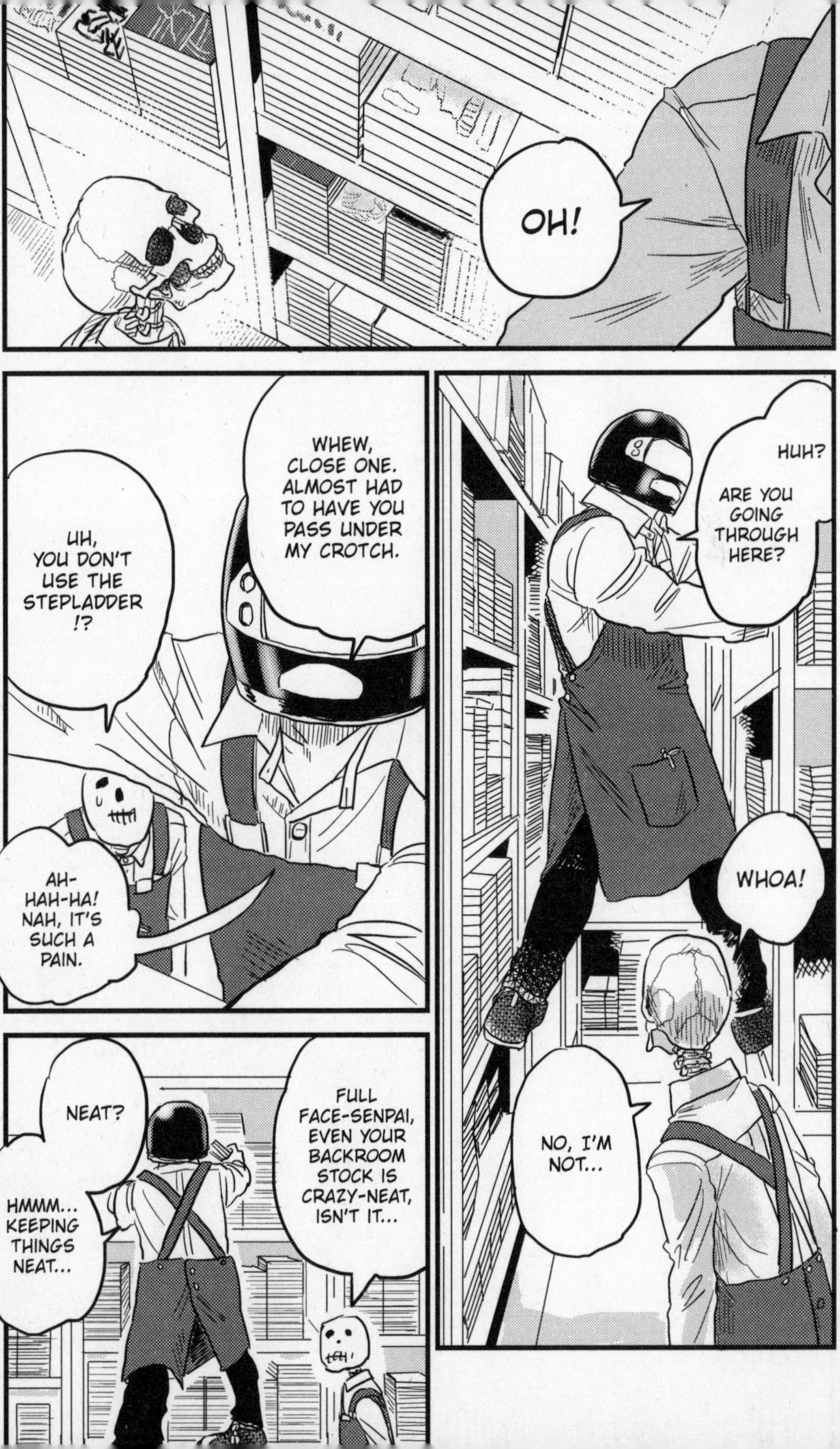
OH!
HUH?
ARE YOU GOING THROUGH HERE?
WHOA!
NO, I'M NOT...
WHEW, CLOSE ONE. ALMOST HAD TO HAVE YOU PASS UNDER MY CROTCH.
UH, YOU DON'T USE THE STEPLADDER !?
AH-HAH-HA! NAH, IT'S SUCH A PAIN.
FULL FACE-SENPAI, EVEN YOUR BACKROOM STOCK IS CRAZY-NEAT, ISN'T IT...
NEAT?
HMMM... KEEPING THINGS NEAT...

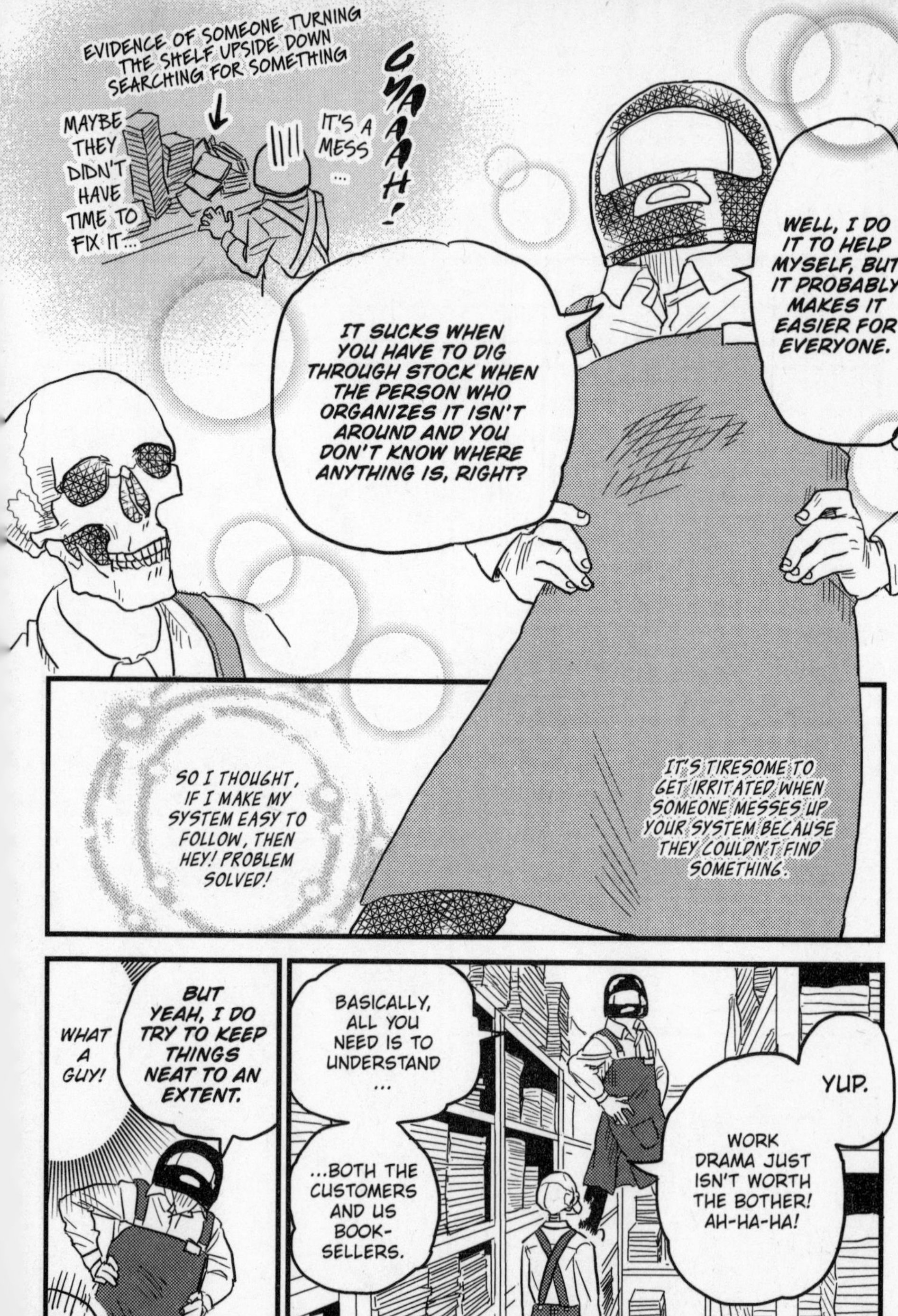
WELL, I DO IT TO HELP MYSELF, BUT IT PROBABLY MAKES IT EASIER FOR EVERYONE.
IT SUCKS WHEN YOU HAVE TO DIG THROUGH STOCK WHEN THE PERSON WHO ORGANIZES IT ISN'T AROUND AND YOU DON'T KNOW WHERE ANYTHING IS, RIGHT?
EVIDENCE OF SOMEONE TURNING THE SHELF UPSIDE DOWN SEARCHING FOR SOMETHING
GYAAAAH!
IT'S A MESS ...
MAYBE THEY DIDN'T HAVE TIME TO FIX IT...
IT'S TIRESOME TO GET IRRITATED WHEN SOMEONE MESSES UP YOUR SYSTEM BECAUSE THEY COULDN'T FIND SOMETHING.
SO I THOUGHT, IF I MAKE MY SYSTEM EASY TO FOLLOW, THEN HEY! PROBLEM SOLVED!
BASICALLY, ALL YOU NEED IS TO UNDERSTAND ...
...BOTH THE CUSTOMERS AND US BOOK-SELLERS.
YUP.
WORK DRAMA JUST ISN'T WORTH THE BOTHER! AH-HA-HA!
BUT YEAH, I DO TRY TO KEEP THINGS NEAT TO AN EXTENT.
WHAT A GUY!

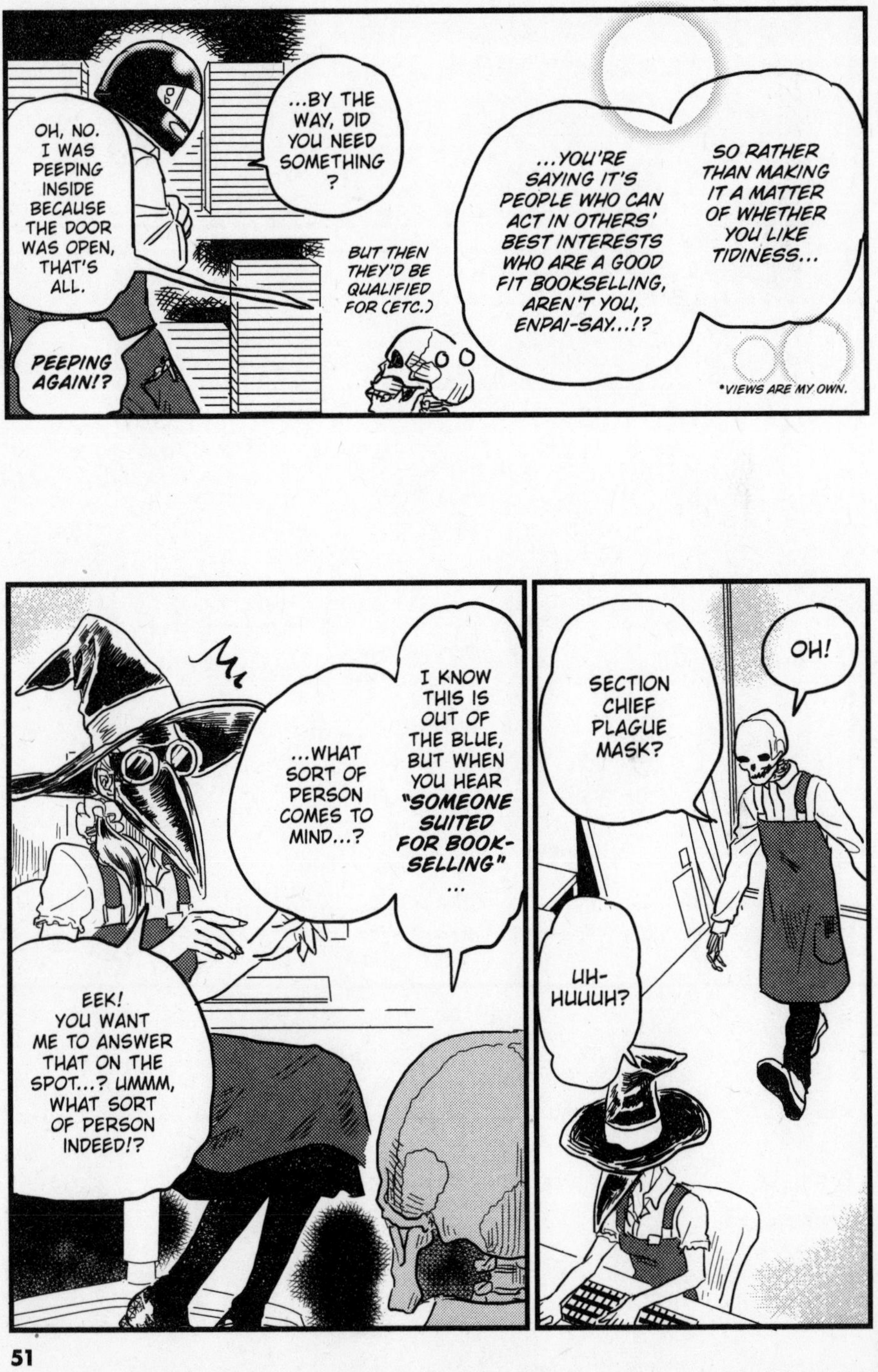
SO RATHER THAN MAKING IT A MATTER OF WHETHER YOU LIKE TIDINESS...
...YOU'RE SAYING IT'S PEOPLE WHO CAN ACT IN OTHERS' BEST INTERESTS WHO ARE A GOOD FIT BOOKSELLING, AREN'T YOU, ENPAI-SAY...!?
BUT THEN THEY'D BE QUALIFIED FOR (ETC.)
...BY THE WAY, DID YOU NEED SOMETHING?
OH, NO. I WAS PEEPING INSIDE BECAUSE THE DOOR WAS OPEN, THAT'S ALL.
PEEPING AGAIN!?
*VIEWS ARE MY OWN.
OH!
SECTION CHIEF PLAGUE MASK?
UH-HUUUH?
I KNOW THIS IS OUT OF THE BLUE, BUT WHEN YOU HEAR "SOMEONE SUITED FOR BOOK-SELLING"...
...WHAT SORT OF PERSON COMES TO MIND...?
EEK! YOU WANT ME TO ANSWER THAT ON THE SPOT...? UMMM, WHAT SORT OF PERSON INDEED!?

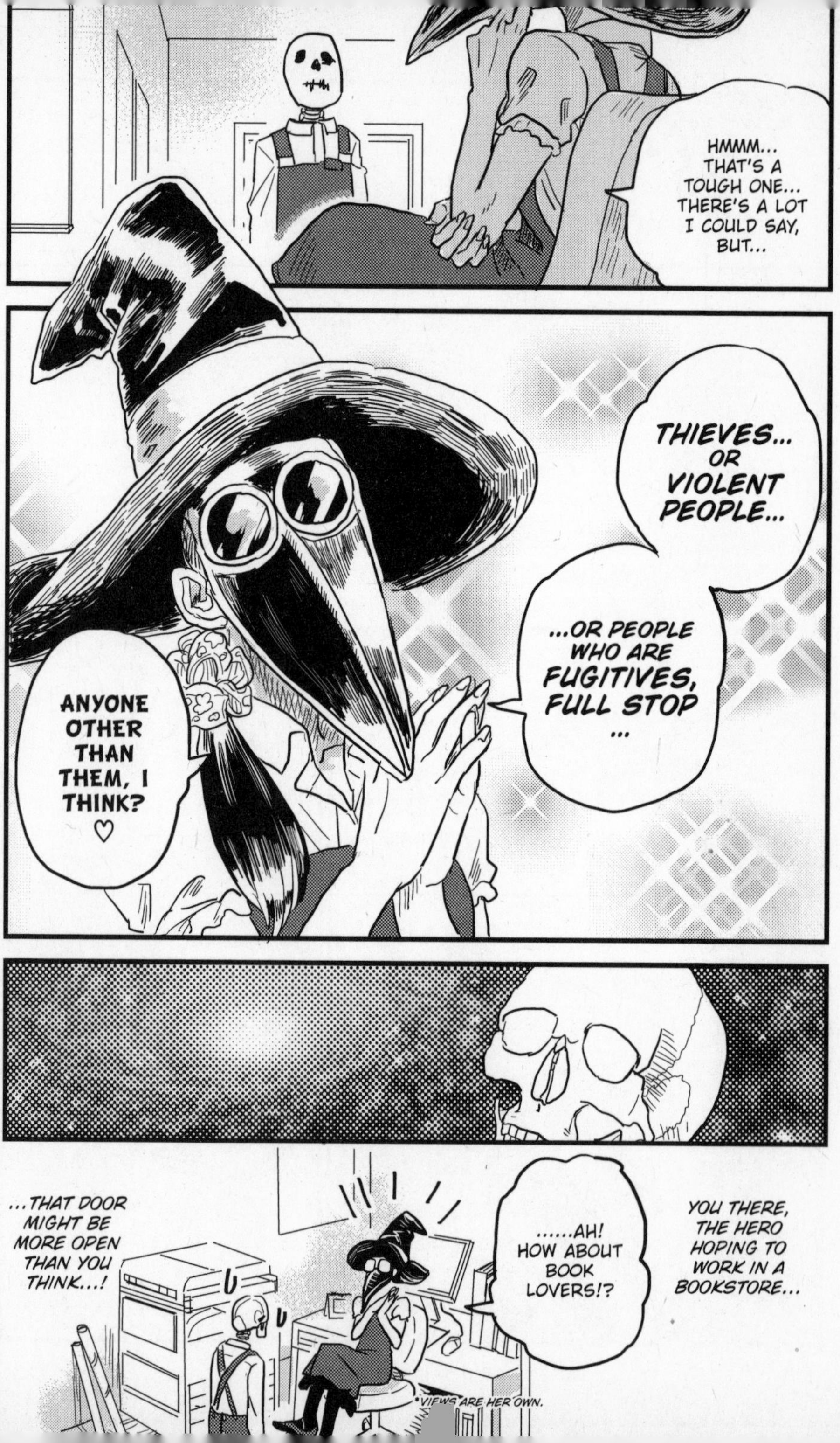
HMMM... THAT'S A TOUGH ONE... THERE'S A LOT I COULD SAY, BUT...
THIEVES... OR VIOLENT PEOPLE...
...OR PEOPLE WHO ARE FUGITIVES, FULL STOP ...
ANYONE OTHER THAN THEM, I THINK? ♡
YOU THERE, THE HERO HOPING TO WORK IN A BOOKSTORE...
......AH! HOW ABOUT BOOK LOVERS!?
...THAT DOOR MIGHT BE MORE OPEN THAN YOU THINK...!
*VIEWS ARE HER OWN.

Skull-face
Bookseller
Honda-san

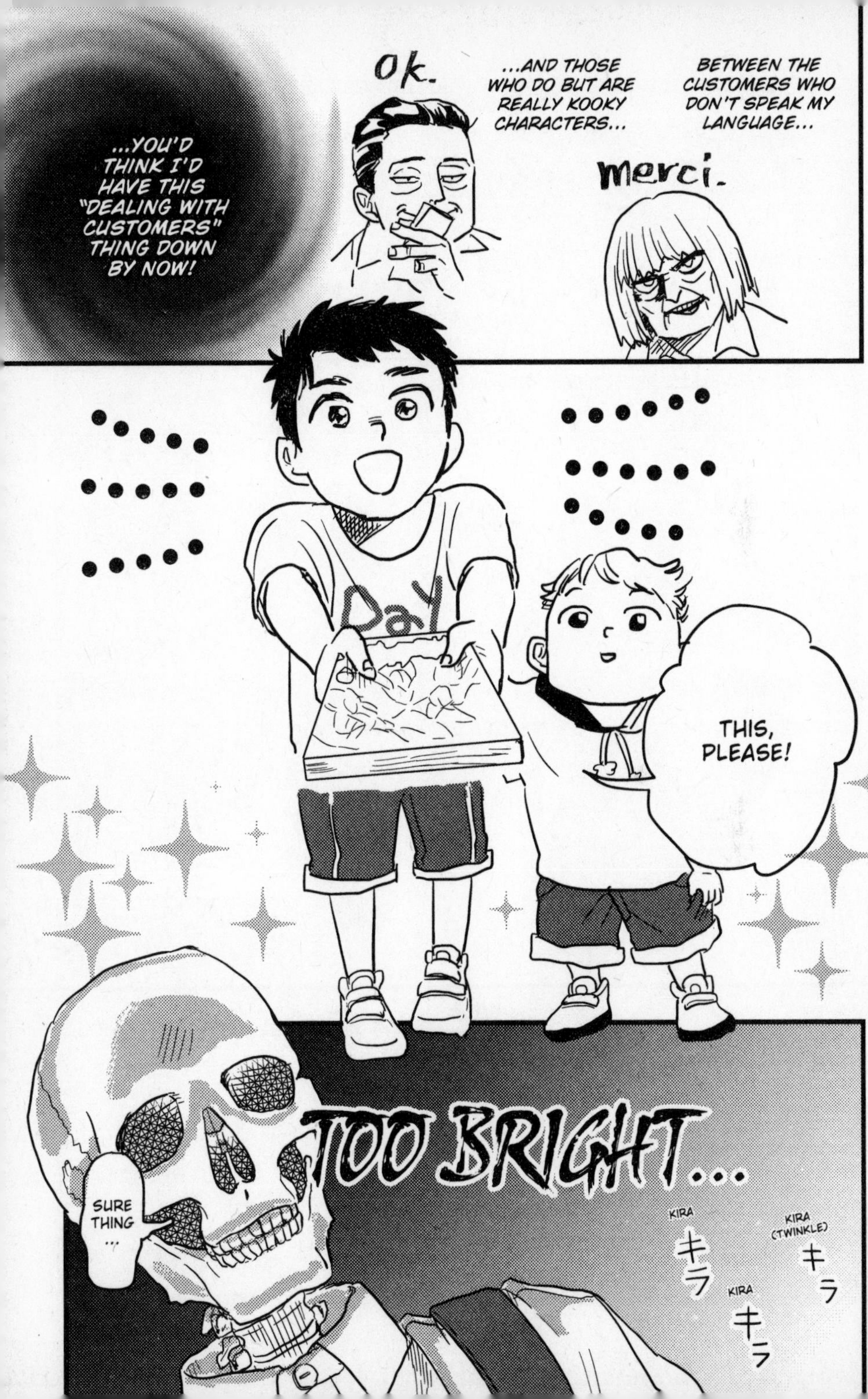
BETWEEN THE CUSTOMERS WHO DON'T SPEAK MY LANGUAGE...
merci.
...AND THOSE WHO DO BUT ARE REALLY KOOKY CHARACTERS...
ok.
...YOU'D THINK I'D HAVE THIS "DEALING WITH CUSTOMERS" THING DOWN BY NOW!
....
....
THIS, PLEASE!
KIRA キラ
KIRA (TWINKLE) キラ
KIRA キラ
TOO BRIGHT...
SURE THING ...

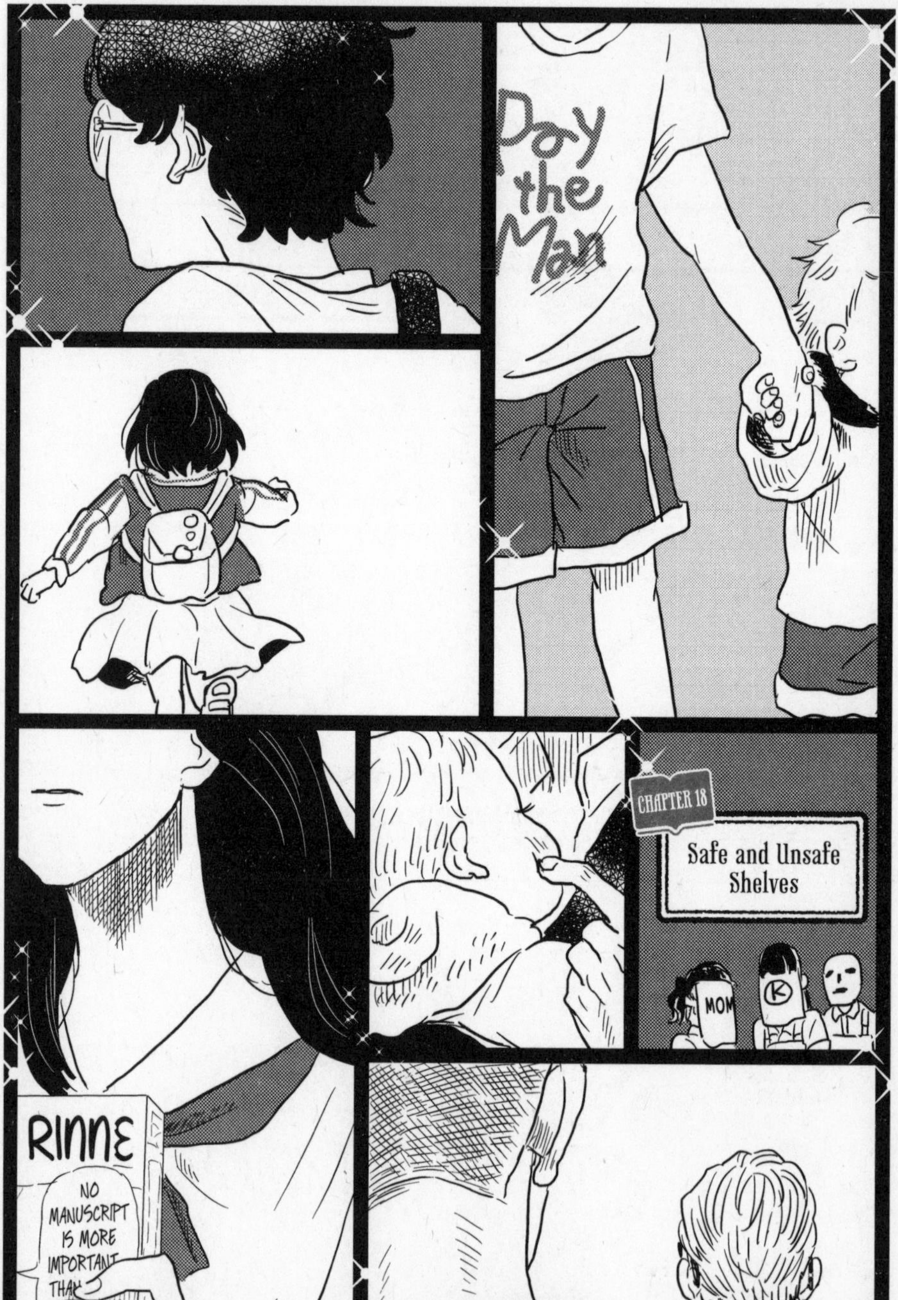
Day the Man
CHAPTER 18
Safe and Unsafe Shelves
MOM
K
RINNE
NO MANUSCRIPT IS MORE IMPORTANT THAN BIG BOOBS

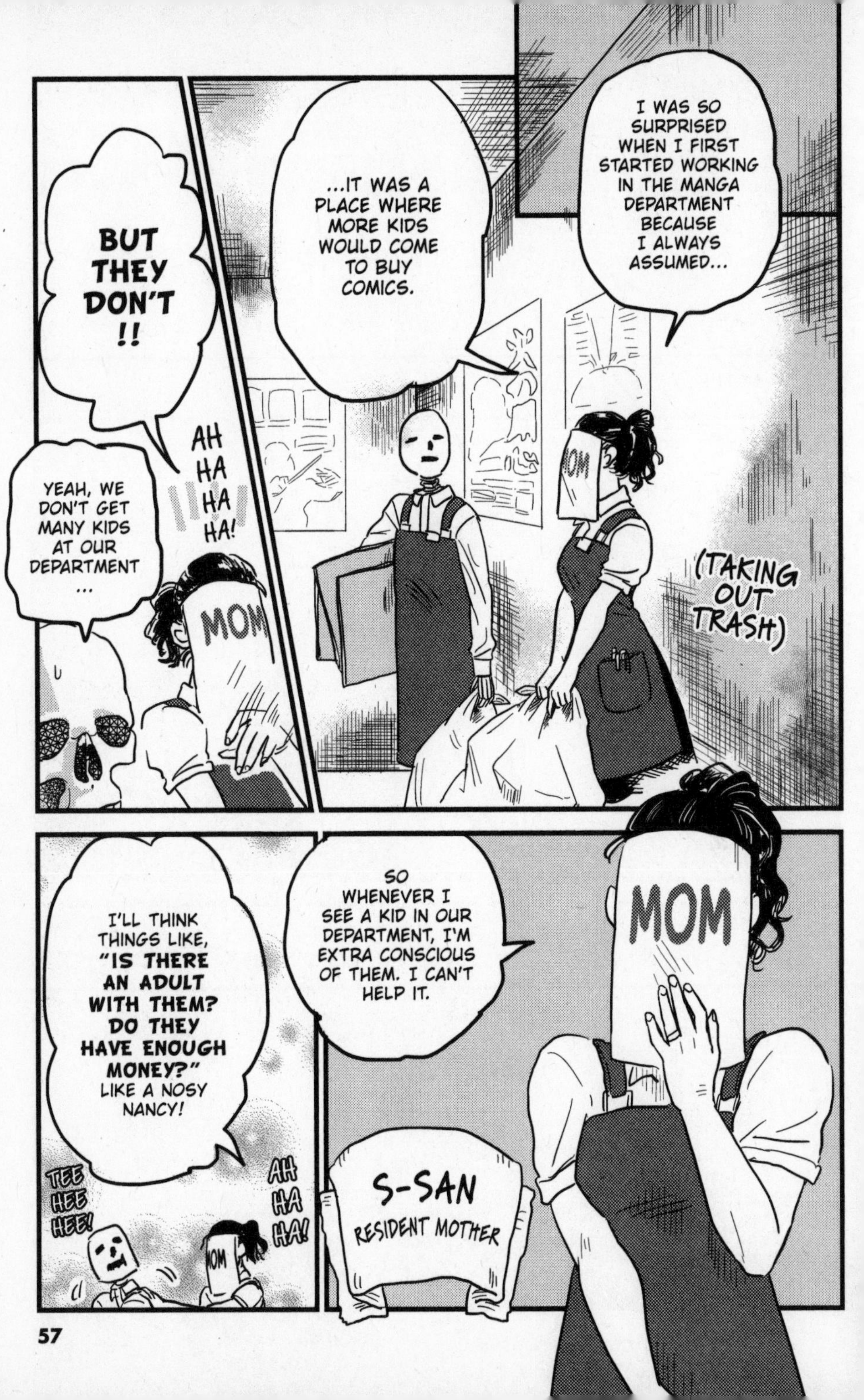
I WAS SO SURPRISED WHEN I FIRST STARTED WORKING IN THE MANGA DEPARTMENT BECAUSE I ALWAYS ASSUMED...
...IT WAS A PLACE WHERE MORE KIDS WOULD COME TO BUY COMICS.
MOM
(TAKING OUT TRASH)
BUT THEY DON'T!!
AH HA HA HA!
YEAH, WE DON'T GET MANY KIDS AT OUR DEPARTMENT...
MOM
SO WHENEVER I SEE A KID IN OUR DEPARTMENT, I'M EXTRA CONSCIOUS OF THEM. I CAN'T HELP IT.
MOM
S-SAN
RESIDENT MOTHER
I'LL THINK THINGS LIKE, "IS THERE AN ADULT WITH THEM? DO THEY HAVE ENOUGH MONEY?" LIKE A NOSY NANCY!
AH HA HA!
MOM
TEE HEE HEE!

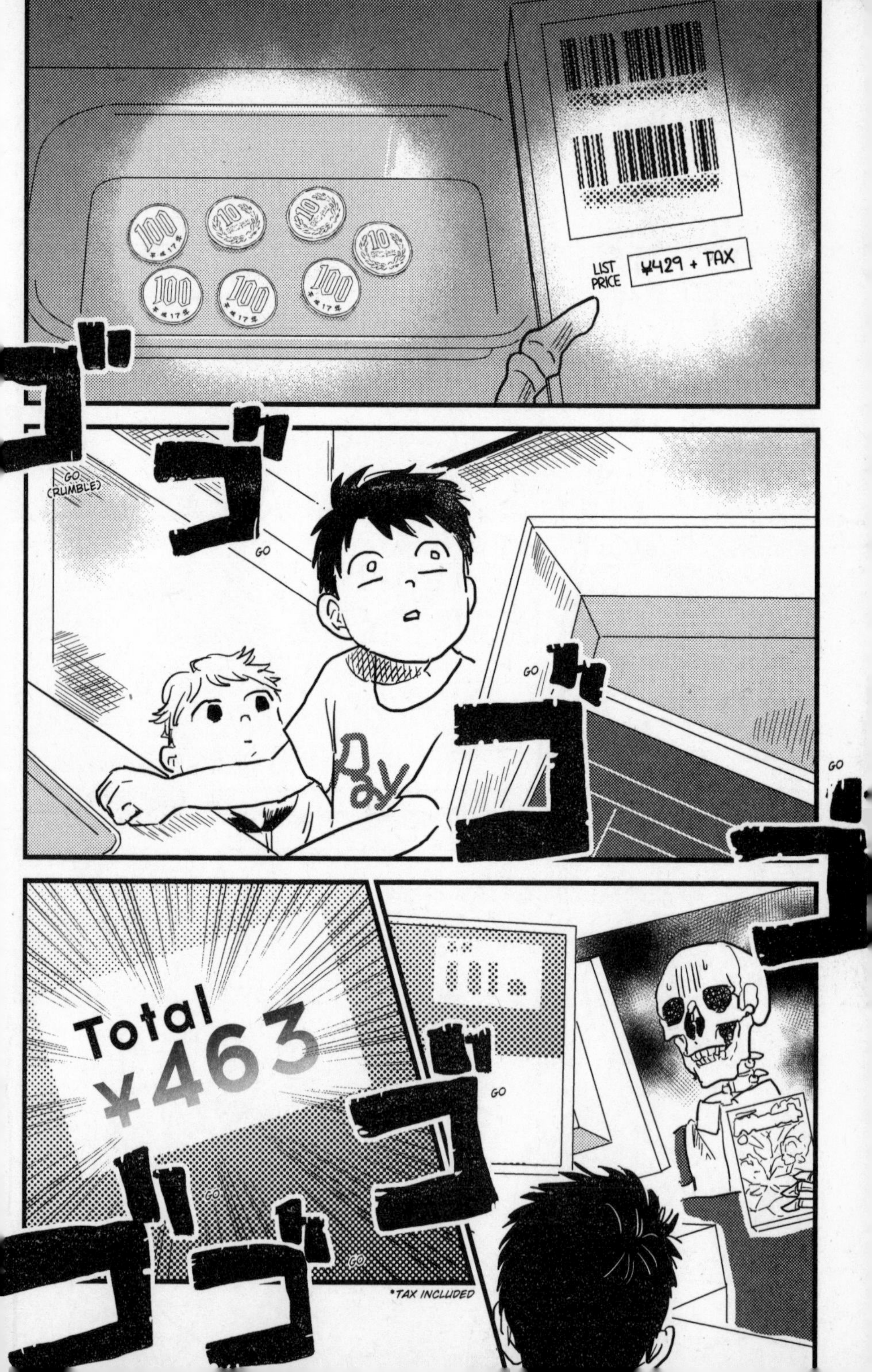
LIST PRICE
¥429 + TAX
ゴ
ゴ
GO (RUMBLE)
GO
ゴ
GO
ゴ
GO
ゴ
GO
ゴ
GO
GO
Total ¥463
*TAX INCLUDED

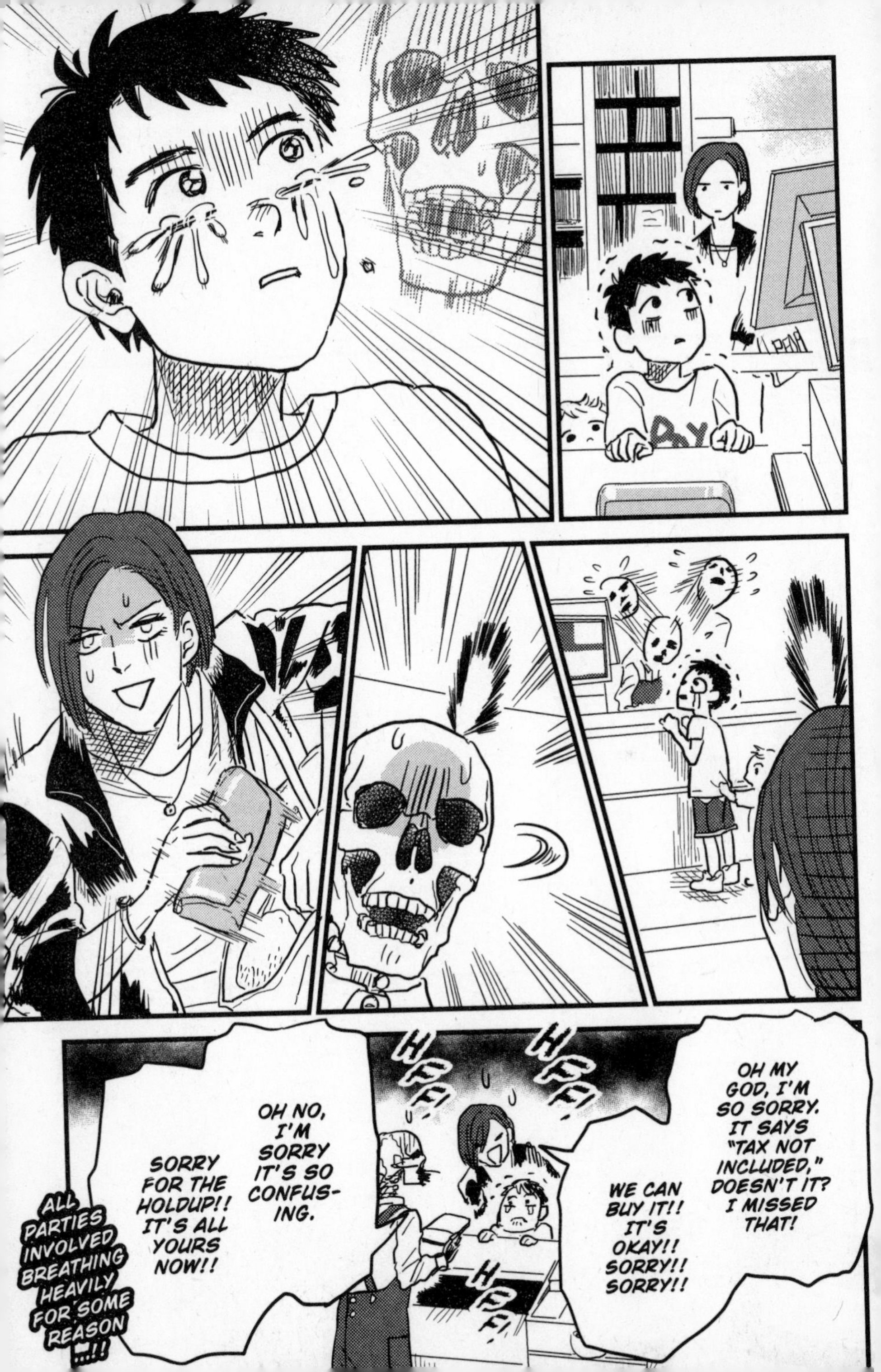
OH MY GOD, I'M SO SORRY. IT SAYS "TAX NOT INCLUDED," DOESN'T IT? I MISSED THAT!
WE CAN BUY IT!! IT'S OKAY!! SORRY!! SORRY!!
HFF! HFF!
HFF!
OH NO, I'M SORRY IT'S SO CONFUS-ING.
SORRY FOR THE HOLDUP!! IT'S ALL YOURS NOW!!
ALL PARTIES INVOLVED BREATHING HEAVILY FOR SOME REASON…!!

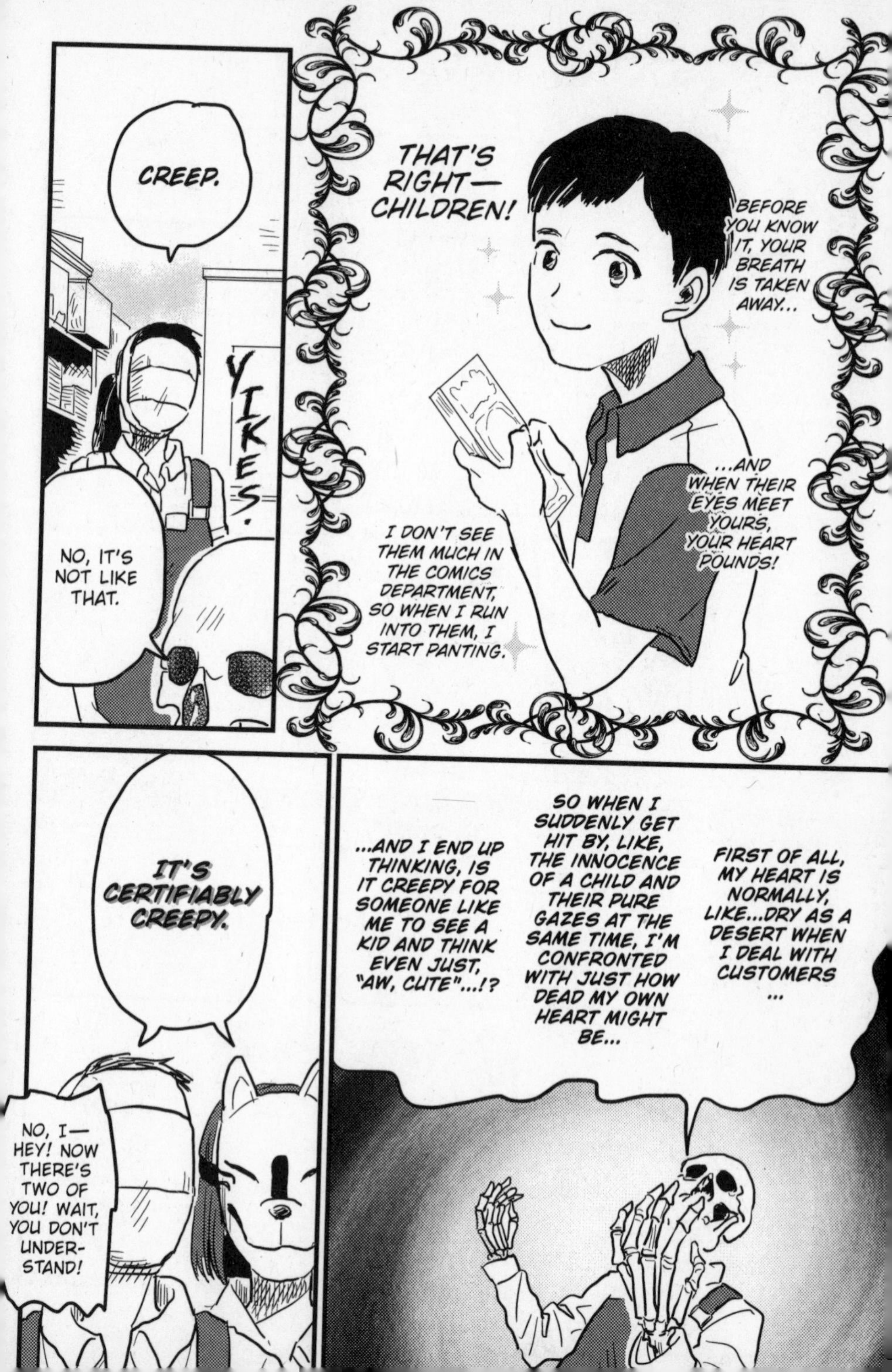

BEFORE YOU KNOW IT, YOUR BREATH IS TAKEN AWAY...
THAT'S RIGHT—CHILDREN!
...AND WHEN THEIR EYES MEET YOURS, YOUR HEART POUNDS!
I DON'T SEE THEM MUCH IN THE COMICS DEPARTMENT, SO WHEN I RUN INTO THEM, I START PANTING.
CREEP.
YIKES.
NO, IT'S NOT LIKE THAT.
FIRST OF ALL, MY HEART IS NORMALLY, LIKE...DRY AS A DESERT WHEN I DEAL WITH CUSTOMERS ...
SO WHEN I SUDDENLY GET HIT BY, LIKE, THE INNOCENCE OF A CHILD AND THEIR PURE GAZES AT THE SAME TIME, I'M CONFRONTED WITH JUST HOW DEAD MY OWN HEART MIGHT BE...
...AND I END UP THINKING, IS IT CREEPY FOR SOMEONE LIKE ME TO SEE A KID AND THINK EVEN JUST, "AW, CUTE"...!?
IT'S CERTIFIABLY CREEPY.
NO, I— HEY! NOW THERE'S TWO OF YOU! WAIT, YOU DON'T UNDER-STAND!

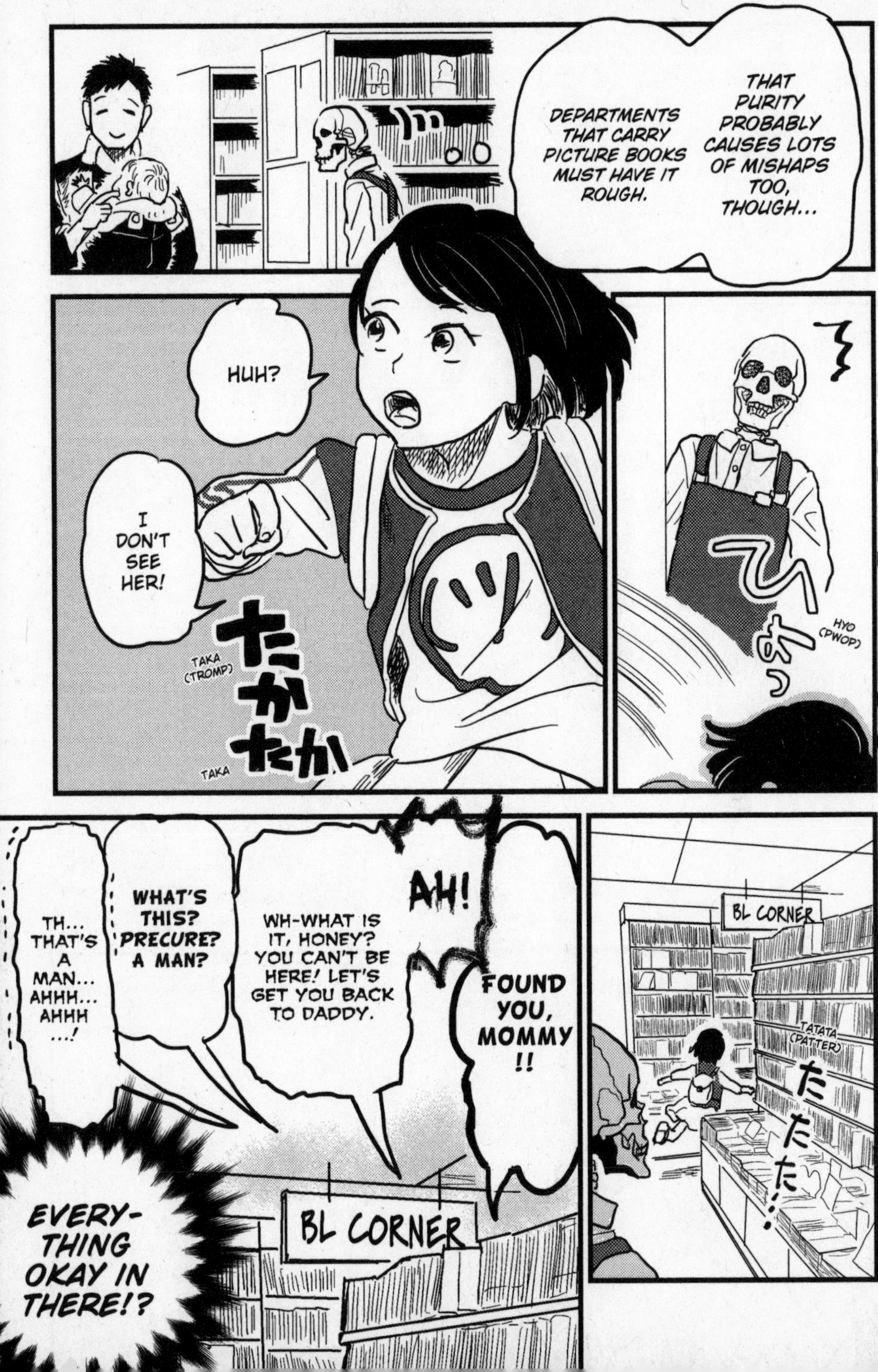
DEPARTMENTS THAT CARRY PICTURE BOOKS MUST HAVE IT ROUGH.
THAT PURITY PROBABLY CAUSES LOTS OF MISHAPS TOO, THOUGH...
HYO (PWOP)
HUH?
I DON'T SEE HER!
TAKA (TROMP)
TAKA
BL CORNER
TATATA (PATTER)
FOUND YOU, MOMMY!!
AH!
WH-WHAT IS IT, HONEY? YOU CAN'T BE HERE! LET'S GET YOU BACK TO DADDY.
WHAT'S THIS? PRECURE? A MAN?
TH... THAT'S A MAN... AHHH... AHHH...!
BL CORNER
EVERY-THING OKAY IN THERE!?

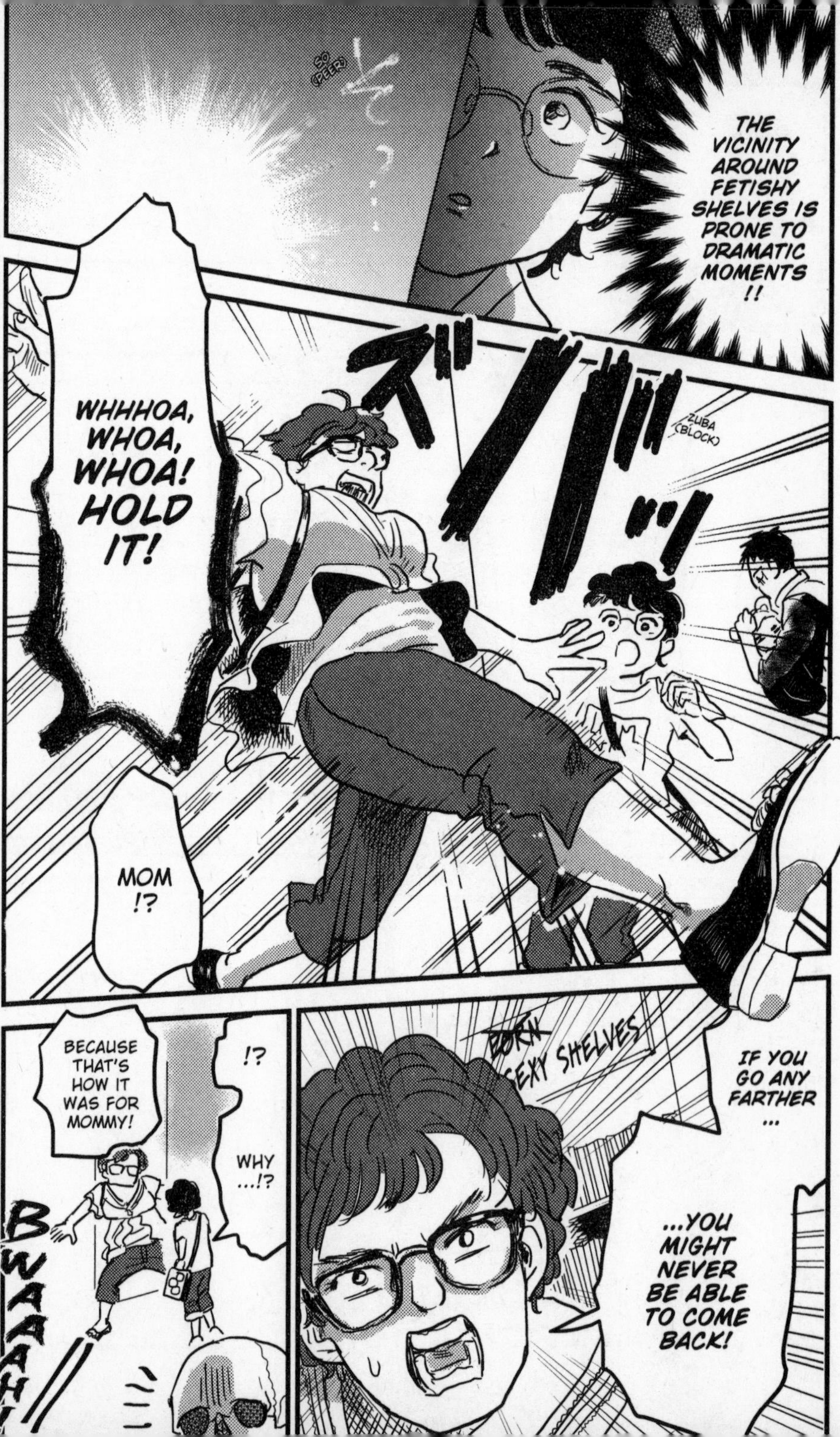
THE VICINITY AROUND FETISHY SHELVES IS PRONE TO DRAMATIC MOMENTS !!
SO (PEER)
ZUBA (BLOCK)
WHHHOA, WHOA, WHOA! HOLD IT!
MOM !?
PORN SEXY SHELVES
IF YOU GO ANY FARTHER ...
...YOU MIGHT NEVER BE ABLE TO COME BACK!
!?
WHY ...!?
BECAUSE THAT'S HOW IT WAS FOR MOMMY!
BWAAAAH!!

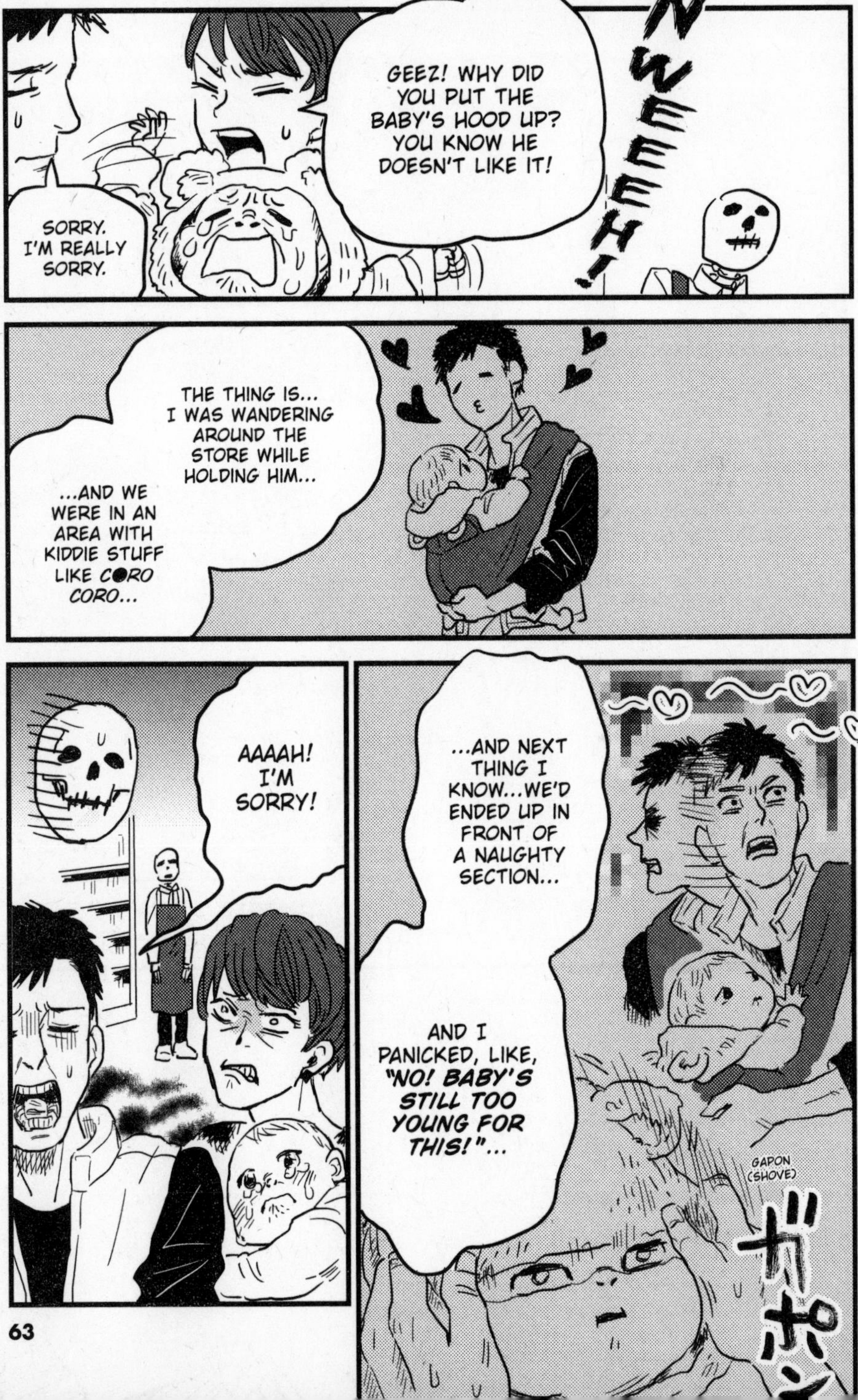
NWEEEH!
GEEZ! WHY DID YOU PUT THE BABY'S HOOD UP? YOU KNOW HE DOESN'T LIKE IT!
SORRY. I'M REALLY SORRY.
THE THING IS... I WAS WANDERING AROUND THE STORE WHILE HOLDING HIM...
...AND WE WERE IN AN AREA WITH KIDDIE STUFF LIKE *C●RO CORO*...
...AND NEXT THING I KNOW...WE'D ENDED UP IN FRONT OF A NAUGHTY SECTION...
AND I PANICKED, LIKE, *"NO! BABY'S STILL TOO YOUNG FOR THIS!"*...
GAPON (SHOVE)
ガポン
AAAAH! I'M SORRY!

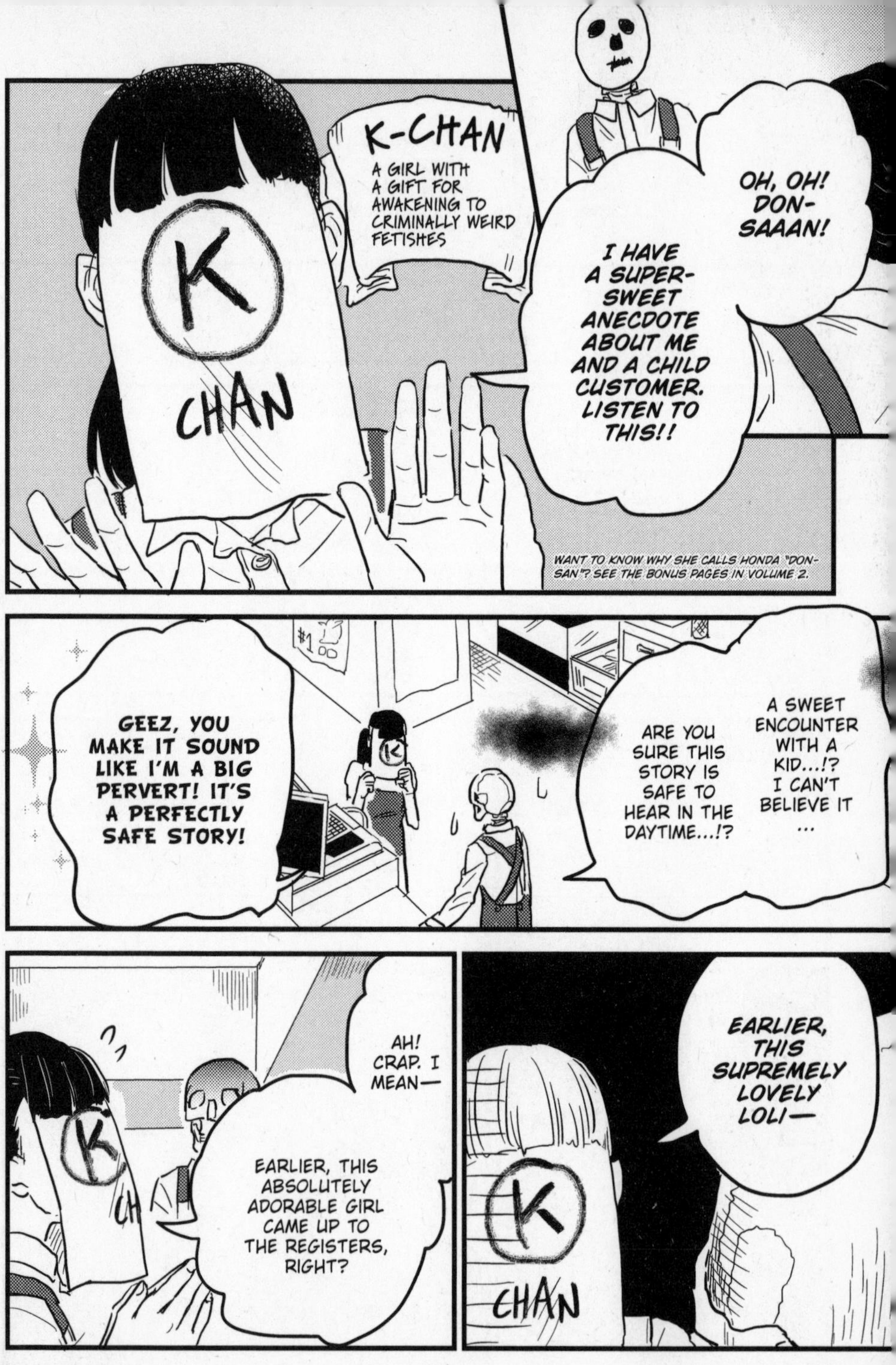
OH, OH! DON-SAAAN!
I HAVE A SUPER-SWEET ANECDOTE ABOUT ME AND A CHILD CUSTOMER. LISTEN TO THIS!!
K-CHAN
A GIRL WITH A GIFT FOR AWAKENING TO CRIMINALLY WEIRD FETISHES
K CHAN
WANT TO KNOW WHY SHE CALLS HONDA "DON-SAN"? SEE THE BONUS PAGES IN VOLUME 2.
A SWEET ENCOUNTER WITH A KID...!? I CAN'T BELIEVE IT ...
ARE YOU SURE THIS STORY IS SAFE TO HEAR IN THE DAYTIME...!?
GEEZ, YOU MAKE IT SOUND LIKE I'M A BIG PERVERT! IT'S A PERFECTLY SAFE STORY!
EARLIER, THIS SUPREMELY LOVELY LOLI—
K CHAN
AH! CRAP. I MEAN—
EARLIER, THIS ABSOLUTELY ADORABLE GIRL CAME UP TO THE REGISTERS, RIGHT?

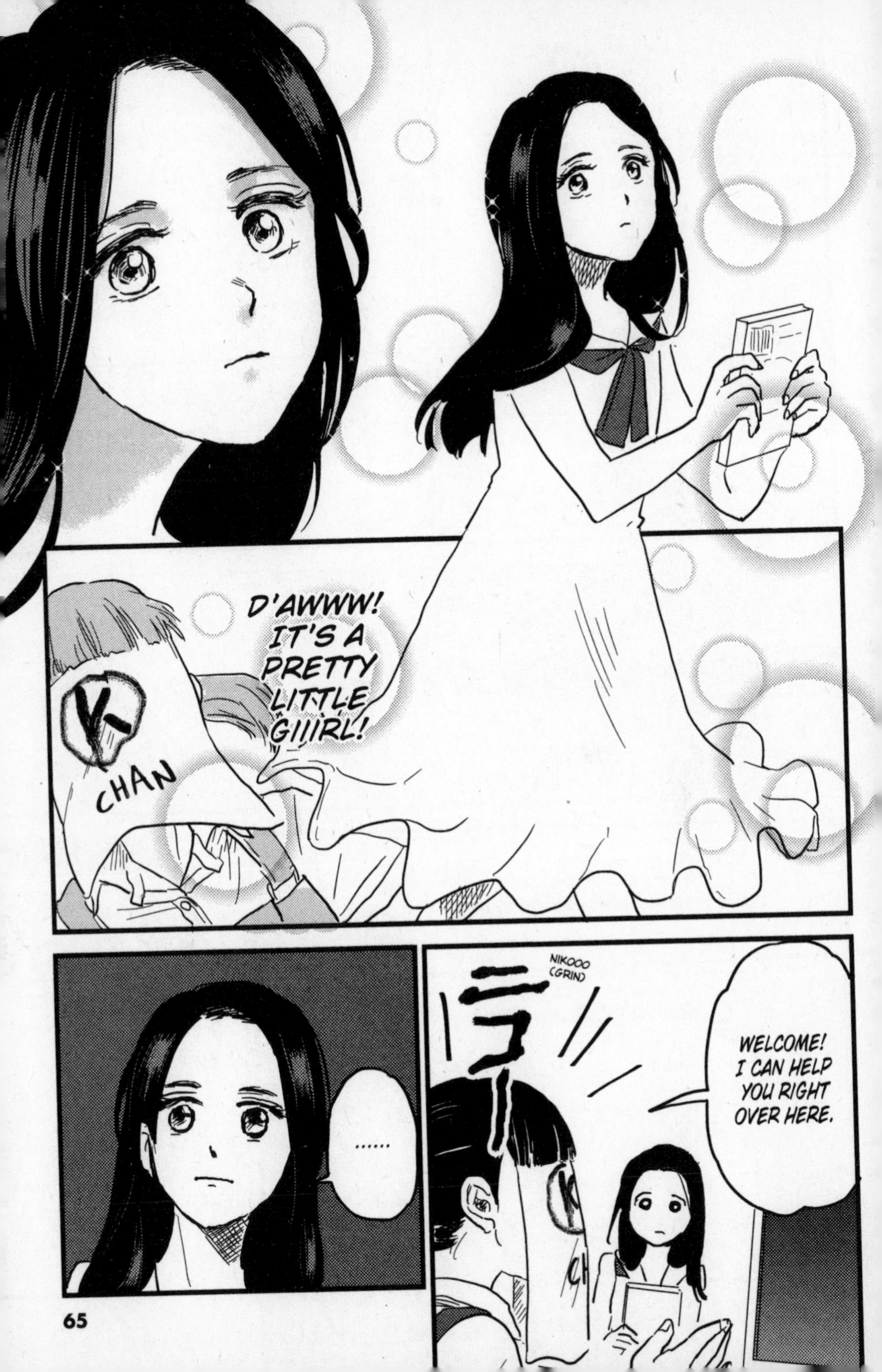
D'AWWW! IT'S A PRETTY LITTLE GIIIRL!
K-CHAN
NIKOOO (GRIN)
WELCOME! I CAN HELP YOU RIGHT OVER HERE.
......

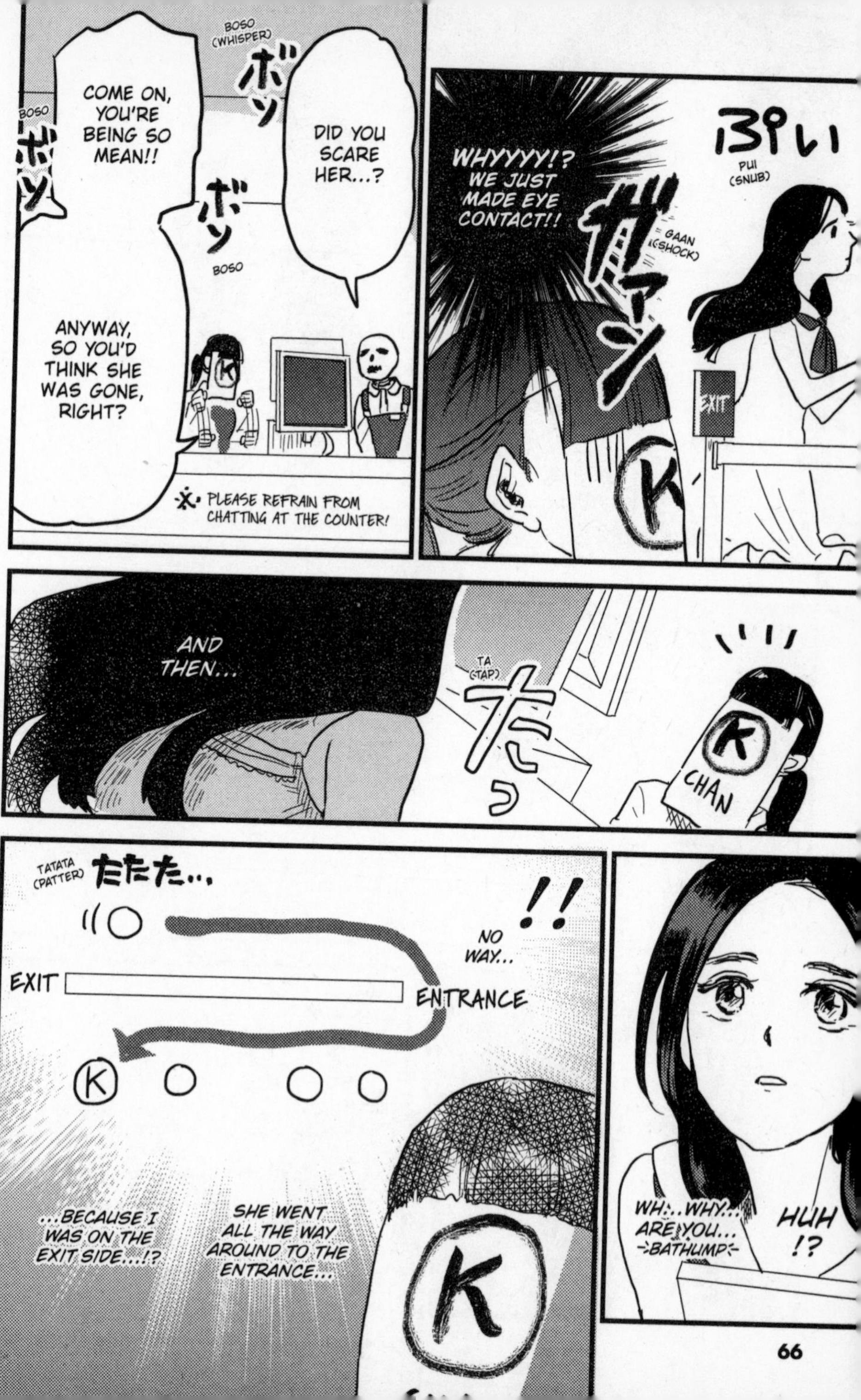
ぷい
PUI (SNUB)
ガーン
GAAN (SHOCK)
WHYYYY!? WE JUST MADE EYE CONTACT!!
BOSO (WHISPER)
ボソ
DID YOU SCARE HER...?
ボソ
BOSO
COME ON, YOU'RE BEING SO MEAN!!
ボソ
BOSO
ANYWAY, SO YOU'D THINK SHE WAS GONE, RIGHT?
EXIT
※ PLEASE REFRAIN FROM CHATTING AT THE COUNTER!
K CHAN
TA (TAP)
たっ
AND THEN...
HUH !?
WH...WHY... ARE YOU...
BATHUMP
!!
NO WAY...
TATATA (PATTER)
たたた...
EXIT
ENTRANCE
K
SHE WENT ALL THE WAY AROUND TO THE ENTRANCE...
...BECAUSE I WAS ON THE EXIT SIDE...!?

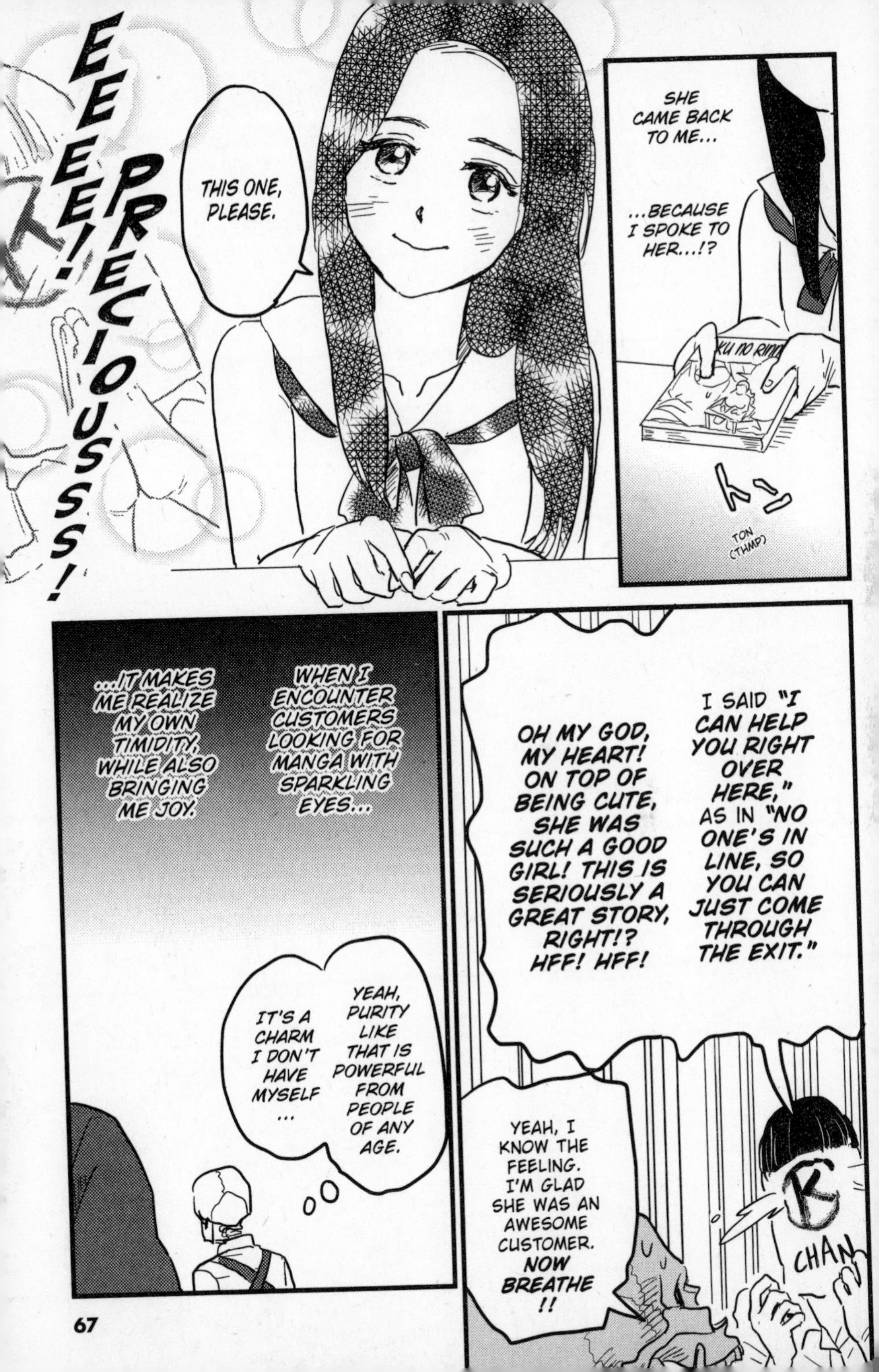
SHE CAME BACK TO ME...
...BECAUSE I SPOKE TO HER...!?
TON (THMP)
THIS ONE, PLEASE.
EEEE! PRECIOUSSSS!
I SAID "I CAN HELP YOU RIGHT OVER HERE," AS IN "NO ONE'S IN LINE, SO YOU CAN JUST COME THROUGH THE EXIT."
OH MY GOD, MY HEART! ON TOP OF BEING CUTE, SHE WAS SUCH A GOOD GIRL! THIS IS SERIOUSLY A GREAT STORY, RIGHT!? HFF! HFF!
YEAH, I KNOW THE FEELING. I'M GLAD SHE WAS AN AWESOME CUSTOMER. NOW BREATHE!!
CHAN
WHEN I ENCOUNTER CUSTOMERS LOOKING FOR MANGA WITH SPARKLING EYES...
...IT MAKES ME REALIZE MY OWN TIMIDITY, WHILE ALSO BRINGING ME JOY.
YEAH, PURITY LIKE THAT IS POWERFUL FROM PEOPLE OF ANY AGE.
IT'S A CHARM I DON'T HAVE MYSELF...

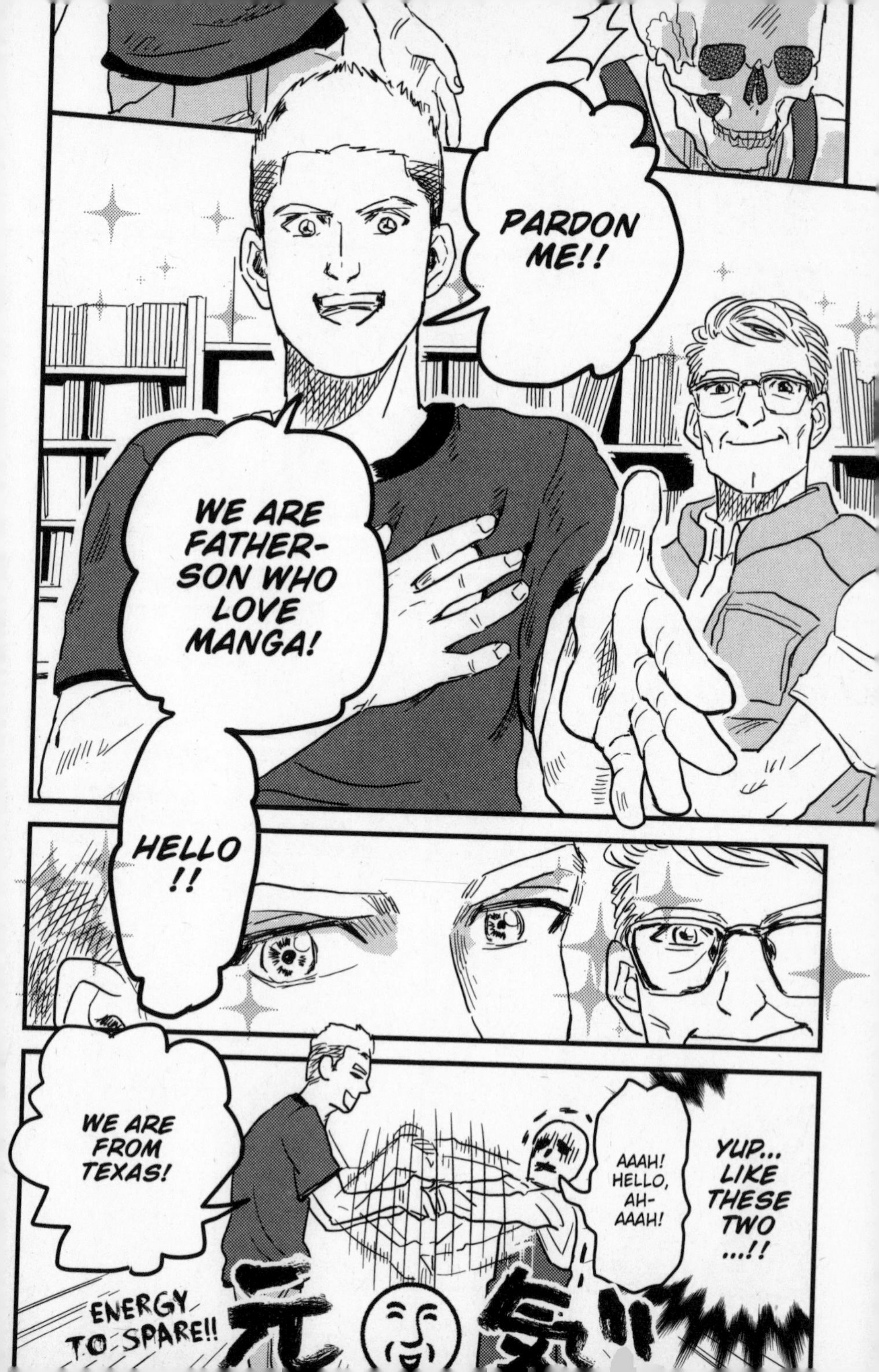
PARDON ME!!
WE ARE FATHER-SON WHO LOVE MANGA!
HELLO !!
YUP... LIKE THESE TWO ...!!
AAAH! HELLO, AH-AAAH!
WE ARE FROM TEXAS!
ENERGY TO SPARE!!
元気!!

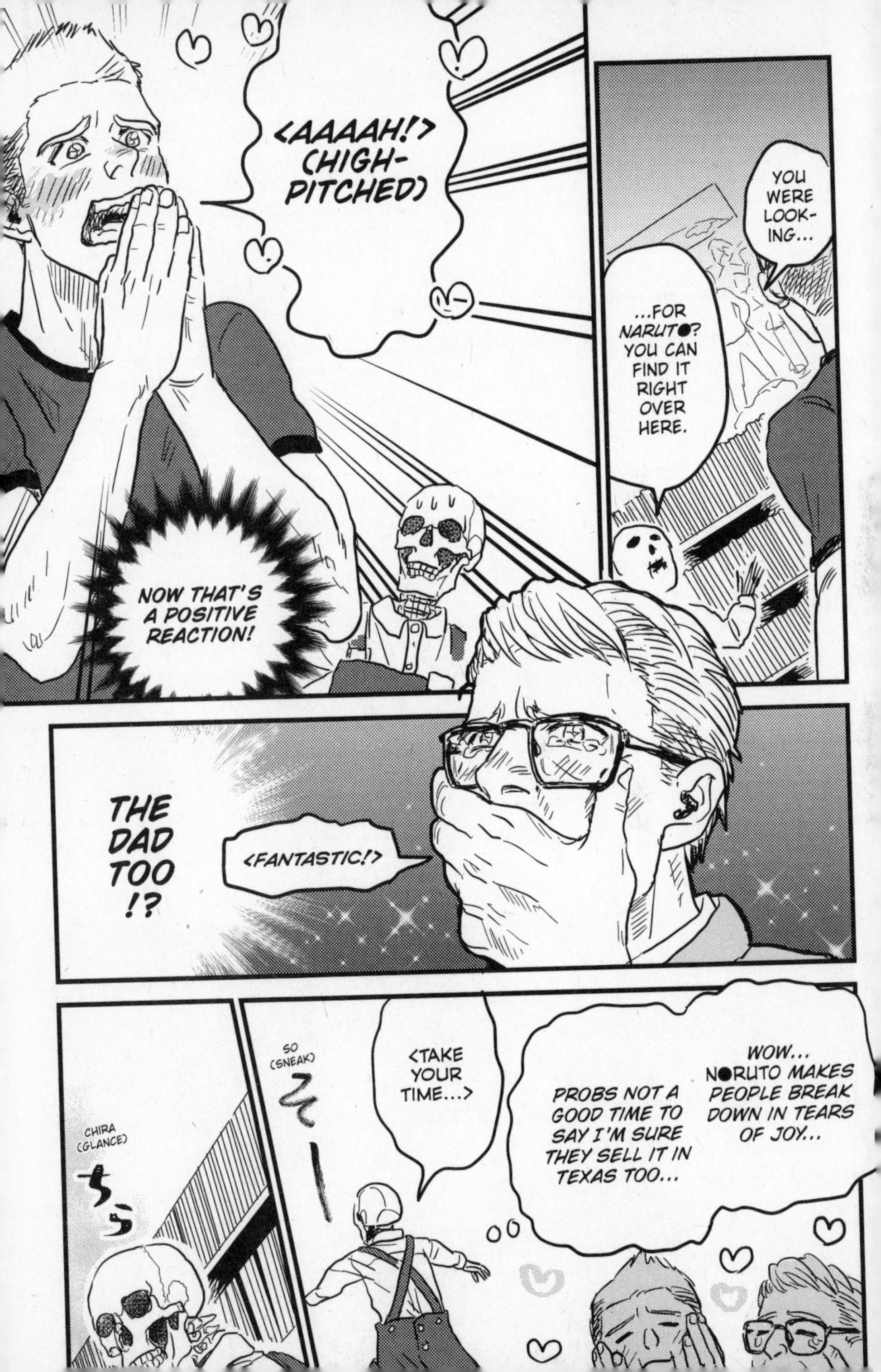
YOU WERE LOOKING...
...FOR NARUT●? YOU CAN FIND IT RIGHT OVER HERE.
<AAAAH!> (HIGH-PITCHED)
NOW THAT'S A POSITIVE REACTION!
<FANTASTIC!>
THE DAD TOO!?
WOW... N●RUTO MAKES PEOPLE BREAK DOWN IN TEARS OF JOY...
PROBS NOT A GOOD TIME TO SAY I'M SURE THEY SELL IT IN TEXAS TOO...
<TAKE YOUR TIME...>
SO (SNEAK)
CHIRA (GLANCE)

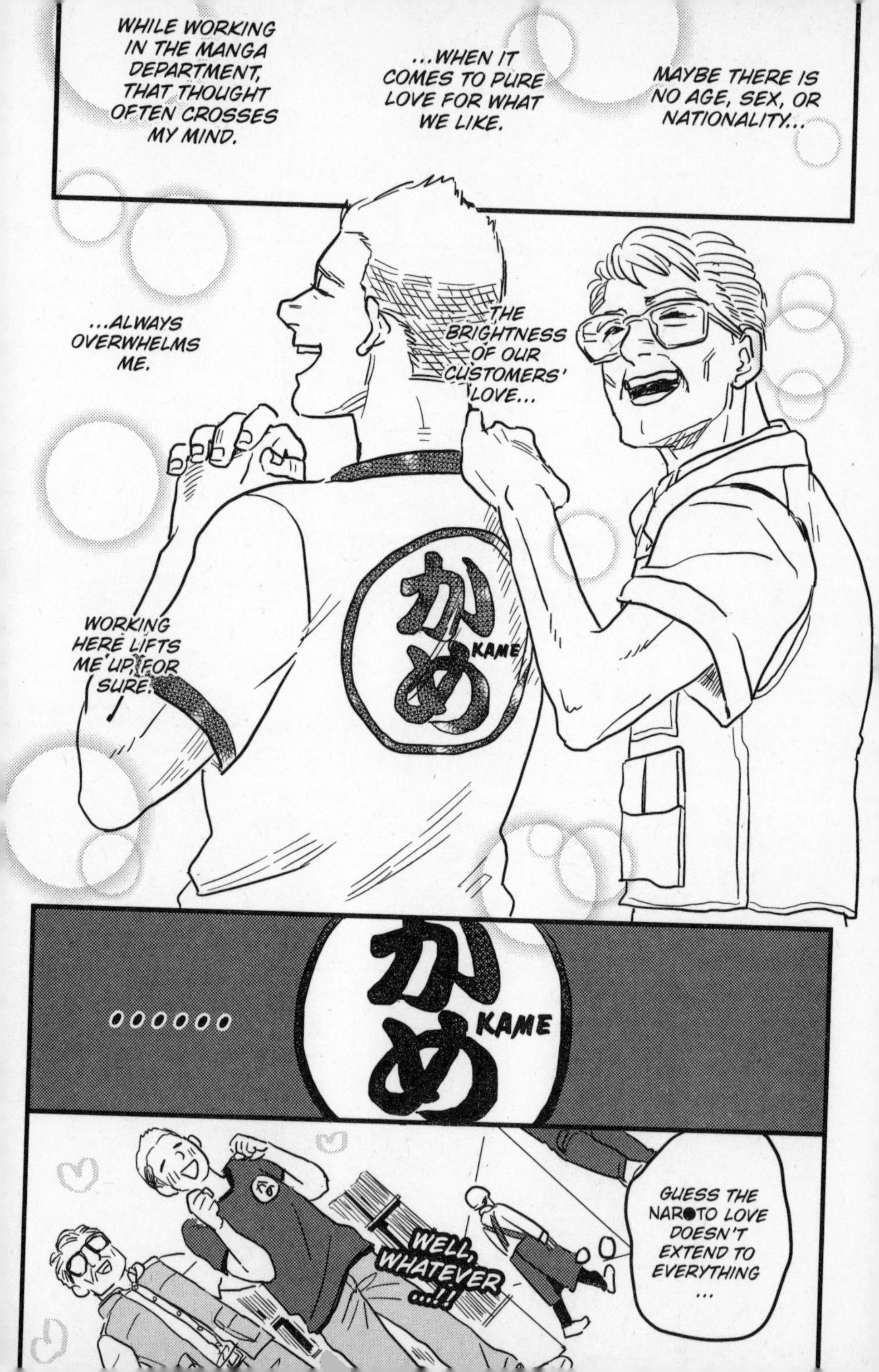
MAYBE THERE IS NO AGE, SEX, OR NATIONALITY...
...WHEN IT COMES TO PURE LOVE FOR WHAT WE LIKE.
WHILE WORKING IN THE MANGA DEPARTMENT, THAT THOUGHT OFTEN CROSSES MY MIND.
THE BRIGHTNESS OF OUR CUSTOMERS' LOVE...
...ALWAYS OVERWHELMS ME.
かめ KAME
WORKING HERE LIFTS ME UP, FOR SURE.
かめ KAME
OOOOOO
GUESS THE NAR●TO LOVE DOESN'T EXTEND TO EVERYTHING ...
WELL, WHATEVER ...!!

Skull-face
Bookseller
Honda-san

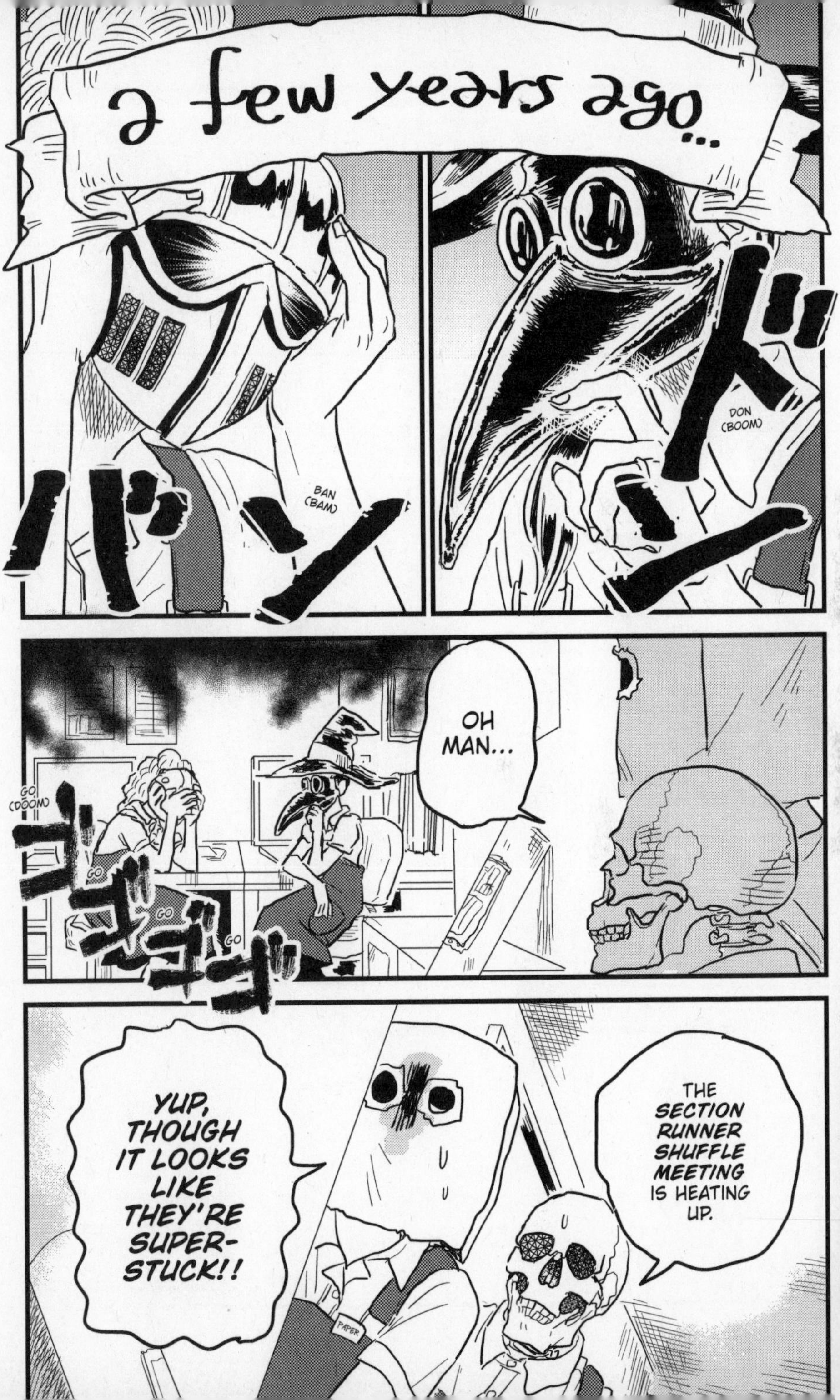
a few years ago...
DON (BOOM)
BAN (BAM)
OH MAN...
GO (DOOM)
GO
GO
GO
THE SECTION RUNNER SHUFFLE MEETING IS HEATING UP.
YUP, THOUGH IT LOOKS LIKE THEY'RE SUPER-STUCK!!
PAPER

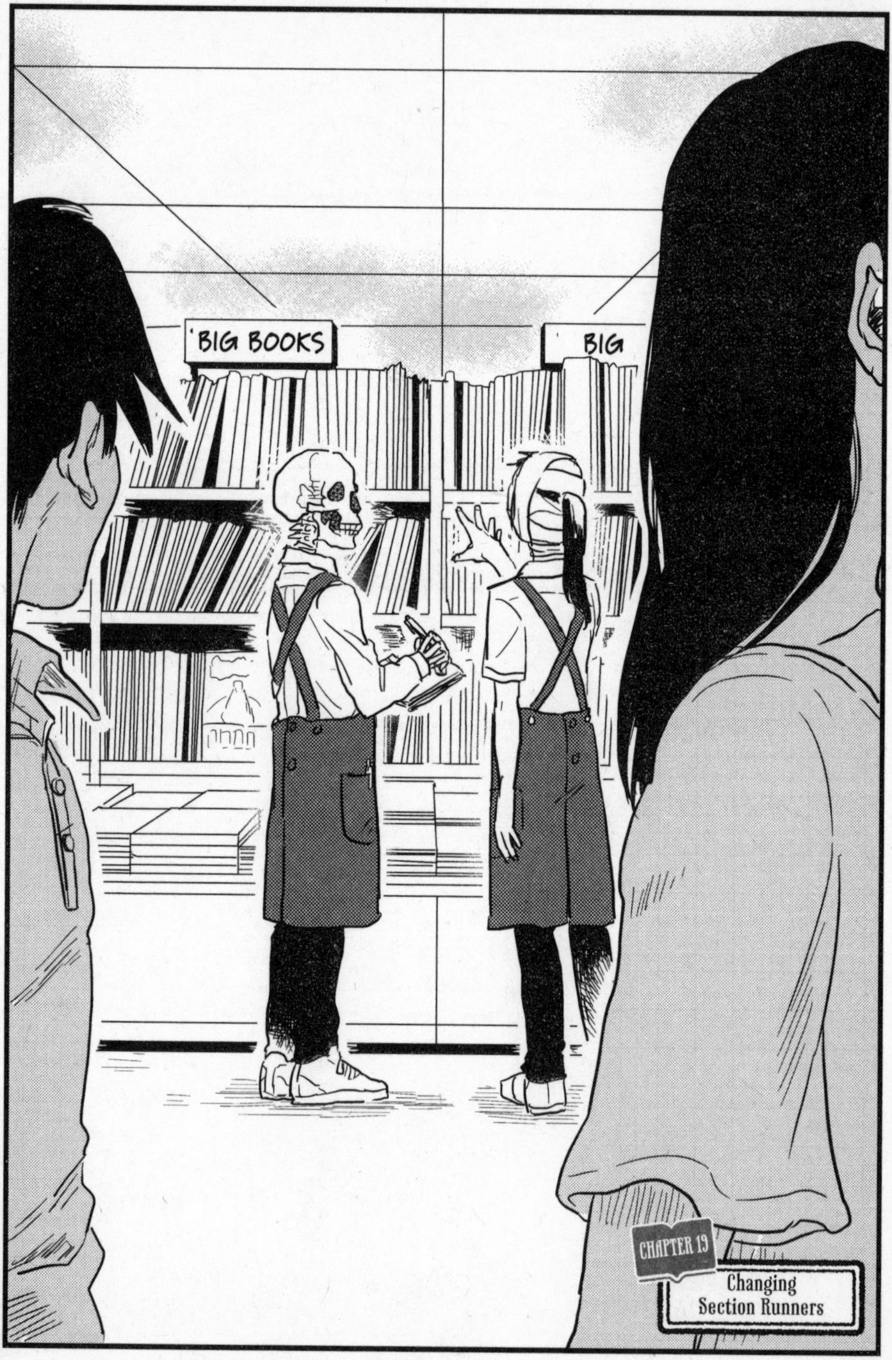
BIG BOOKS
BIG
CHAPTER 19
Changing Section Runners

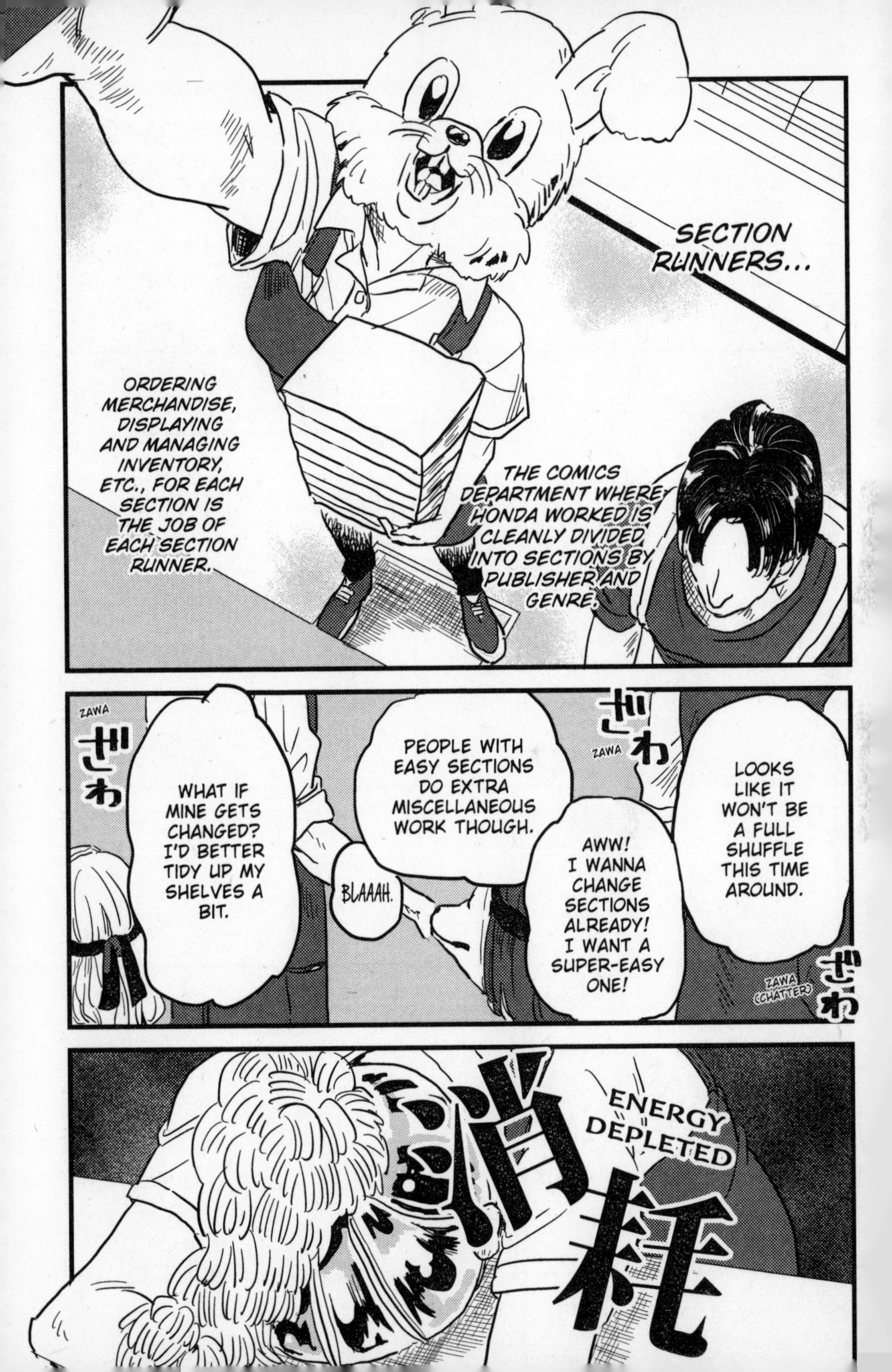
SECTION RUNNERS...
THE COMICS DEPARTMENT WHERE HONDA WORKED IS CLEANLY DIVIDED INTO SECTIONS BY PUBLISHER AND GENRE.
ORDERING MERCHANDISE, DISPLAYING AND MANAGING INVENTORY, ETC., FOR EACH SECTION IS THE JOB OF EACH SECTION RUNNER.
ざわ
ZAWA (CHATTER)
LOOKS LIKE IT WON'T BE A FULL SHUFFLE THIS TIME AROUND.
ざわ
ZAWA
AWW! I WANNA CHANGE SECTIONS ALREADY! I WANT A SUPER-EASY ONE!
PEOPLE WITH EASY SECTIONS DO EXTRA MISCELLANEOUS WORK THOUGH.
BLAAAH.
WHAT IF MINE GETS CHANGED? I'D BETTER TIDY UP MY SHELVES A BIT.
ZAWA
ざわ
消耗
ENERGY DEPLETED

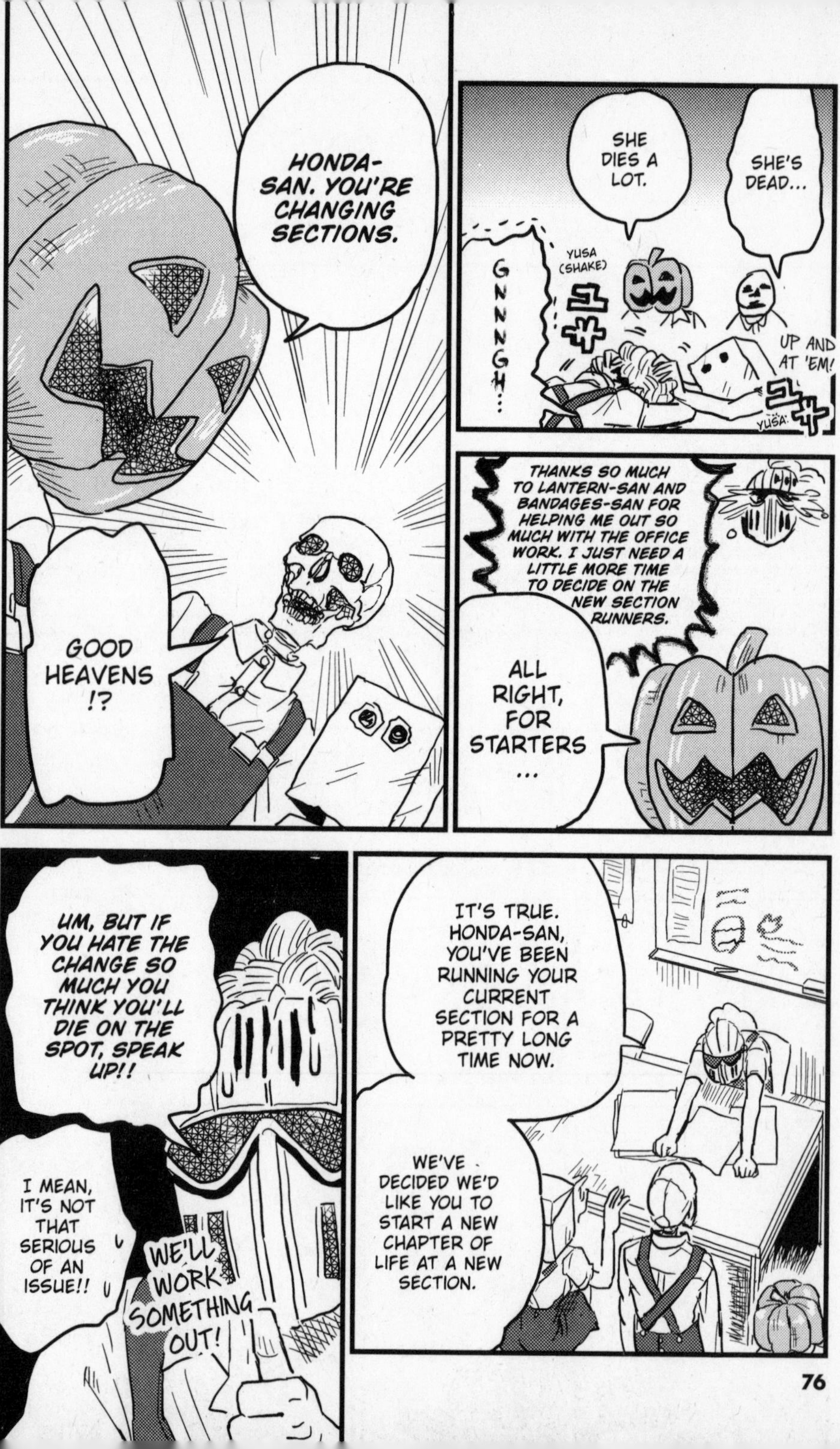
SHE'S DEAD...
SHE DIES A LOT.
UP AND AT 'EM!
YUSA
YUSA (SHAKE)
GNNNGH...
THANKS SO MUCH TO LANTERN-SAN AND BANDAGES-SAN FOR HELPING ME OUT SO MUCH WITH THE OFFICE WORK. I JUST NEED A LITTLE MORE TIME TO DECIDE ON THE NEW SECTION RUNNERS.
ALL RIGHT, FOR STARTERS...
HONDA-SAN. YOU'RE CHANGING SECTIONS.
GOOD HEAVENS!?
IT'S TRUE. HONDA-SAN, YOU'VE BEEN RUNNING YOUR CURRENT SECTION FOR A PRETTY LONG TIME NOW.
WE'VE DECIDED WE'D LIKE YOU TO START A NEW CHAPTER OF LIFE AT A NEW SECTION.
UM, BUT IF YOU HATE THE CHANGE SO MUCH YOU THINK YOU'LL DIE ON THE SPOT, SPEAK UP!!
I MEAN, IT'S NOT THAT SERIOUS OF AN ISSUE!!
WE'LL WORK SOMETHING OUT!

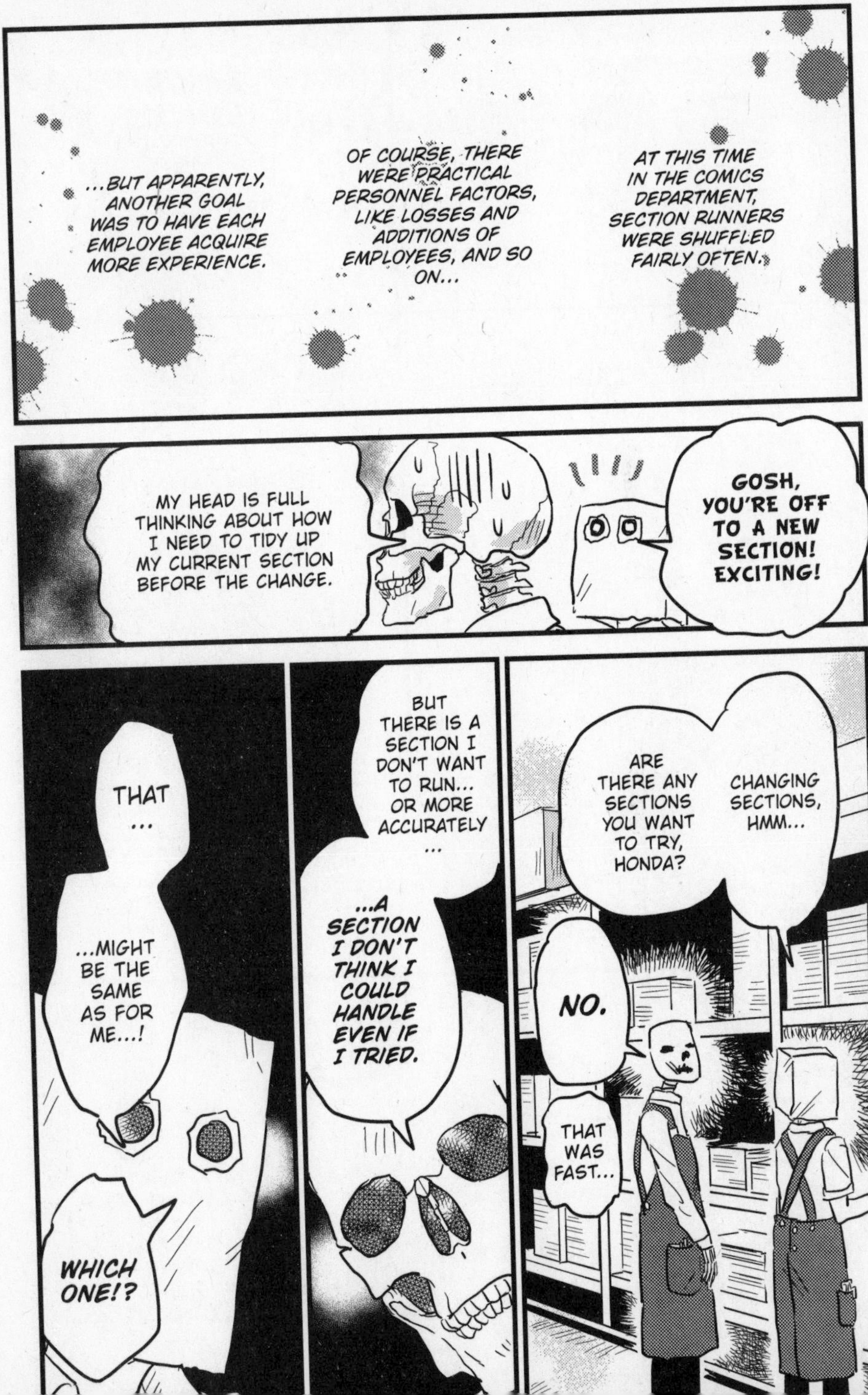
AT THIS TIME IN THE COMICS DEPARTMENT, SECTION RUNNERS WERE SHUFFLED FAIRLY OFTEN.
OF COURSE, THERE WERE PRACTICAL PERSONNEL FACTORS, LIKE LOSSES AND ADDITIONS OF EMPLOYEES, AND SO ON...
...BUT APPARENTLY, ANOTHER GOAL WAS TO HAVE EACH EMPLOYEE ACQUIRE MORE EXPERIENCE.
GOSH, YOU'RE OFF TO A NEW SECTION! EXCITING!
MY HEAD IS FULL THINKING ABOUT HOW I NEED TO TIDY UP MY CURRENT SECTION BEFORE THE CHANGE.
CHANGING SECTIONS, HMM...
ARE THERE ANY SECTIONS YOU WANT TO TRY, HONDA?
NO.
THAT WAS FAST...
BUT THERE IS A SECTION I DON'T WANT TO RUN... OR MORE ACCURATELY...
...A SECTION I DON'T THINK I COULD HANDLE EVEN IF I TRIED.
THAT...
...MIGHT BE THE SAME AS FOR ME...!
WHICH ONE!?

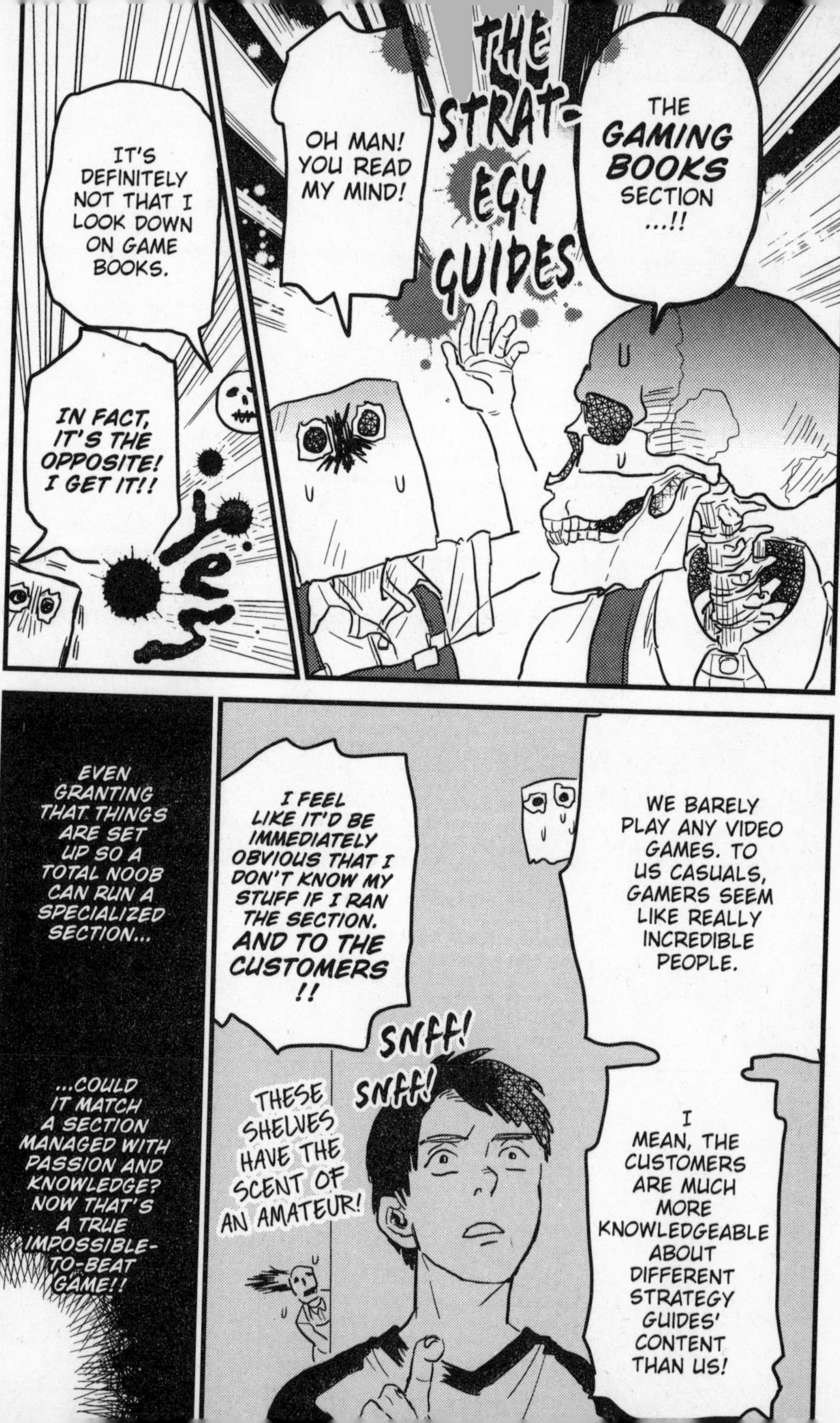
THE GAMING BOOKS SECTION ...!!
THE STRAT-EGY GUIDES
OH MAN! YOU READ MY MIND!
IT'S DEFINITELY NOT THAT I LOOK DOWN ON GAME BOOKS.
IN FACT, IT'S THE OPPOSITE! I GET IT!!
yes
WE BARELY PLAY ANY VIDEO GAMES. TO US CASUALS, GAMERS SEEM LIKE REALLY INCREDIBLE PEOPLE.
I FEEL LIKE IT'D BE IMMEDIATELY OBVIOUS THAT I DON'T KNOW MY STUFF IF I RAN THE SECTION. AND TO THE CUSTOMERS !!
I MEAN, THE CUSTOMERS ARE MUCH MORE KNOWLEDGEABLE ABOUT DIFFERENT STRATEGY GUIDES' CONTENT THAN US!
SNFF! SNFF!
THESE SHELVES HAVE THE SCENT OF AN AMATEUR!
EVEN GRANTING THAT THINGS ARE SET UP SO A TOTAL NOOB CAN RUN A SPECIALIZED SECTION...
...COULD IT MATCH A SECTION MANAGED WITH PASSION AND KNOWLEDGE? NOW THAT'S A TRUE IMPOSSIBLE-TO-BEAT GAME!!

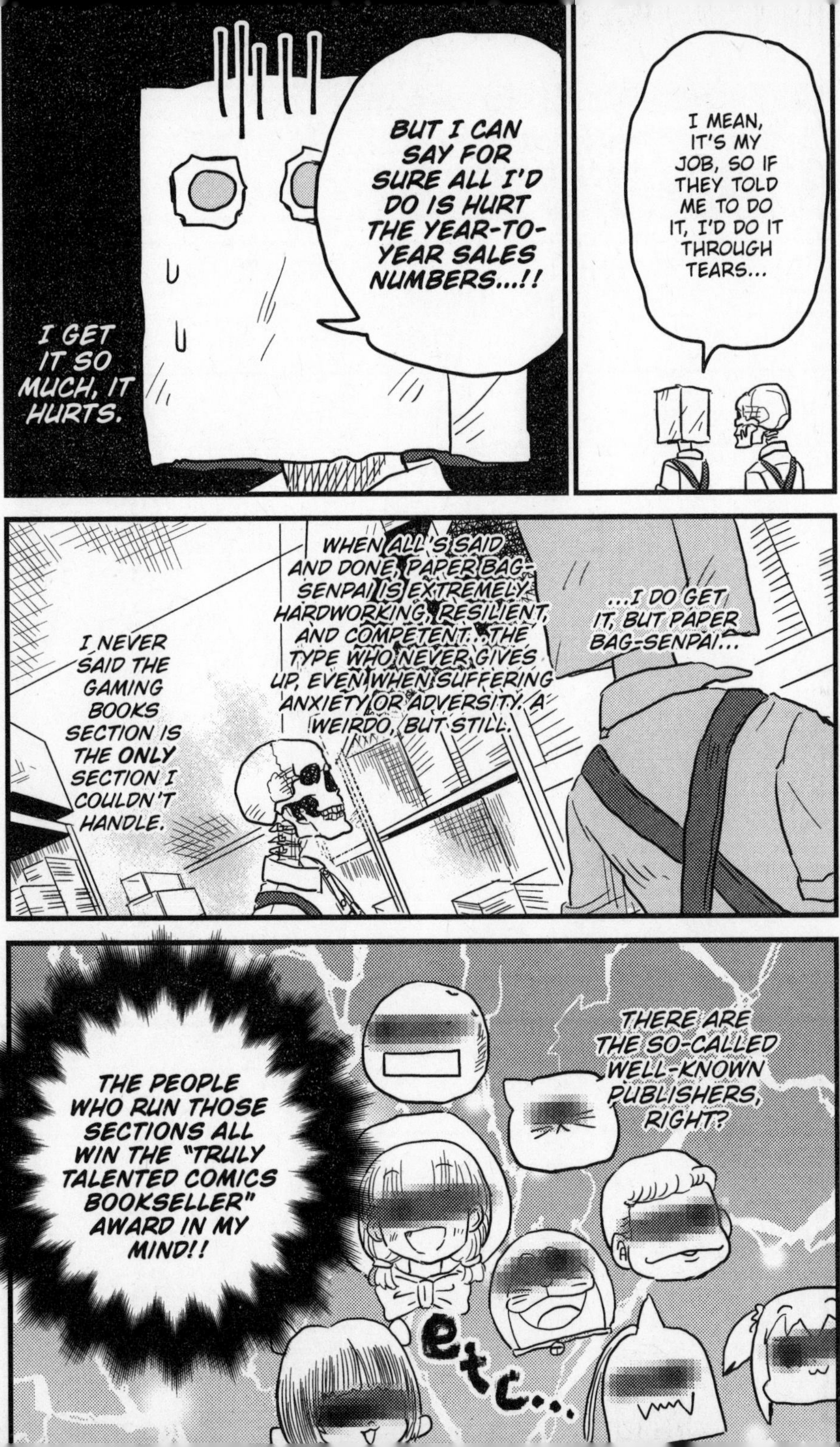
I MEAN, IT'S MY JOB, SO IF THEY TOLD ME TO DO IT, I'D DO IT THROUGH TEARS...
BUT I CAN SAY FOR SURE ALL I'D DO IS HURT THE YEAR-TO-YEAR SALES NUMBERS...!!
I GET IT SO MUCH, IT HURTS.
...I DO GET IT, BUT PAPER BAG-SENPAI...
WHEN ALL'S SAID AND DONE, PAPER BAG-SENPAI IS EXTREMELY HARDWORKING, RESILIENT, AND COMPETENT. THE TYPE WHO NEVER GIVES UP, EVEN WHEN SUFFERING ANXIETY OR ADVERSITY. A WEIRDO, BUT STILL.
I NEVER SAID THE GAMING BOOKS SECTION IS THE ONLY SECTION I COULDN'T HANDLE.
THERE ARE THE SO-CALLED WELL-KNOWN PUBLISHERS, RIGHT?
THE PEOPLE WHO RUN THOSE SECTIONS ALL WIN THE "TRULY TALENTED COMICS BOOKSELLER" AWARD IN MY MIND!!
etc...

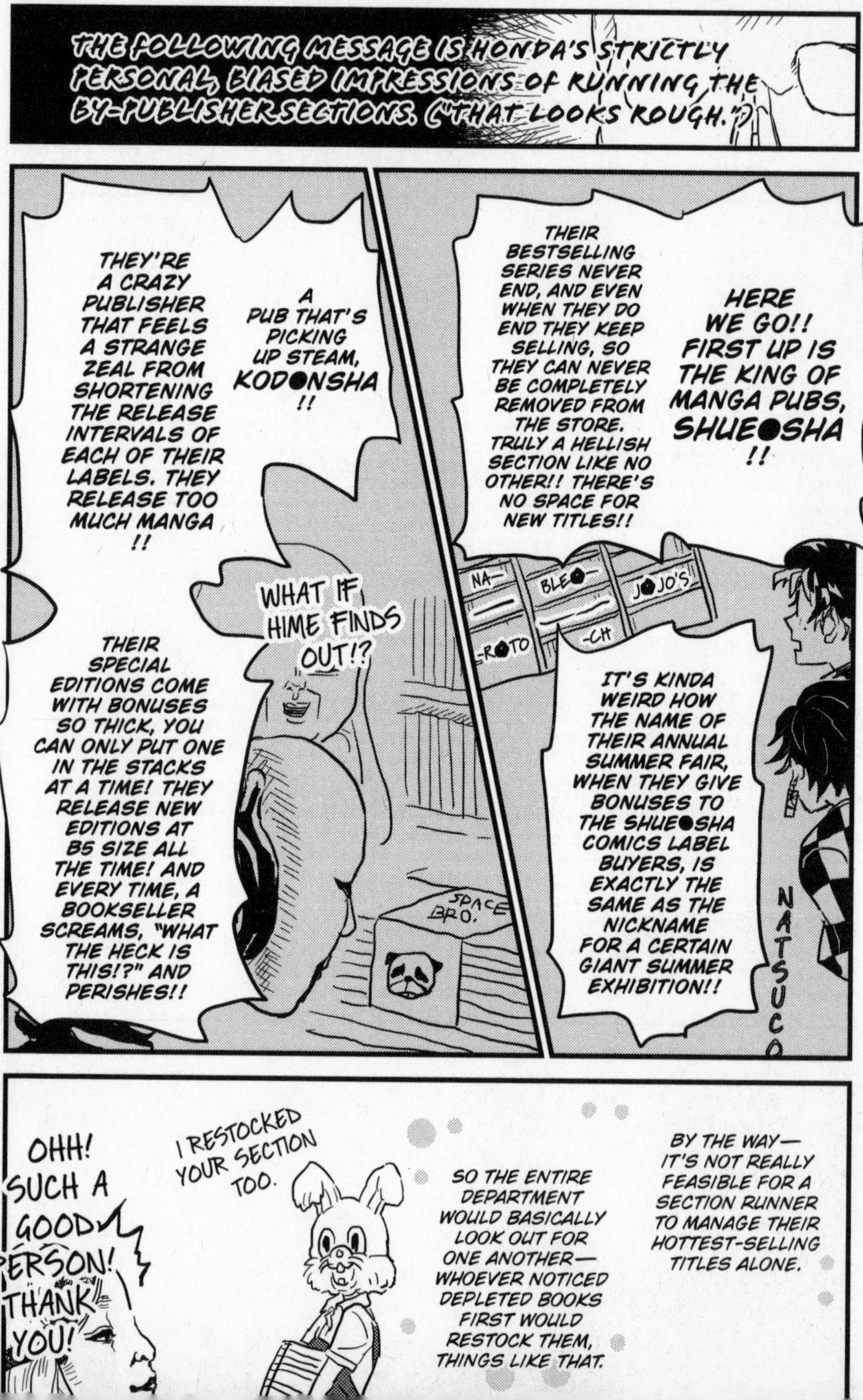
THE FOLLOWING MESSAGE IS HONDA'S STRICTLY PERSONAL, BIASED IMPRESSIONS OF RUNNING THE BY-PUBLISHER SECTIONS. ("THAT LOOKS ROUGH.")
HERE WE GO!! FIRST UP IS THE KING OF MANGA PUBS, SHUE●SHA!!
THEIR BESTSELLING SERIES NEVER END, AND EVEN WHEN THEY DO END THEY KEEP SELLING, SO THEY CAN NEVER BE COMPLETELY REMOVED FROM THE STORE. TRULY A HELLISH SECTION LIKE NO OTHER!! THERE'S NO SPACE FOR NEW TITLES!!
NA-
BLE●-
J●JO'S
-R●TO
-CH
IT'S KINDA WEIRD HOW THE NAME OF THEIR ANNUAL SUMMER FAIR, WHEN THEY GIVE BONUSES TO THE SHUE●SHA COMICS LABEL BUYERS, IS EXACTLY THE SAME AS THE NICKNAME FOR A CERTAIN GIANT SUMMER EXHIBITION!!
NATSUCO
A PUB THAT'S PICKING UP STEAM, KOD●NSHA!!
THEY'RE A CRAZY PUBLISHER THAT FEELS A STRANGE ZEAL FROM SHORTENING THE RELEASE INTERVALS OF EACH OF THEIR LABELS. THEY RELEASE TOO MUCH MANGA!!
WHAT IF HIME FINDS OUT!?
THEIR SPECIAL EDITIONS COME WITH BONUSES SO THICK, YOU CAN ONLY PUT ONE IN THE STACKS AT A TIME! THEY RELEASE NEW EDITIONS AT B5 SIZE ALL THE TIME! AND EVERY TIME, A BOOKSELLER SCREAMS, "WHAT THE HECK IS THIS!?" AND PERISHES!!
SPACE BRO.
BY THE WAY— IT'S NOT REALLY FEASIBLE FOR A SECTION RUNNER TO MANAGE THEIR HOTTEST-SELLING TITLES ALONE.
SO THE ENTIRE DEPARTMENT WOULD BASICALLY LOOK OUT FOR ONE ANOTHER— WHOEVER NOTICED DEPLETED BOOKS FIRST WOULD RESTOCK THEM, THINGS LIKE THAT.
I RESTOCKED YOUR SECTION TOO.
OHH! SUCH A GOOD PERSON! THANK YOU!

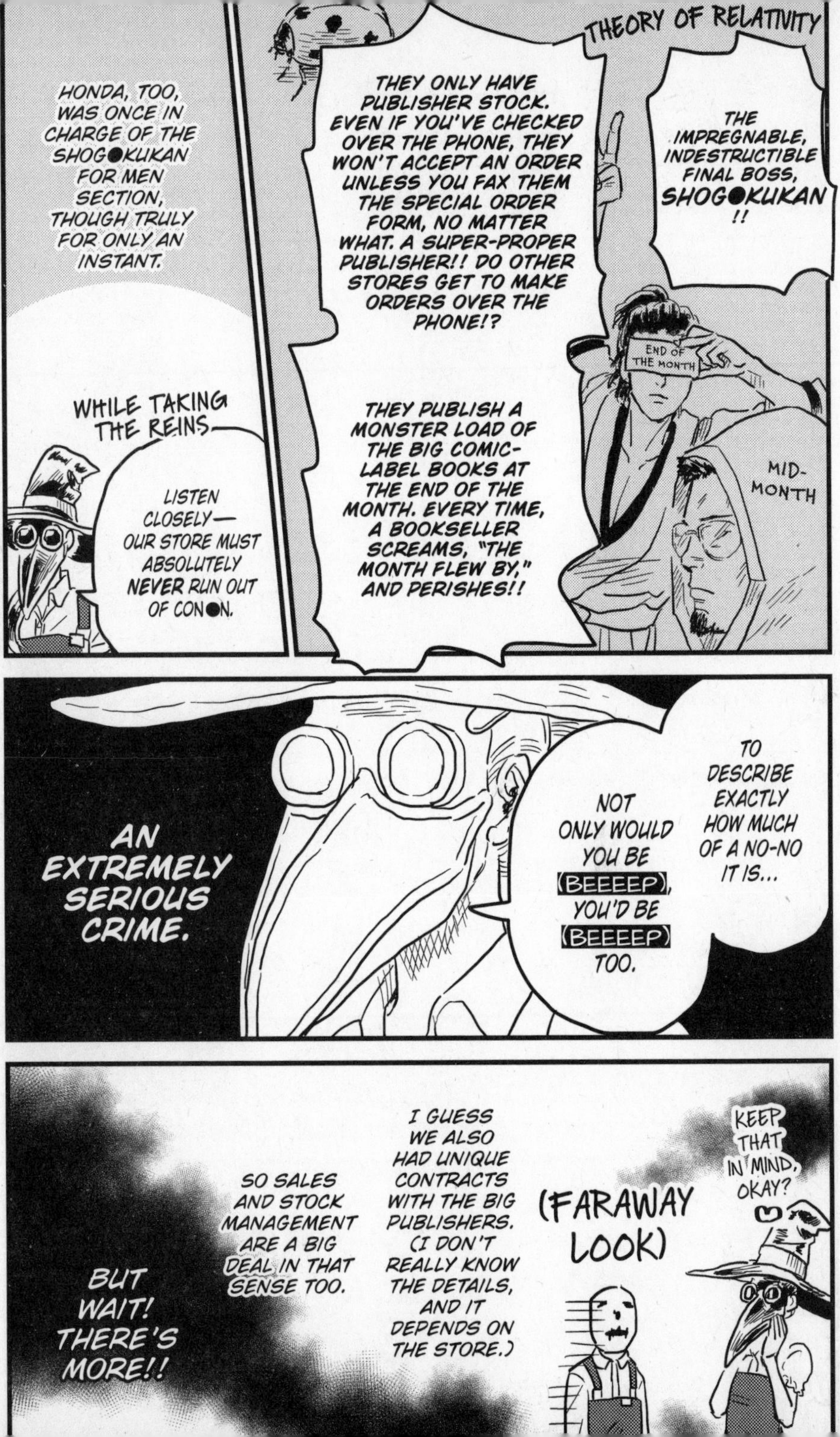
THEORY OF RELATIVITY
THE IMPREGNABLE, INDESTRUCTIBLE FINAL BOSS, SHOGOKUKAN!!
THEY ONLY HAVE PUBLISHER STOCK. EVEN IF YOU'VE CHECKED OVER THE PHONE, THEY WON'T ACCEPT AN ORDER UNLESS YOU FAX THEM THE SPECIAL ORDER FORM, NO MATTER WHAT. A SUPER-PROPER PUBLISHER!! DO OTHER STORES GET TO MAKE ORDERS OVER THE PHONE!?
THEY PUBLISH A MONSTER LOAD OF THE BIG COMIC-LABEL BOOKS AT THE END OF THE MONTH. EVERY TIME, A BOOKSELLER SCREAMS, "THE MONTH FLEW BY," AND PERISHES!!
END OF THE MONTH
MID-MONTH
HONDA, TOO, WAS ONCE IN CHARGE OF THE SHOGOKUKAN FOR MEN SECTION, THOUGH TRULY FOR ONLY AN INSTANT.
WHILE TAKING THE REINS
LISTEN CLOSELY— OUR STORE MUST ABSOLUTELY NEVER RUN OUT OF CONAN.
RUN OUT = TO BE SOLD OUT
TO DESCRIBE EXACTLY HOW MUCH OF A NO-NO IT IS...
NOT ONLY WOULD YOU BE (BEEEEP), YOU'D BE (BEEEEP) TOO.
AN EXTREMELY SERIOUS CRIME.
KEEP THAT IN MIND, OKAY?
(FARAWAY LOOK)
I GUESS WE ALSO HAD UNIQUE CONTRACTS WITH THE BIG PUBLISHERS. (I DON'T REALLY KNOW THE DETAILS, AND IT DEPENDS ON THE STORE.)
SO SALES AND STOCK MANAGEMENT ARE A BIG DEAL IN THAT SENSE TOO.
BUT WAIT! THERE'S MORE!!

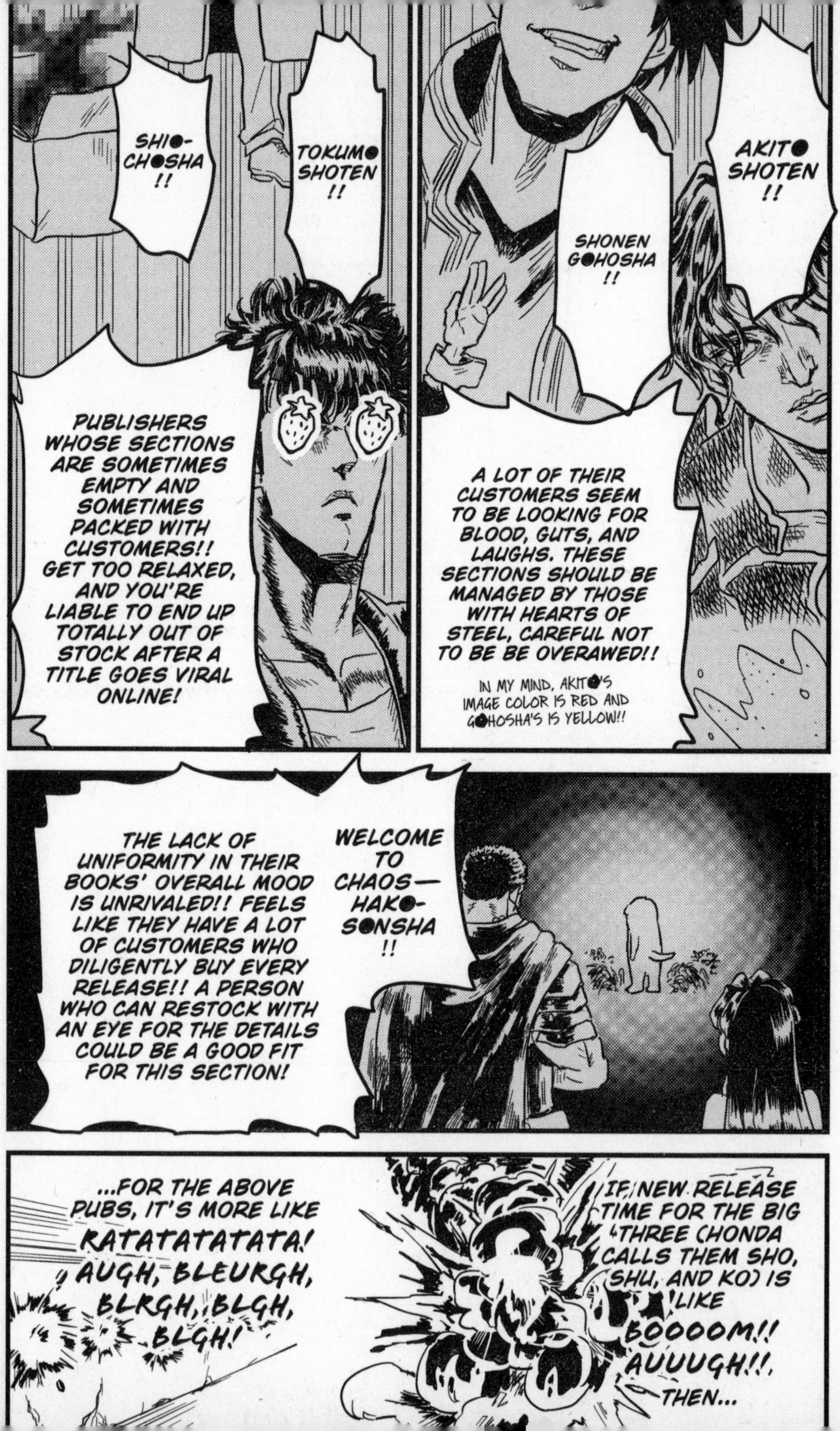
AKIT● SHOTEN!!
SHONEN G●HOSHA!!
A LOT OF THEIR CUSTOMERS SEEM TO BE LOOKING FOR BLOOD, GUTS, AND LAUGHS. THESE SECTIONS SHOULD BE MANAGED BY THOSE WITH HEARTS OF STEEL, CAREFUL NOT TO BE BE OVERAWED!!
IN MY MIND, AKIT●'S IMAGE COLOR IS RED AND G●HOSHA'S IS YELLOW!!
TOKUM● SHOTEN!!
SHI●-CH●SHA!!
PUBLISHERS WHOSE SECTIONS ARE SOMETIMES EMPTY AND SOMETIMES PACKED WITH CUSTOMERS!! GET TOO RELAXED, AND YOU'RE LIABLE TO END UP TOTALLY OUT OF STOCK AFTER A TITLE GOES VIRAL ONLINE!
WELCOME TO CHAOS—HAK●-S●NSHA!!
THE LACK OF UNIFORMITY IN THEIR BOOKS' OVERALL MOOD IS UNRIVALED!! FEELS LIKE THEY HAVE A LOT OF CUSTOMERS WHO DILIGENTLY BUY EVERY RELEASE!! A PERSON WHO CAN RESTOCK WITH AN EYE FOR THE DETAILS COULD BE A GOOD FIT FOR THIS SECTION!
IF NEW RELEASE TIME FOR THE BIG THREE (HONDA CALLS THEM SHO, SHU, AND KO) IS LIKE BOOOOM!! AUUUGH!! THEN...
...FOR THE ABOVE PUBS, IT'S MORE LIKE RATATATATATA! AUGH, BLEURGH, BLRGH, BLGH, BLGH!

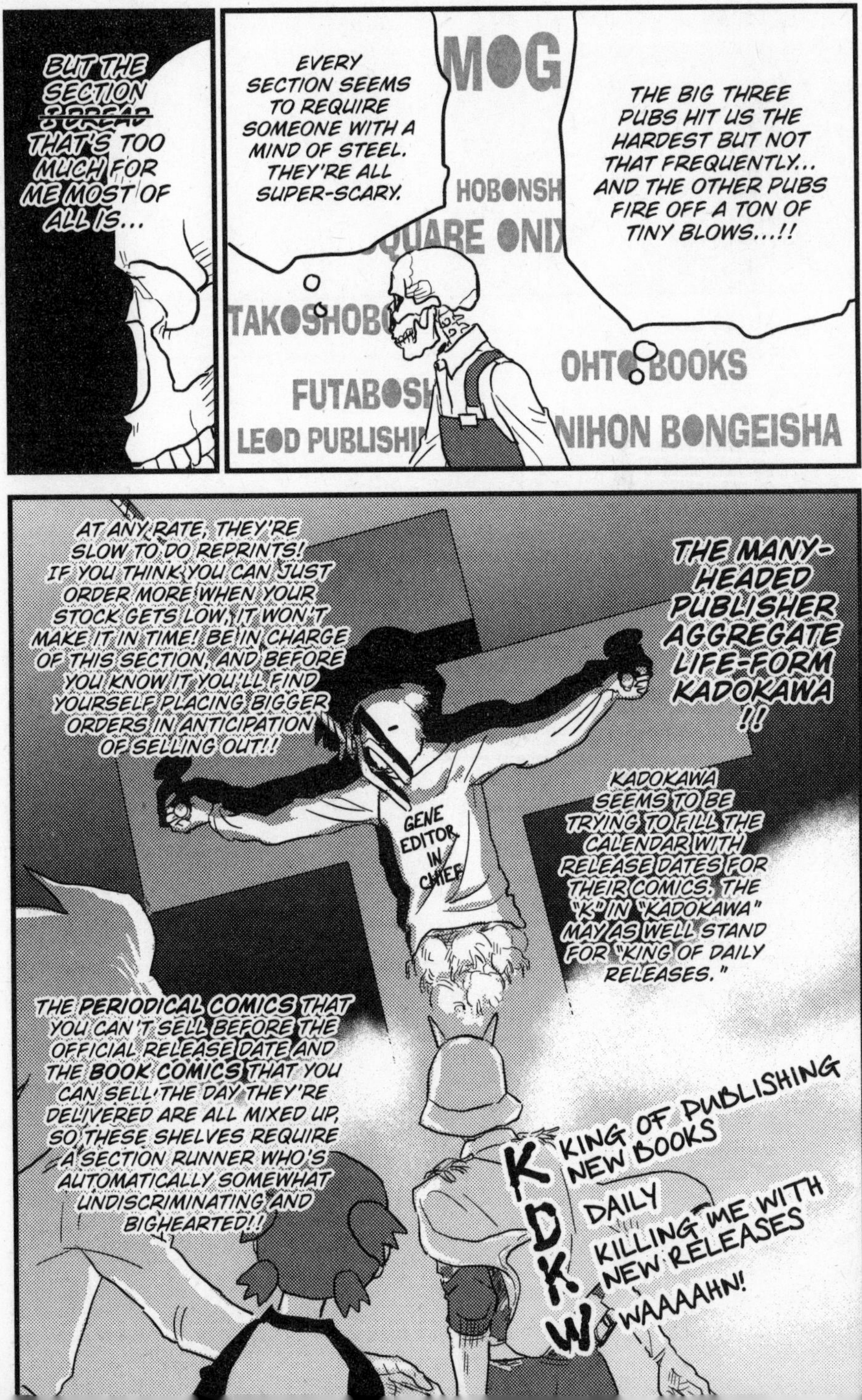

THE BIG THREE PUBS HIT US THE HARDEST BUT NOT THAT FREQUENTLY... AND THE OTHER PUBS FIRE OFF A TON OF TINY BLOWS...!!
EVERY SECTION SEEMS TO REQUIRE SOMEONE WITH A MIND OF STEEL. THEY'RE ALL SUPER-SCARY.
MOG
HOBONSH
QUARE ONIX
TAKOSHOBO
OHTO BOOKS
FUTABOSH
NIHON BONGEISHA
LEOD PUBLISHI
BUT THE SECTION I DREAD THAT'S TOO MUCH FOR ME MOST OF ALL IS...
THE MANY-HEADED PUBLISHER AGGREGATE LIFE-FORM KADOKAWA!!
AT ANY RATE, THEY'RE SLOW TO DO REPRINTS! IF YOU THINK YOU CAN JUST ORDER MORE WHEN YOUR STOCK GETS LOW, IT WON'T MAKE IT IN TIME! BE IN CHARGE OF THIS SECTION, AND BEFORE YOU KNOW IT YOU'LL FIND YOURSELF PLACING BIGGER ORDERS IN ANTICIPATION OF SELLING OUT!!
GENE EDITOR IN CHIEF
KADOKAWA SEEMS TO BE TRYING TO FILL THE CALENDAR WITH RELEASE DATES FOR THEIR COMICS. THE "K" IN "KADOKAWA" MAY AS WELL STAND FOR "KING OF DAILY RELEASES."
THE PERIODICAL COMICS THAT YOU CAN'T SELL BEFORE THE OFFICIAL RELEASE DATE AND THE BOOK COMICS THAT YOU CAN SELL THE DAY THEY'RE DELIVERED ARE ALL MIXED UP, SO THESE SHELVES REQUIRE A SECTION RUNNER WHO'S AUTOMATICALLY SOMEWHAT UNDISCRIMINATING AND BIGHEARTED!!
K KING OF PUBLISHING NEW BOOKS
D DAILY
K KILLING ME WITH NEW RELEASES
W WAAAAHN!

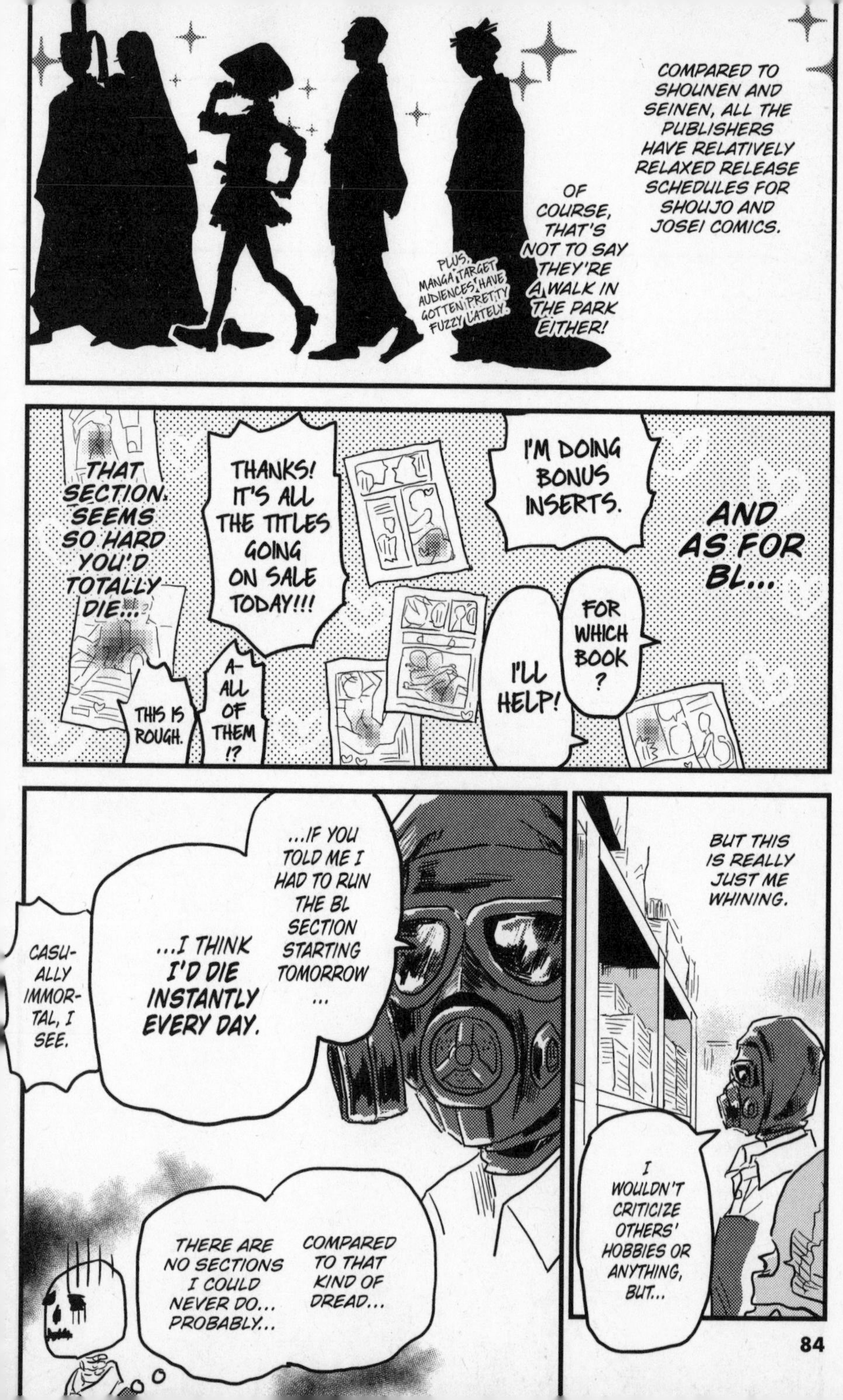
COMPARED TO SHOUNEN AND SEINEN, ALL THE PUBLISHERS HAVE RELATIVELY RELAXED RELEASE SCHEDULES FOR SHOUJO AND JOSEI COMICS.
OF COURSE, THAT'S NOT TO SAY THEY'RE A WALK IN THE PARK EITHER!
PLUS, MANGA TARGET AUDIENCES HAVE GOTTEN PRETTY FUZZY LATELY.
AND AS FOR BL...
I'M DOING BONUS INSERTS.
FOR WHICH BOOK?
I'LL HELP!
THANKS! IT'S ALL THE TITLES GOING ON SALE TODAY!!!
A-ALL OF THEM!?
THAT SECTION SEEMS SO HARD YOU'D TOTALLY DIE...
THIS IS ROUGH.
BUT THIS IS REALLY JUST ME WHINING.
I WOULDN'T CRITICIZE OTHERS' HOBBIES OR ANYTHING, BUT...
...IF YOU TOLD ME I HAD TO RUN THE BL SECTION STARTING TOMORROW...
...I THINK I'D DIE INSTANTLY EVERY DAY.
CASU-ALLY IMMOR-TAL, I SEE.
COMPARED TO THAT KIND OF DREAD...
THERE ARE NO SECTIONS I COULD NEVER DO... PROBABLY...

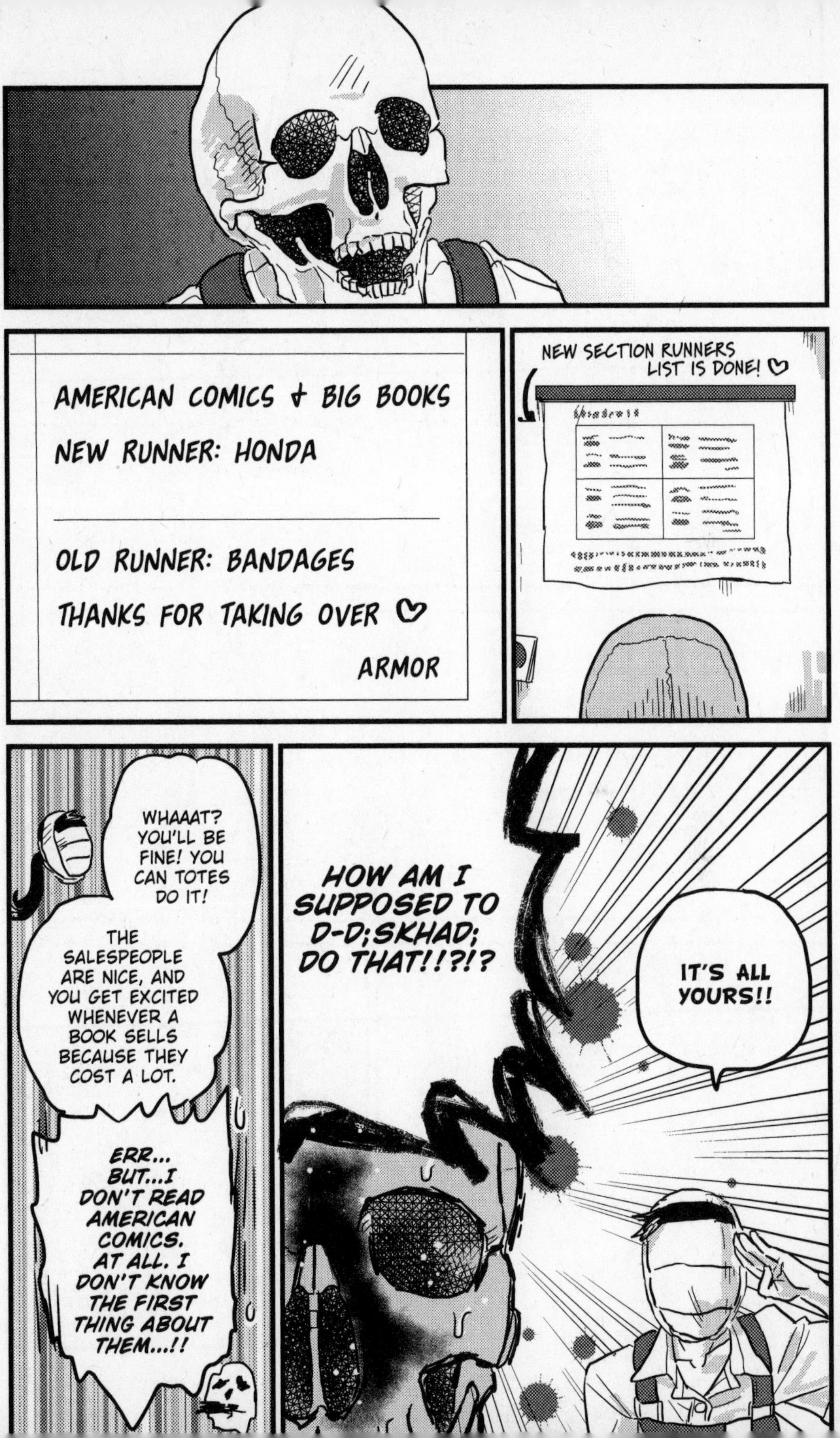
NEW SECTION RUNNERS LIST IS DONE! ♡
AMERICAN COMICS & BIG BOOKS
NEW RUNNER: HONDA
OLD RUNNER: BANDAGES
THANKS FOR TAKING OVER ♡
ARMOR
IT'S ALL YOURS!!
HOW AM I SUPPOSED TO D-D;SKHAD; DO THAT!!?!?
ERR... BUT...I DON'T READ AMERICAN COMICS. AT ALL. I DON'T KNOW THE FIRST THING ABOUT THEM...!!
WHAAAT? YOU'LL BE FINE! YOU CAN TOTES DO IT!
THE SALESPEOPLE ARE NICE, AND YOU GET EXCITED WHENEVER A BOOK SELLS BECAUSE THEY COST A LOT.

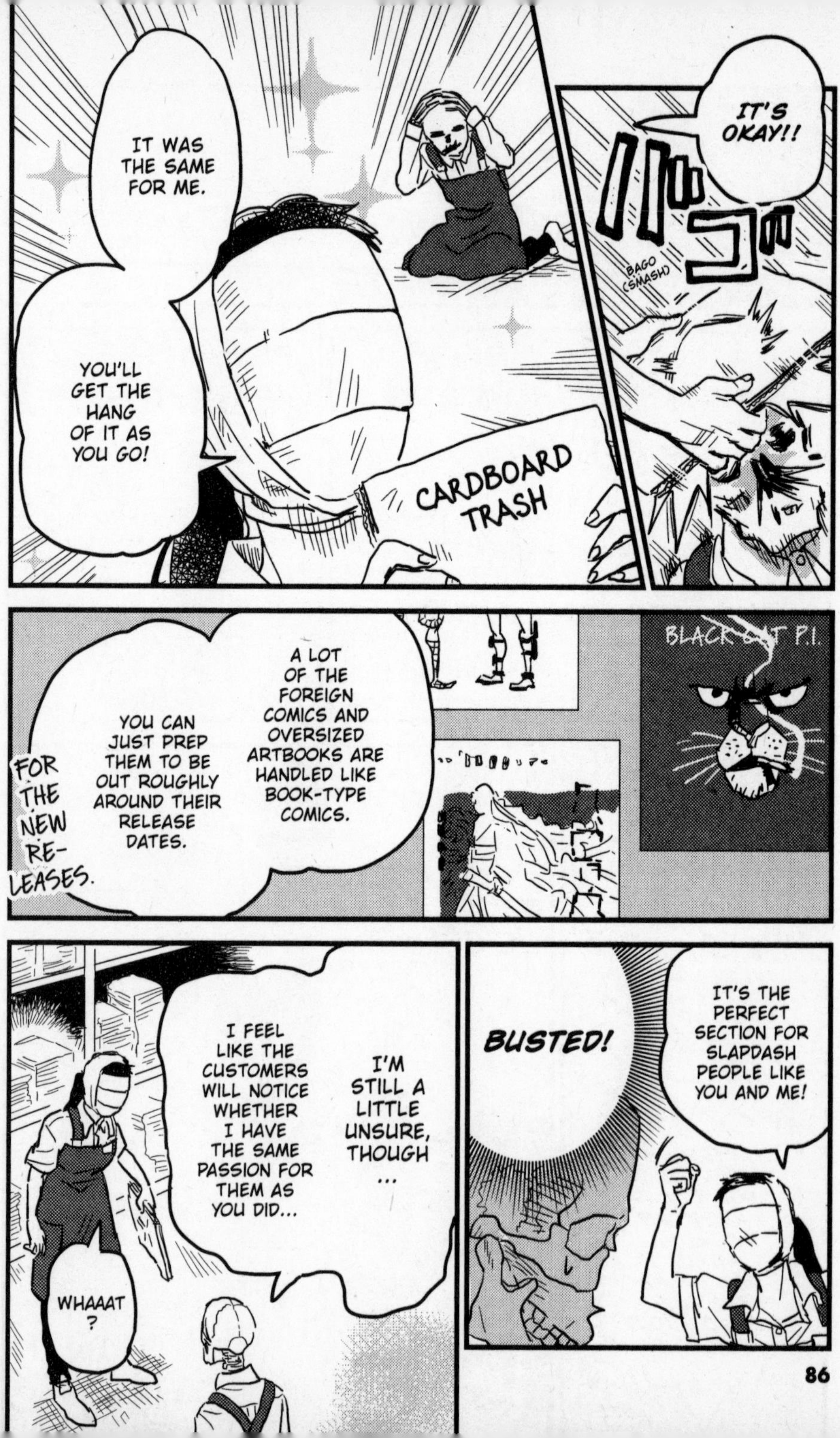
IT'S OKAY!!
BAGO (SMASH)
IT WAS THE SAME FOR ME.
YOU'LL GET THE HANG OF IT AS YOU GO!
CARDBOARD TRASH
A LOT OF THE FOREIGN COMICS AND OVERSIZED ARTBOOKS ARE HANDLED LIKE BOOK-TYPE COMICS.
YOU CAN JUST PREP THEM TO BE OUT ROUGHLY AROUND THEIR RELEASE DATES.
FOR THE NEW RE-LEASES.
IT'S THE PERFECT SECTION FOR SLAPDASH PEOPLE LIKE YOU AND ME!
BUSTED!
I'M STILL A LITTLE UNSURE, THOUGH...
I FEEL LIKE THE CUSTOMERS WILL NOTICE WHETHER I HAVE THE SAME PASSION FOR THEM AS YOU DID...
WHAAAT?

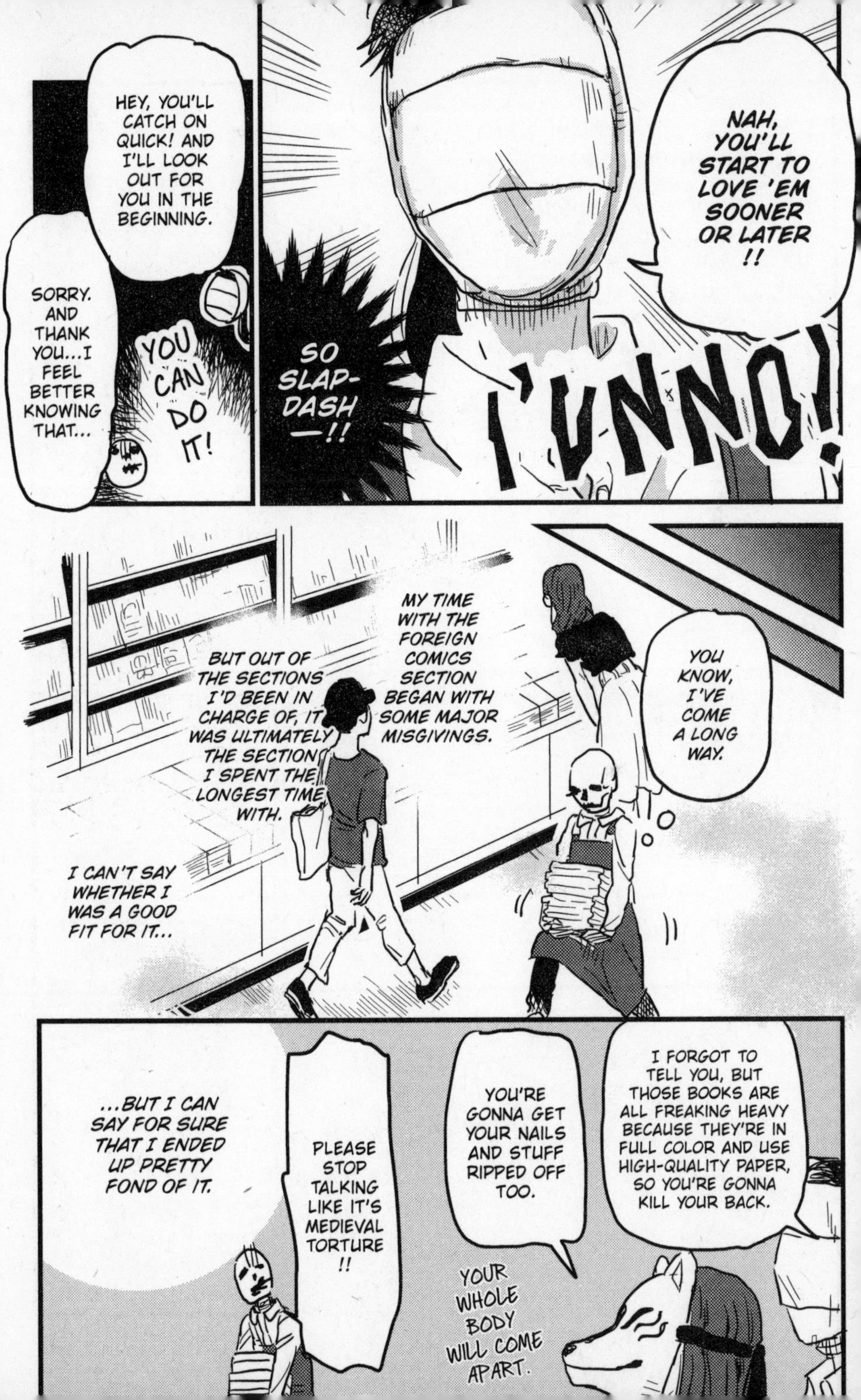
NAH, YOU'LL START TO LOVE 'EM SOONER OR LATER !!
I'UNNO!
SO SLAP-DASH—!!
HEY, YOU'LL CATCH ON QUICK! AND I'LL LOOK OUT FOR YOU IN THE BEGINNING.
SORRY. AND THANK YOU...I FEEL BETTER KNOWING THAT...
YOU CAN DO IT!
YOU KNOW, I'VE COME A LONG WAY.
MY TIME WITH THE FOREIGN COMICS SECTION BEGAN WITH SOME MAJOR MISGIVINGS.
BUT OUT OF THE SECTIONS I'D BEEN IN CHARGE OF, IT WAS ULTIMATELY THE SECTION I SPENT THE LONGEST TIME WITH.
I CAN'T SAY WHETHER I WAS A GOOD FIT FOR IT...
I FORGOT TO TELL YOU, BUT THOSE BOOKS ARE ALL FREAKING HEAVY BECAUSE THEY'RE IN FULL COLOR AND USE HIGH-QUALITY PAPER, SO YOU'RE GONNA KILL YOUR BACK.
YOU'RE GONNA GET YOUR NAILS AND STUFF RIPPED OFF TOO.
YOUR WHOLE BODY WILL COME APART.
PLEASE STOP TALKING LIKE IT'S MEDIEVAL TORTURE !!
...BUT I CAN SAY FOR SURE THAT I ENDED UP PRETTY FOND OF IT.

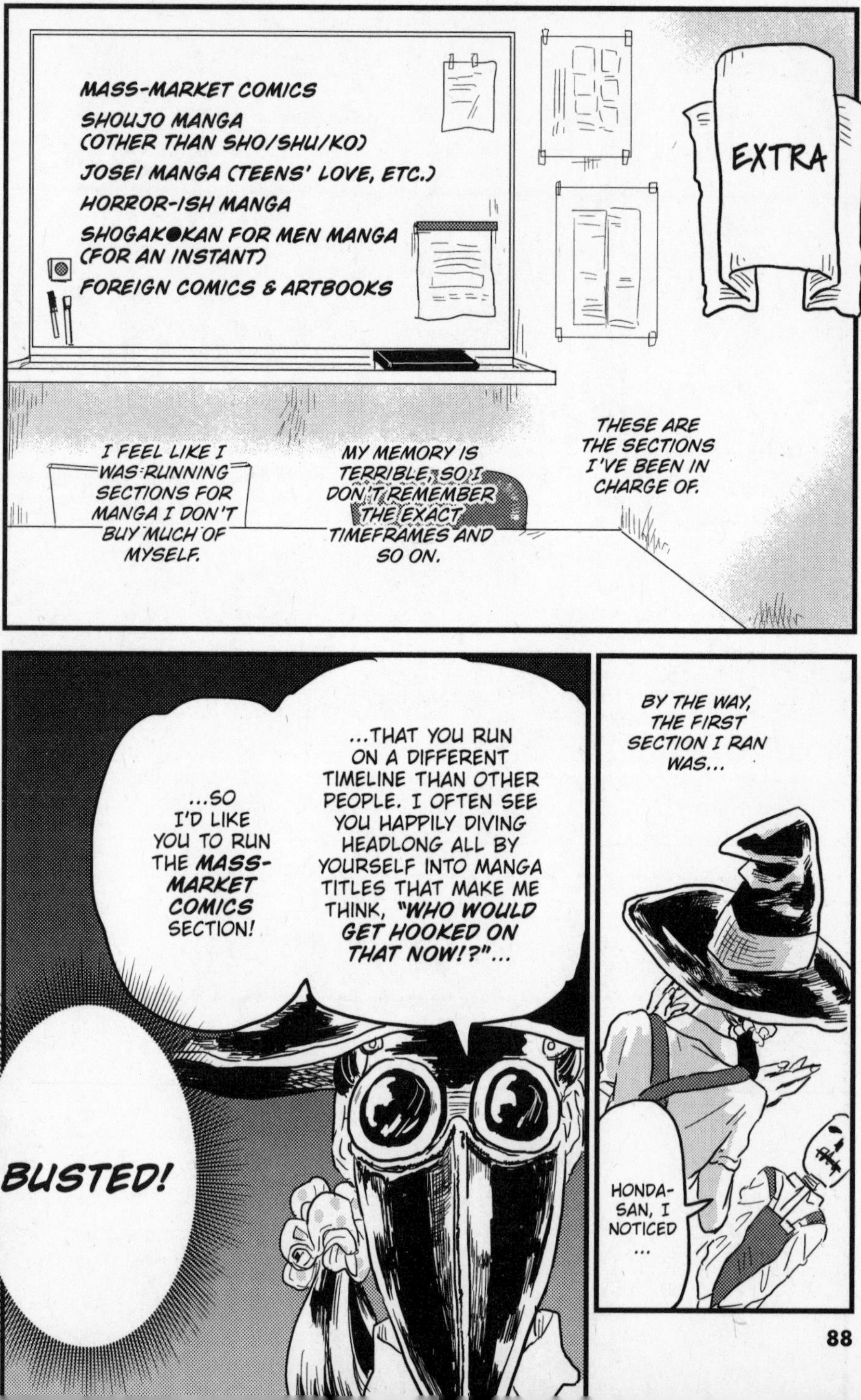
EXTRA
MASS-MARKET COMICS
SHOUJO MANGA (OTHER THAN SHO/SHU/KO)
JOSEI MANGA (TEENS' LOVE, ETC.)
HORROR-ISH MANGA
SHOGAK●KAN FOR MEN MANGA (FOR AN INSTANT)
FOREIGN COMICS & ARTBOOKS
THESE ARE THE SECTIONS I'VE BEEN IN CHARGE OF.
MY MEMORY IS TERRIBLE, SO I DON'T REMEMBER THE EXACT TIMEFRAMES AND SO ON.
I FEEL LIKE I WAS RUNNING SECTIONS FOR MANGA I DON'T BUY MUCH OF MYSELF.
BY THE WAY, THE FIRST SECTION I RAN WAS...
HONDA-SAN, I NOTICED ...
...THAT YOU RUN ON A DIFFERENT TIMELINE THAN OTHER PEOPLE. I OFTEN SEE YOU HAPPILY DIVING HEADLONG ALL BY YOURSELF INTO MANGA TITLES THAT MAKE ME THINK, "WHO WOULD GET HOOKED ON THAT NOW!?"...
...SO I'D LIKE YOU TO RUN THE MASS-MARKET COMICS SECTION!
BUSTED!

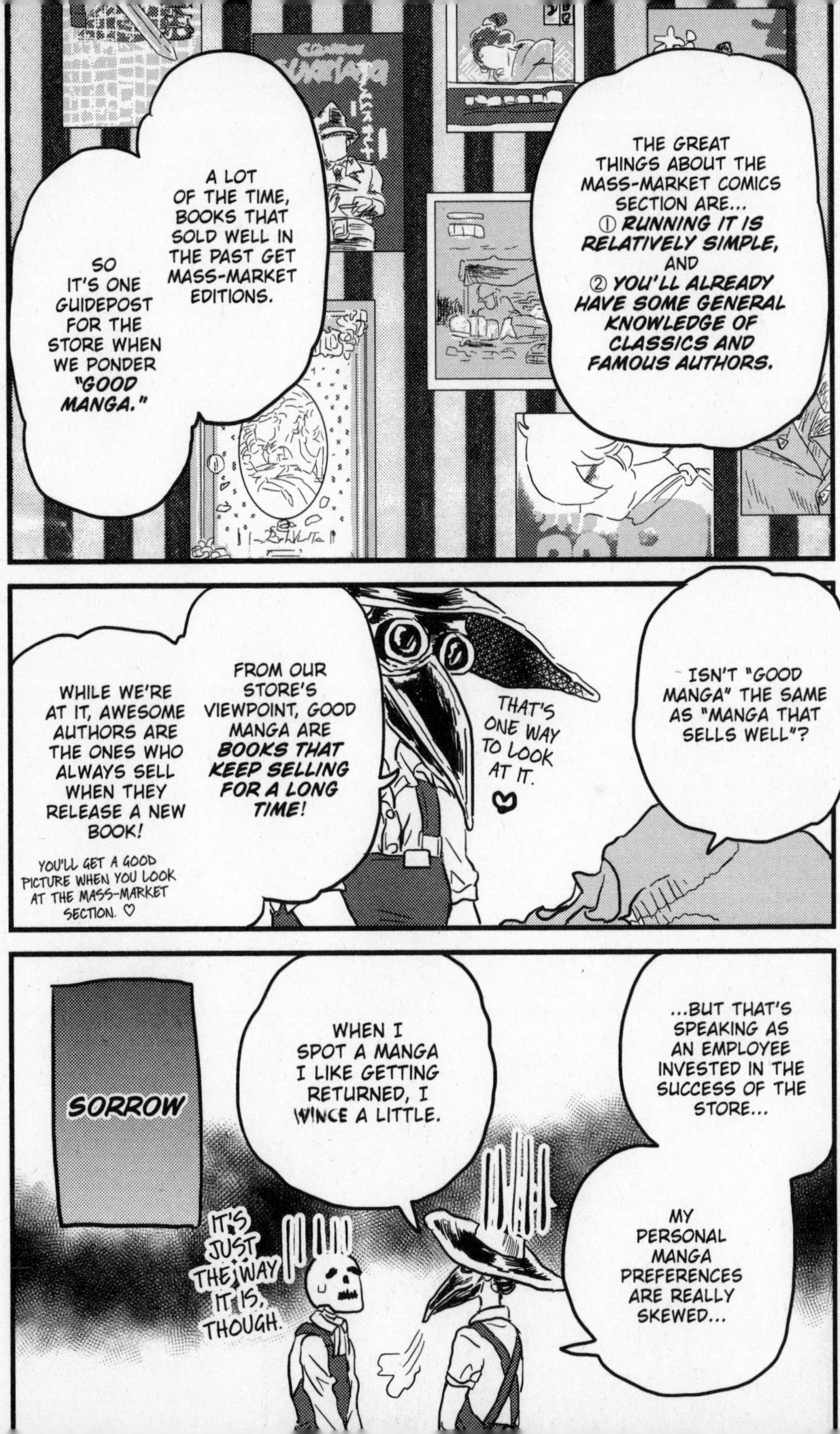
THE GREAT THINGS ABOUT THE MASS-MARKET COMICS SECTION ARE... ① RUNNING IT IS RELATIVELY SIMPLE, AND ② YOU'LL ALREADY HAVE SOME GENERAL KNOWLEDGE OF CLASSICS AND FAMOUS AUTHORS.
A LOT OF THE TIME, BOOKS THAT SOLD WELL IN THE PAST GET MASS-MARKET EDITIONS.
SO IT'S ONE GUIDEPOST FOR THE STORE WHEN WE PONDER "GOOD MANGA."
ISN'T "GOOD MANGA" THE SAME AS "MANGA THAT SELLS WELL"?
THAT'S ONE WAY TO LOOK AT IT. ♥
FROM OUR STORE'S VIEWPOINT, GOOD MANGA ARE BOOKS THAT KEEP SELLING FOR A LONG TIME!
WHILE WE'RE AT IT, AWESOME AUTHORS ARE THE ONES WHO ALWAYS SELL WHEN THEY RELEASE A NEW BOOK!
YOU'LL GET A GOOD PICTURE WHEN YOU LOOK AT THE MASS-MARKET SECTION. ♡
...BUT THAT'S SPEAKING AS AN EMPLOYEE INVESTED IN THE SUCCESS OF THE STORE...
MY PERSONAL MANGA PREFERENCES ARE REALLY SKEWED...
WHEN I SPOT A MANGA I LIKE GETTING RETURNED, I WINCE A LITTLE.
IT'S JUST THE WAY IT IS, THOUGH.
SORROW

Skull-face
Bookseller
Honda-san

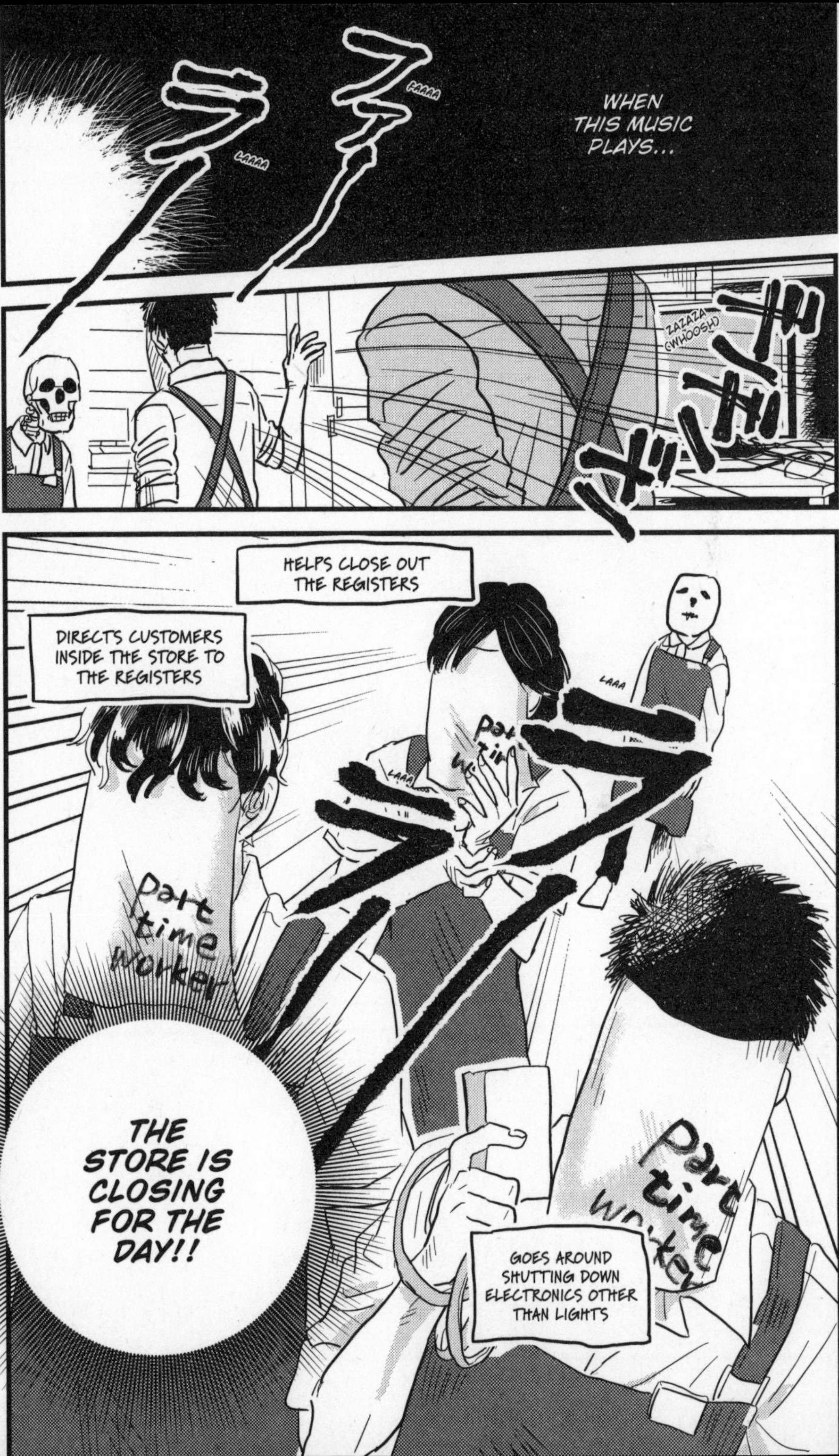

WHEN THIS MUSIC PLAYS...
FAAAA
LAAAA
ZAZAZA (WHOOSH)
HELPS CLOSE OUT THE REGISTERS
DIRECTS CUSTOMERS INSIDE THE STORE TO THE REGISTERS
LAAA
LAAA
Part time worker
Part time worker
THE STORE IS CLOSING FOR THE DAY!!
GOES AROUND SHUTTING DOWN ELECTRONICS OTHER THAN LIGHTS

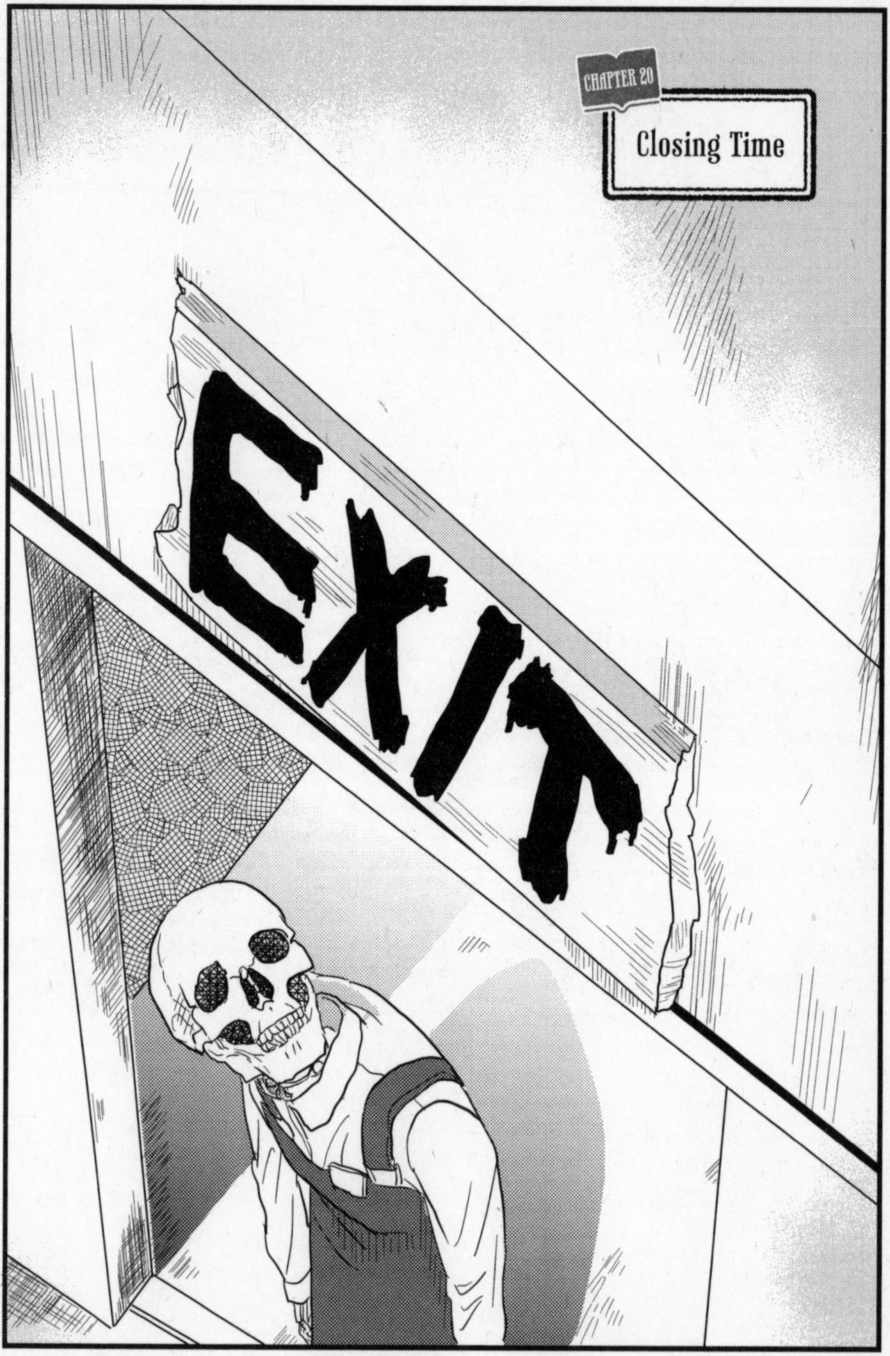
CHAPTER 20
Closing Time
EXIT

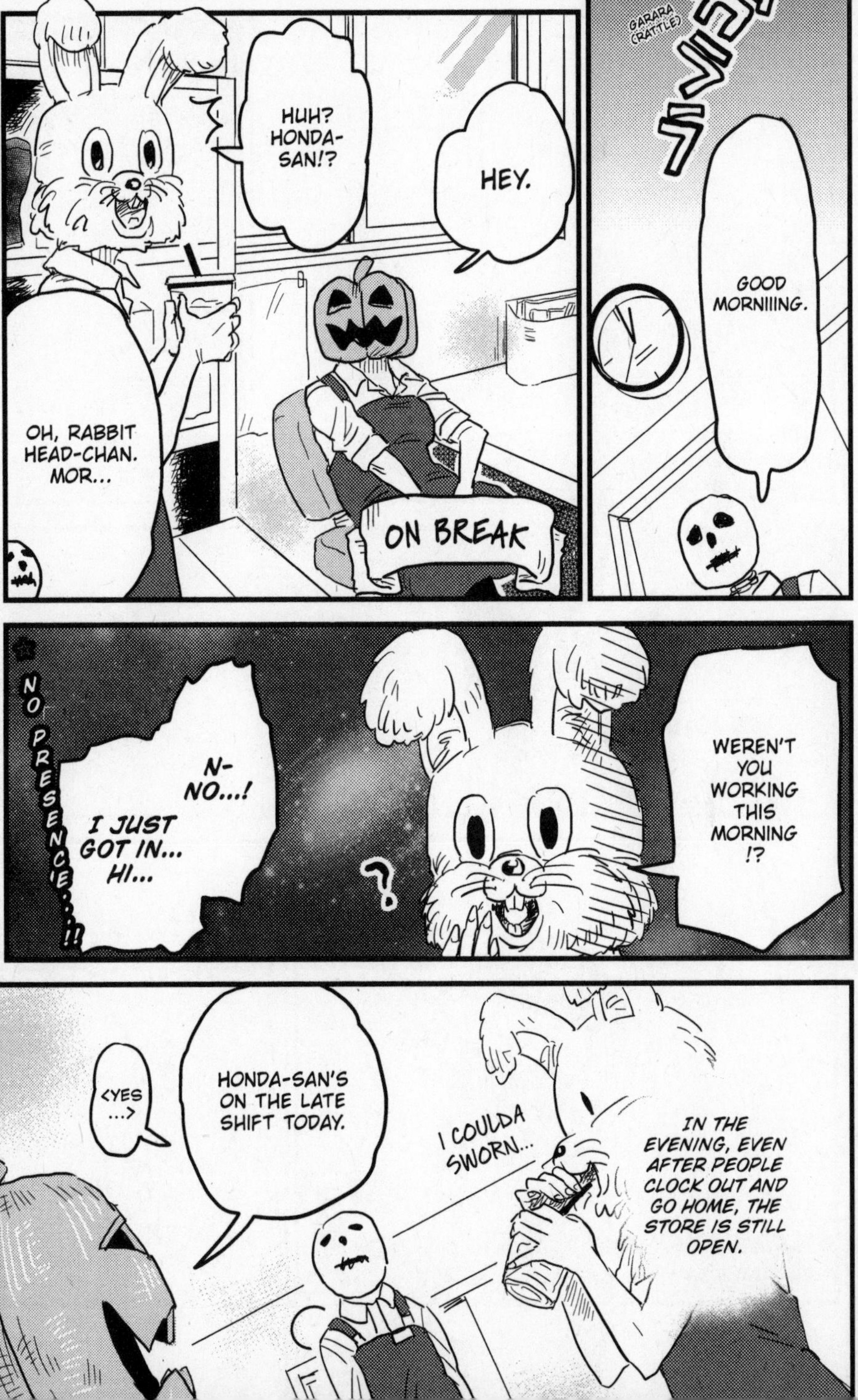
GARARA (RATTLE)
GOOD MORNIIING.
HEY.
HUH? HONDA-SAN!?
OH, RABBIT HEAD-CHAN. MOR...
ON BREAK
WEREN'T YOU WORKING THIS MORNING!?
N-NO...!
I JUST GOT IN... HI...
NO PRESENCE...!!
IN THE EVENING, EVEN AFTER PEOPLE CLOCK OUT AND GO HOME, THE STORE IS STILL OPEN.
I COULDA SWORN...
HONDA-SAN'S ON THE LATE SHIFT TODAY.
<YES ...>

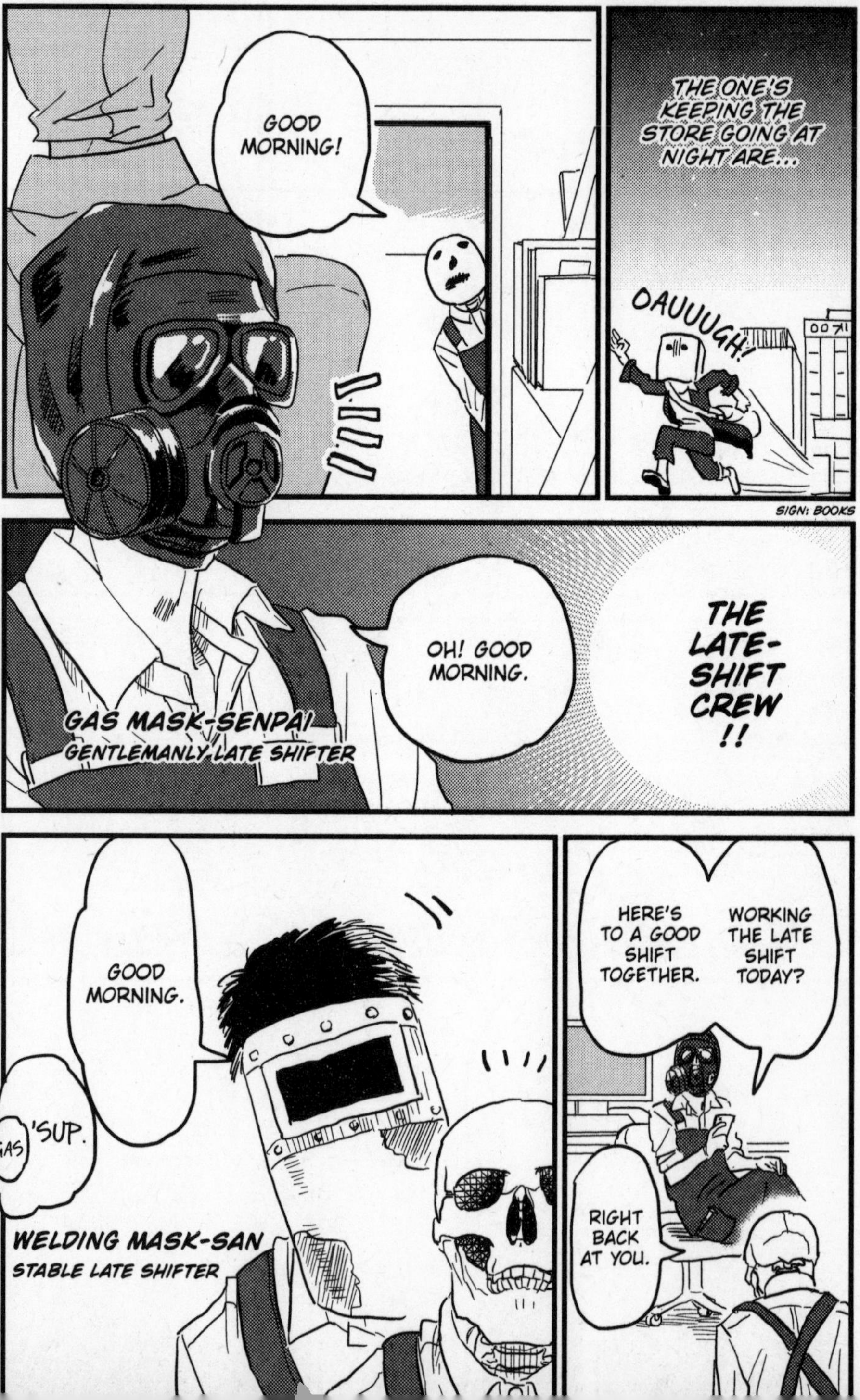
THE ONE'S KEEPING THE STORE GOING AT NIGHT ARE...
OAUUUGH!
GOOD MORNING!
THE LATE-SHIFT CREW!!
OH! GOOD MORNING.
GAS MASK-SENPAI
GENTLEMANLY LATE SHIFTER
WORKING THE LATE SHIFT TODAY?
HERE'S TO A GOOD SHIFT TOGETHER.
RIGHT BACK AT YOU.
GOOD MORNING.
GAS
'SUP.
WELDING MASK-SAN
STABLE LATE SHIFTER
SIGN: BOOKS

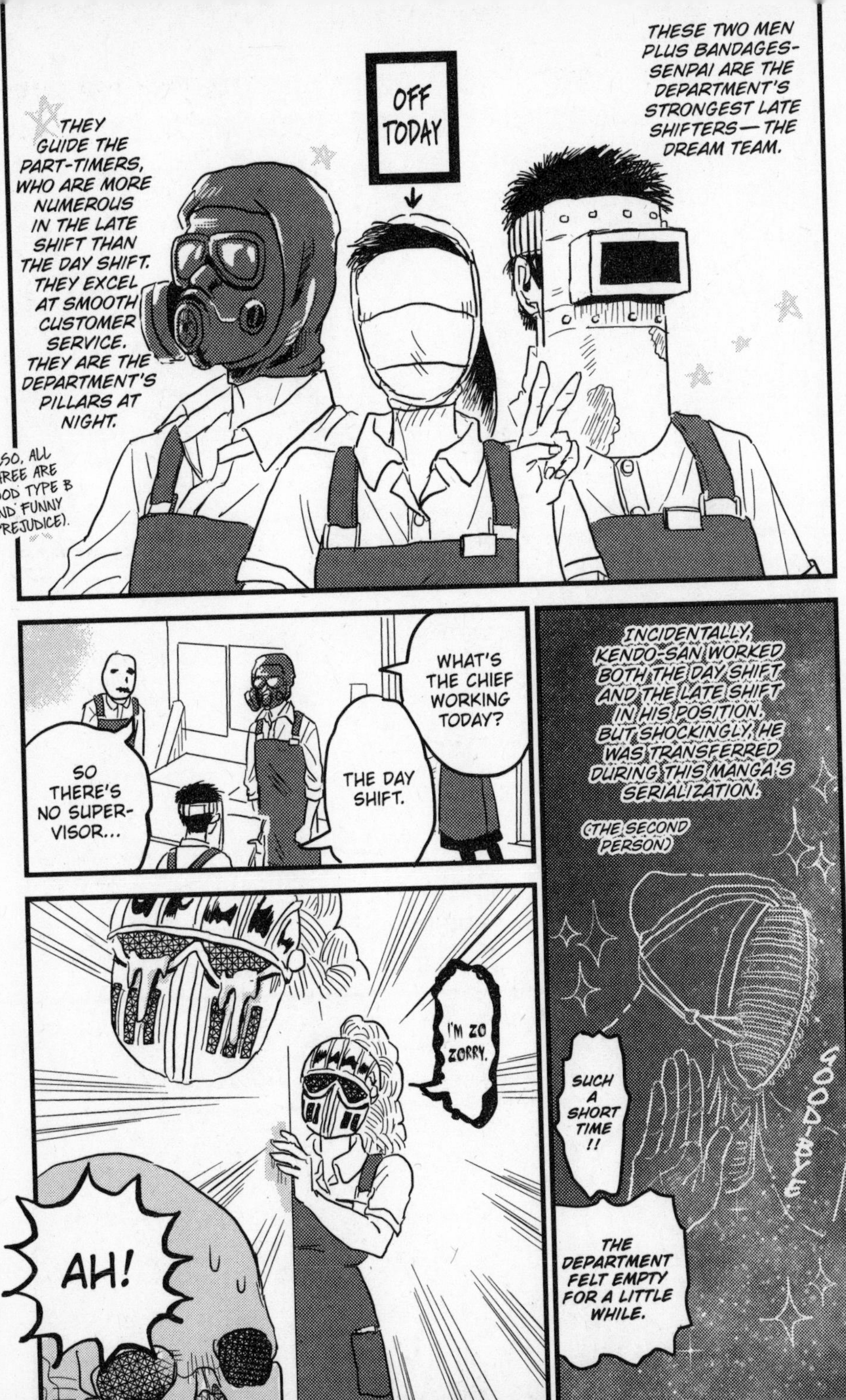
THESE TWO MEN PLUS BANDAGES-SENPAI ARE THE DEPARTMENT'S STRONGEST LATE SHIFTERS—THE DREAM TEAM.
OFF TODAY
THEY GUIDE THE PART-TIMERS, WHO ARE MORE NUMEROUS IN THE LATE SHIFT THAN THE DAY SHIFT. THEY EXCEL AT SMOOTH CUSTOMER SERVICE. THEY ARE THE DEPARTMENT'S PILLARS AT NIGHT.
ALSO, ALL THREE ARE BLOOD TYPE B AND FUNNY (PREJUDICE).
INCIDENTALLY, KENDO-SAN WORKED BOTH THE DAY SHIFT AND THE LATE SHIFT IN HIS POSITION. BUT SHOCKINGLY, HE WAS TRANSFERRED DURING THIS MANGA'S SERIALIZATION.
(THE SECOND PERSON)
GOOD-BYE
SUCH A SHORT TIME!!
THE DEPARTMENT FELT EMPTY FOR A LITTLE WHILE.
WHAT'S THE CHIEF WORKING TODAY?
THE DAY SHIFT.
SO THERE'S NO SUPER-VISOR...
I'M ZO ZORRY.
AH!

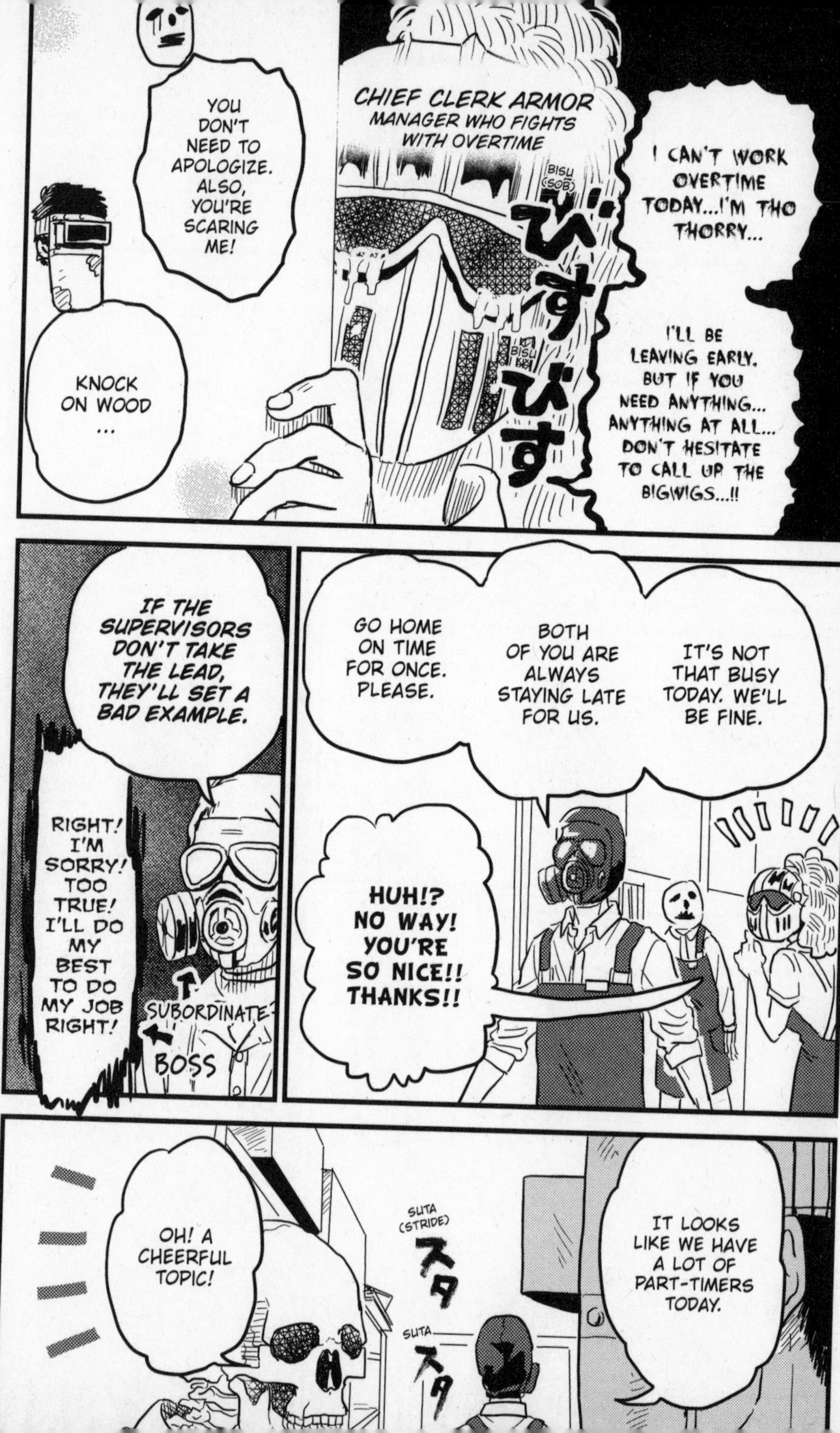
I CAN'T WORK OVERTIME TODAY...I'M THO THORRY...
CHIEF CLERK ARMOR
MANAGER WHO FIGHTS WITH OVERTIME
BISU (SOB)
びすびす
BISU
びす
I'LL BE LEAVING EARLY. BUT IF YOU NEED ANYTHING... ANYTHING AT ALL... DON'T HESITATE TO CALL UP THE BIGWIGS...!!
YOU DON'T NEED TO APOLOGIZE. ALSO, YOU'RE SCARING ME!
KNOCK ON WOOD ...
IT'S NOT THAT BUSY TODAY. WE'LL BE FINE.
BOTH OF YOU ARE ALWAYS STAYING LATE FOR US.
GO HOME ON TIME FOR ONCE. PLEASE.
HUH!? NO WAY! YOU'RE SO NICE!! THANKS!!
IF THE SUPERVISORS DON'T TAKE THE LEAD, THEY'LL SET A BAD EXAMPLE.
RIGHT! I'M SORRY! TOO TRUE! I'LL DO MY BEST TO DO MY JOB RIGHT!
SUBORDINATE
BOSS
IT LOOKS LIKE WE HAVE A LOT OF PART-TIMERS TODAY.
SUTA (STRIDE)
スタ
SUTA
スタ
OH! A CHEERFUL TOPIC!

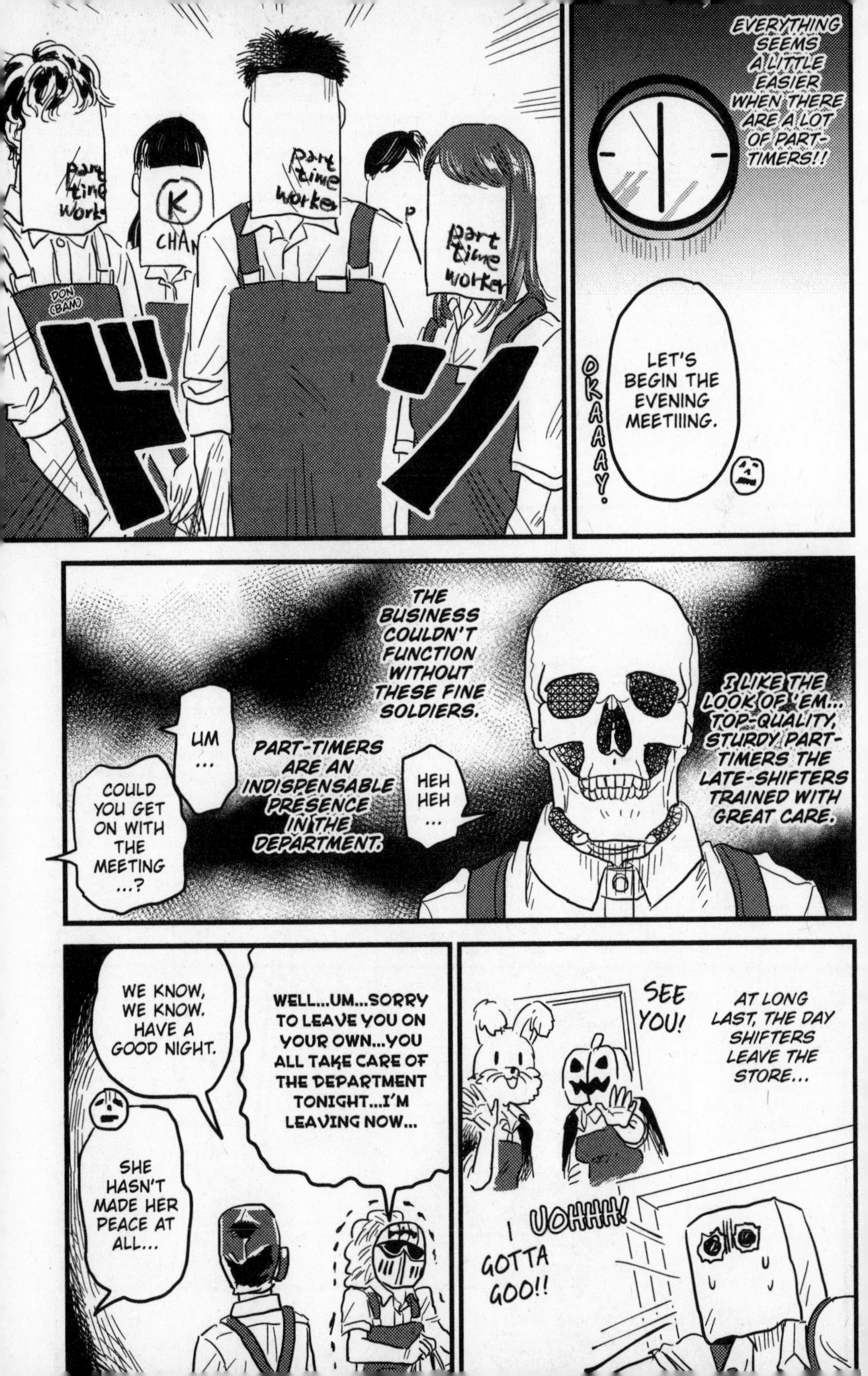
EVERYTHING SEEMS A LITTLE EASIER WHEN THERE ARE A LOT OF PART-TIMERS!!
LET'S BEGIN THE EVENING MEETIIING.
OKAAAAY.
part time work
K
CHAN
part time worker
part time worker
DON (BAM)
I LIKE THE LOOK OF 'EM... TOP-QUALITY, STURDY PART-TIMERS THE LATE-SHIFTERS TRAINED WITH GREAT CARE.
THE BUSINESS COULDN'T FUNCTION WITHOUT THESE FINE SOLDIERS.
HEH HEH ...
PART-TIMERS ARE AN INDISPENSABLE PRESENCE IN THE DEPARTMENT.
UM ...
COULD YOU GET ON WITH THE MEETING ...?
AT LONG LAST, THE DAY SHIFTERS LEAVE THE STORE...
SEE YOU!
UOHHHH!
I GOTTA GOO!!
WELL...UM...SORRY TO LEAVE YOU ON YOUR OWN...YOU ALL TAKE CARE OF THE DEPARTMENT TONIGHT...I'M LEAVING NOW...
WE KNOW, WE KNOW. HAVE A GOOD NIGHT.
SHE HASN'T MADE HER PEACE AT ALL...

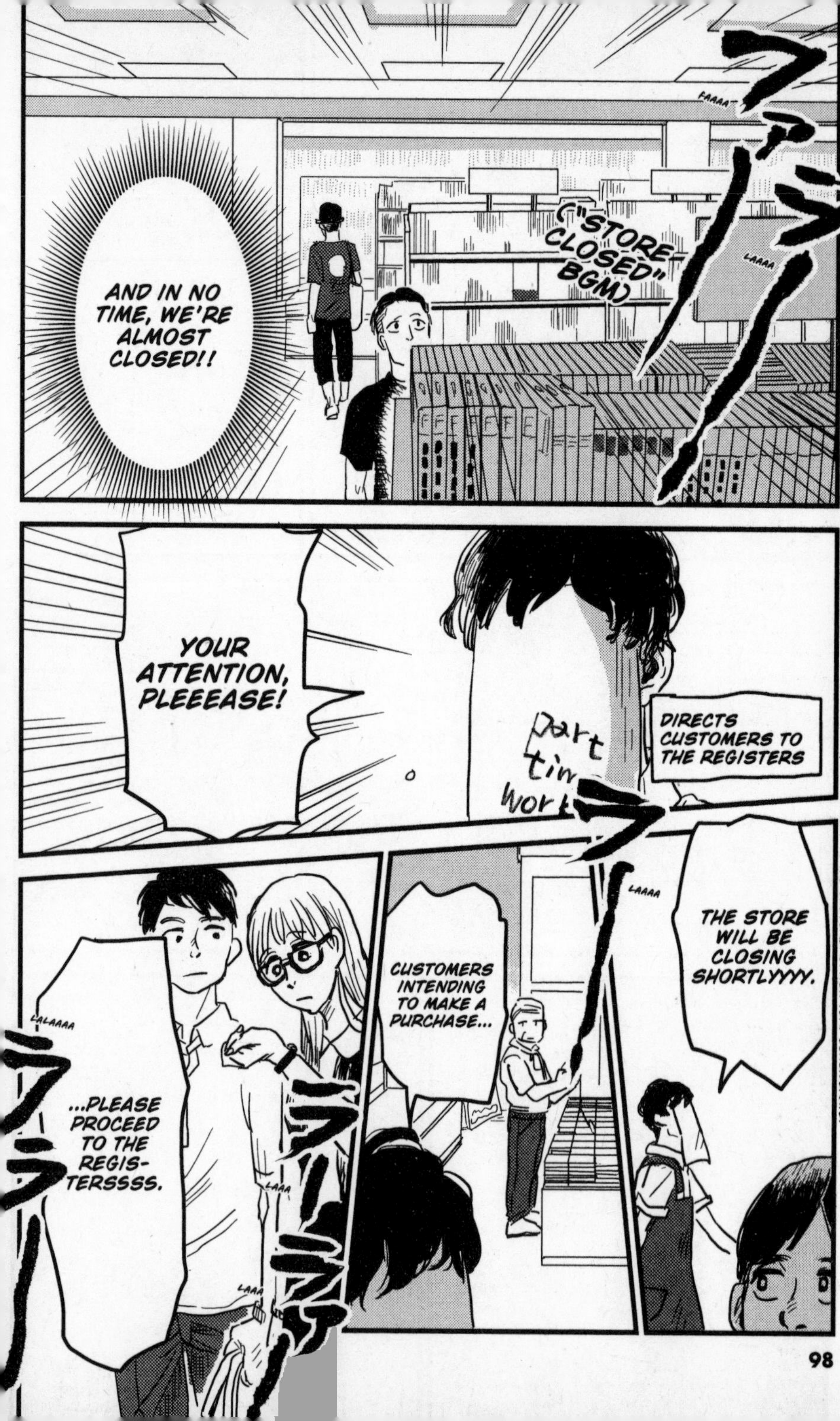
FAAAA
LAAAA
("STORE CLOSED" BGM)
AND IN NO TIME, WE'RE ALMOST CLOSED!!
DIRECTS CUSTOMERS TO THE REGISTERS
YOUR ATTENTION, PLEEEASE!
LAAAA
THE STORE WILL BE CLOSING SHORTLYYYY.
CUSTOMERS INTENDING TO MAKE A PURCHASE...
LALAAAA
...PLEASE PROCEED TO THE REGIS-TERSSSS.
LAAA
LAAA

CLOSING ANNOUNCEMENT...IF SPOKEN TO DIRECTLY, CUSTOMERS CAN THINK, "HUH? THEY'RE TRYING TO KICK ME OUT? WHAT'S WRONG WITH THIS INSULTING STORE?" SO WE WERE TAUGHT TO MAKE THIS ANNOUNCEMENT TOWARD THE AIR, BUT AUDIBLE TO THE CUSTOMERS. HOW VERY CONSIDERATE.

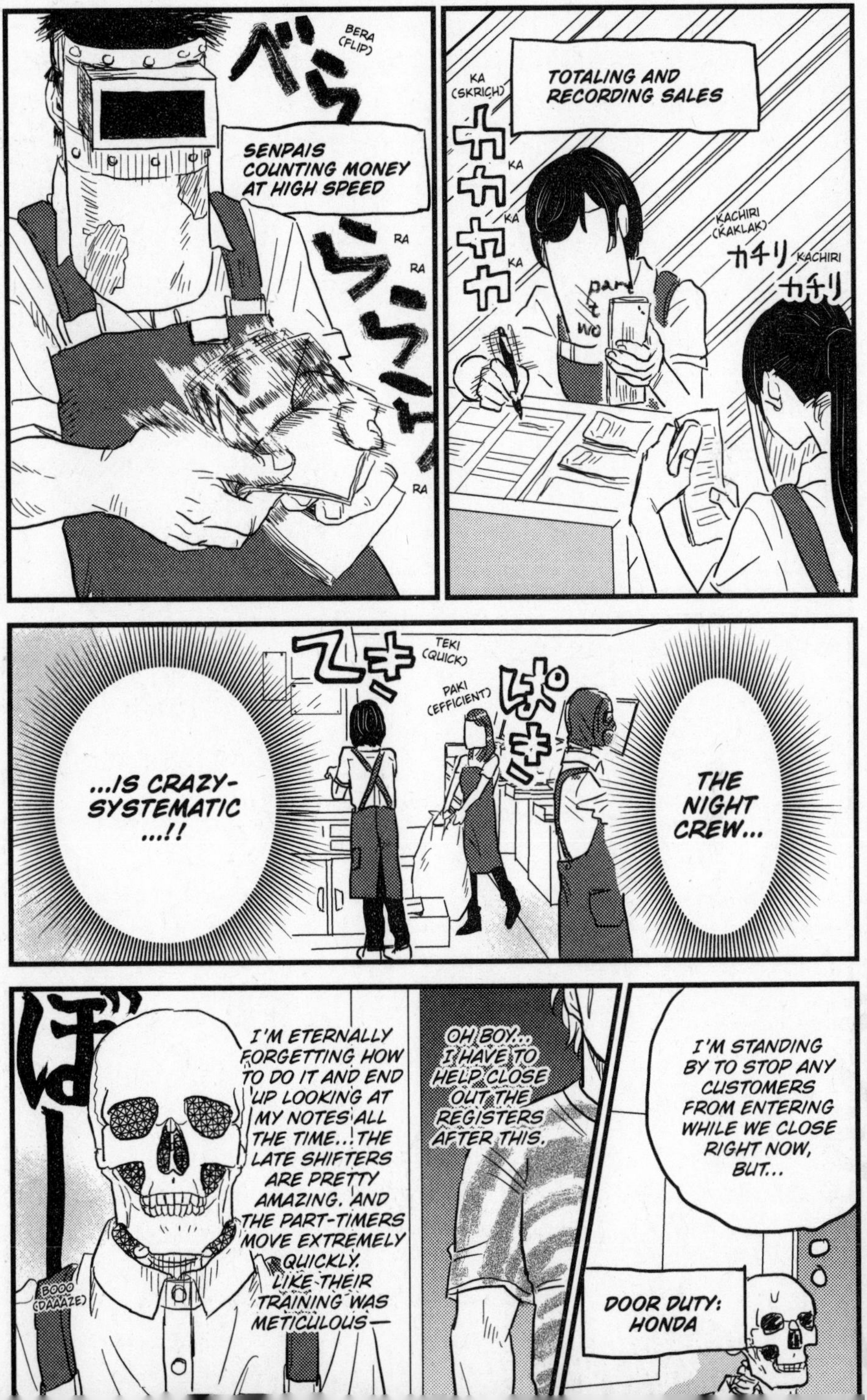
TOTALING AND RECORDING SALES
KA (SKRICH)
カカカカ
KA
KA
KA
KACHIRI (KAKLAK)
カチリ
KACHIRI
カチリ
SENPAIS COUNTING MONEY AT HIGH SPEED
BERA (FLIP)
べらららら
RA
RA
RA
THE NIGHT CREW...
ぱき
PAKI (EFFICIENT)
てき
TEKI (QUICK)
...IS CRAZY-SYSTEMATIC ...!!
I'M STANDING BY TO STOP ANY CUSTOMERS FROM ENTERING WHILE WE CLOSE RIGHT NOW, BUT...
DOOR DUTY: HONDA
OH BOY... I HAVE TO HELP CLOSE OUT THE REGISTERS AFTER THIS.
I'M ETERNALLY FORGETTING HOW TO DO IT AND END UP LOOKING AT MY NOTES ALL THE TIME... THE LATE SHIFTERS ARE PRETTY AMAZING. AND THE PART-TIMERS MOVE EXTREMELY QUICKLY. LIKE THEIR TRAINING WAS METICULOUS—
ぼ
BOOO (DAAAZE)

HONDA-SAN!!

HUH?

EXCUSE ME! I'M SO SORRY!

WE'VE CLOSED FOR THE DA—

AH!

OH SNAP! I LET CUSTOMERS IN!

YEEEEK!

THEY LOOK LIKE HOLLYWOOD STAAAARS!

<PLEASE COME AGAIN. THANK YOU VERY MUCH!! GOOD NIGHT!! HAVE A GOOD NIGHT!!>

HEY, THAT WAS PRETTY GOOD!! SAID THAT LAST BIT TWICE, BUT...

...THAT SHOULD GET THE MESSAGE ACROSS...!!

NNGH! NO, THIS IS NOT THE TIME!

AWAKEN, ENGLISH CONVERSATION ABILITIES!!

<IT'S TIME TO CLOSE.>

UMM, <SORRY>!!

ALMOST! <NOW>!!

BA (WHAP)

SORRY! I UNDERSTA— SNRK! PFFF!

HE GOT THE MESSA— AAAAOOO—

SOMETIMES I'LL BREAK OUT SOME DESPERATE ENGLISH ONLY TO FIND OUT THE CUSTOMER WAS A JAPANESE SPEAKER. IT'S ALWAYS A HARD HIT.

THANKS...

DON-SAN, I'LL SWITCH WITH YOU!

MY SINCEREST APOLO-GIESSS!

THE EXIT IS RIGHT OVER THERE!

GOT IT. LOL. PFFT-LOL!

SHA (FWIP)

THE EXIT IS THIS WAY!

THANK YOUUU.

THANK YOU, PLEASE COME AGAIN!

THEY'RE ALL OUT!!

part time worker

BATAN (SHUT)

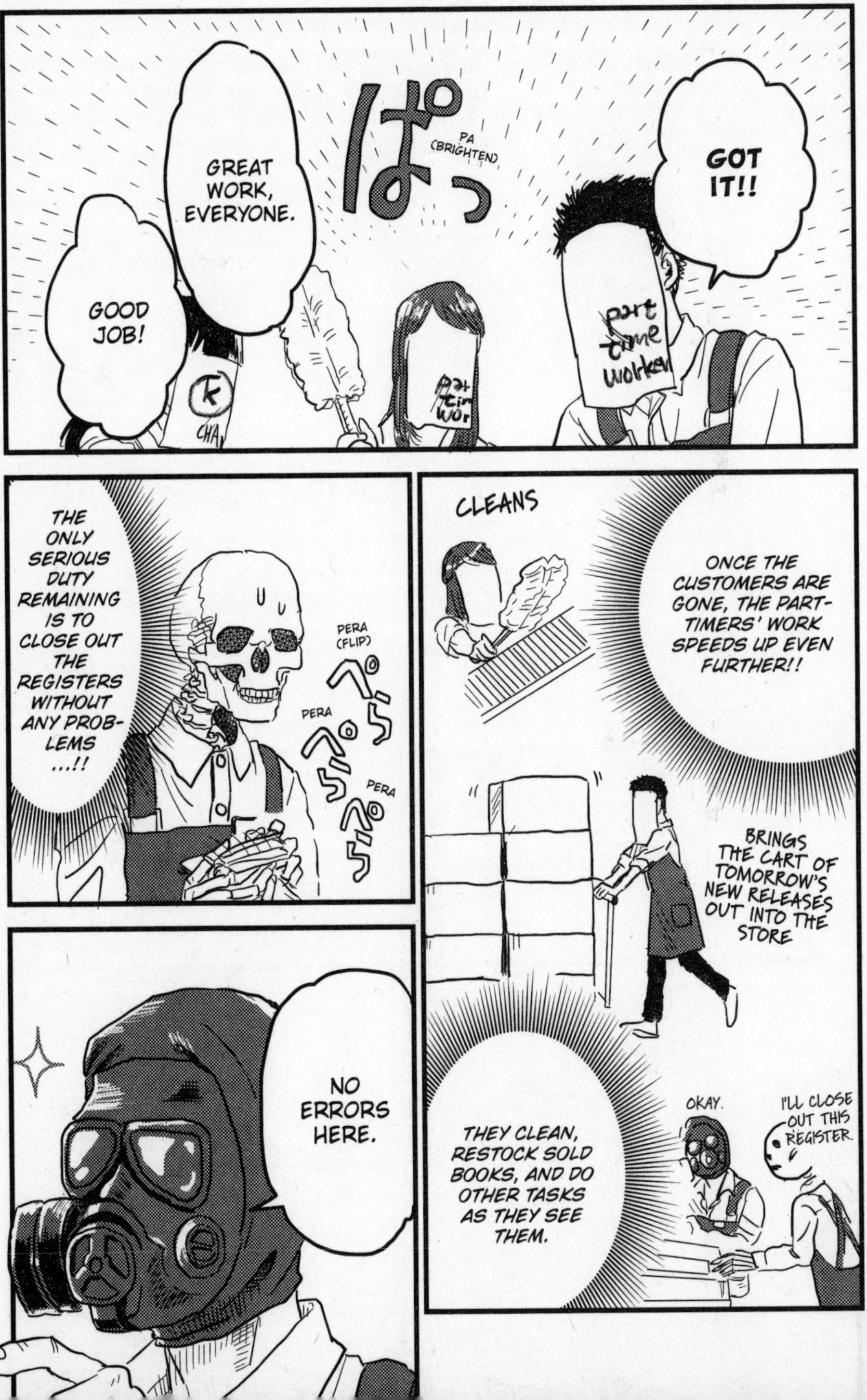
GOT IT!!
part time worker
ぱっ
PA (BRIGHTEN)
GREAT WORK, EVERYONE.
GOOD JOB!
CHA
CLEANS
ONCE THE CUSTOMERS ARE GONE, THE PART-TIMERS' WORK SPEEDS UP EVEN FURTHER!!
BRINGS THE CART OF TOMORROW'S NEW RELEASES OUT INTO THE STORE
I'LL CLOSE OUT THIS REGISTER.
OKAY.
THEY CLEAN, RESTOCK SOLD BOOKS, AND DO OTHER TASKS AS THEY SEE THEM.
THE ONLY SERIOUS DUTY REMAINING IS TO CLOSE OUT THE REGISTERS WITHOUT ANY PROB-LEMS ...!!
PERA (FLIP)
PERA
PERA
NO ERRORS HERE.

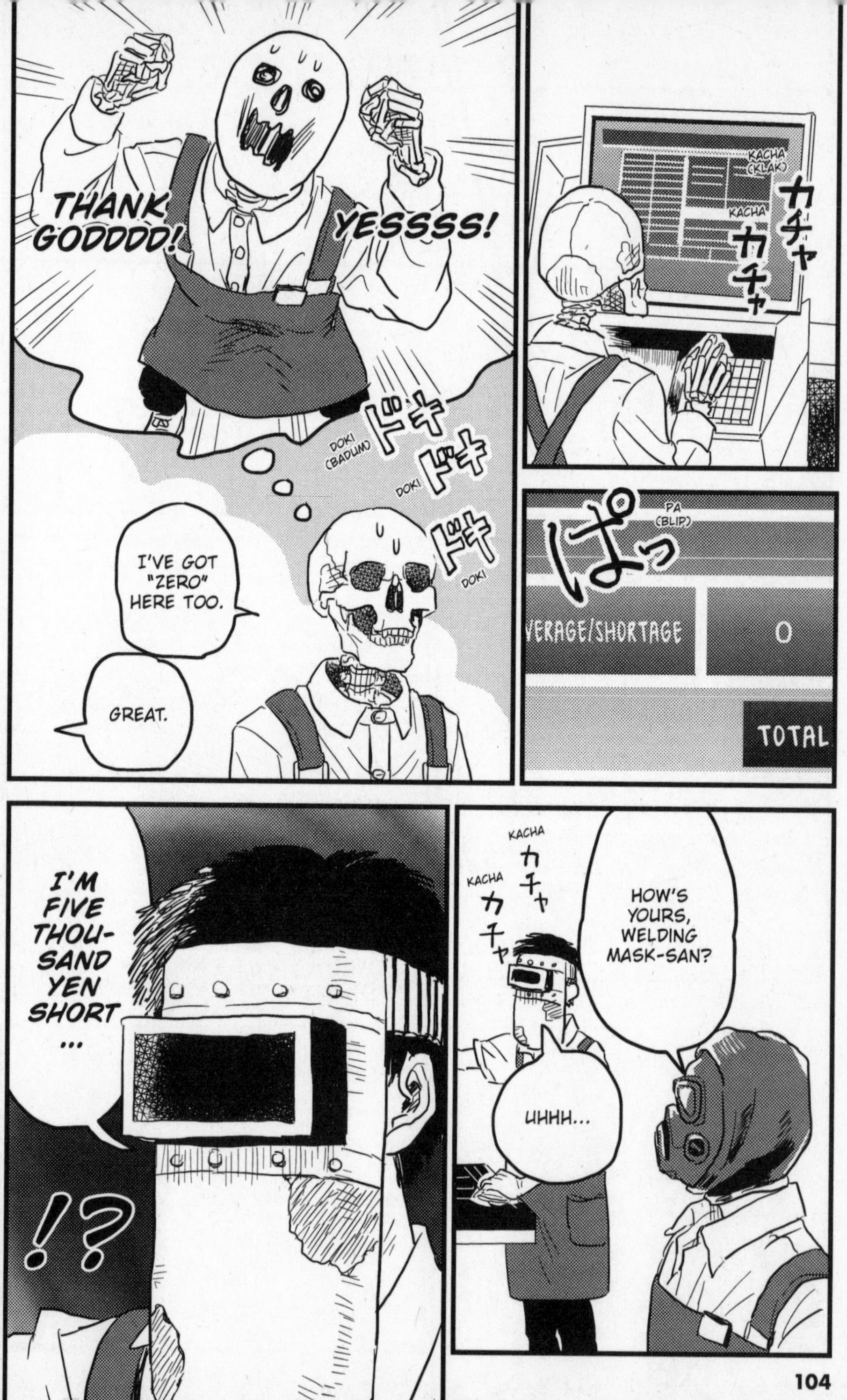
KACHA (KLAK)
カチャ
KACHA
カチャ
PA (BLIP)
ぱっ
VERAGE/SHORTAGE
0
TOTAL
YESSSS!
THANK GODDDD!
ドキ
DOKI (BADUM)
ドキ
DOKI
ドキ
DOKI
I'VE GOT "ZERO" HERE TOO.
GREAT.
KACHA
カチャ
KACHA
カチャ
HOW'S YOURS, WELDING MASK-SAN?
UHHH...
I'M FIVE THOUSAND YEN SHORT...
!?

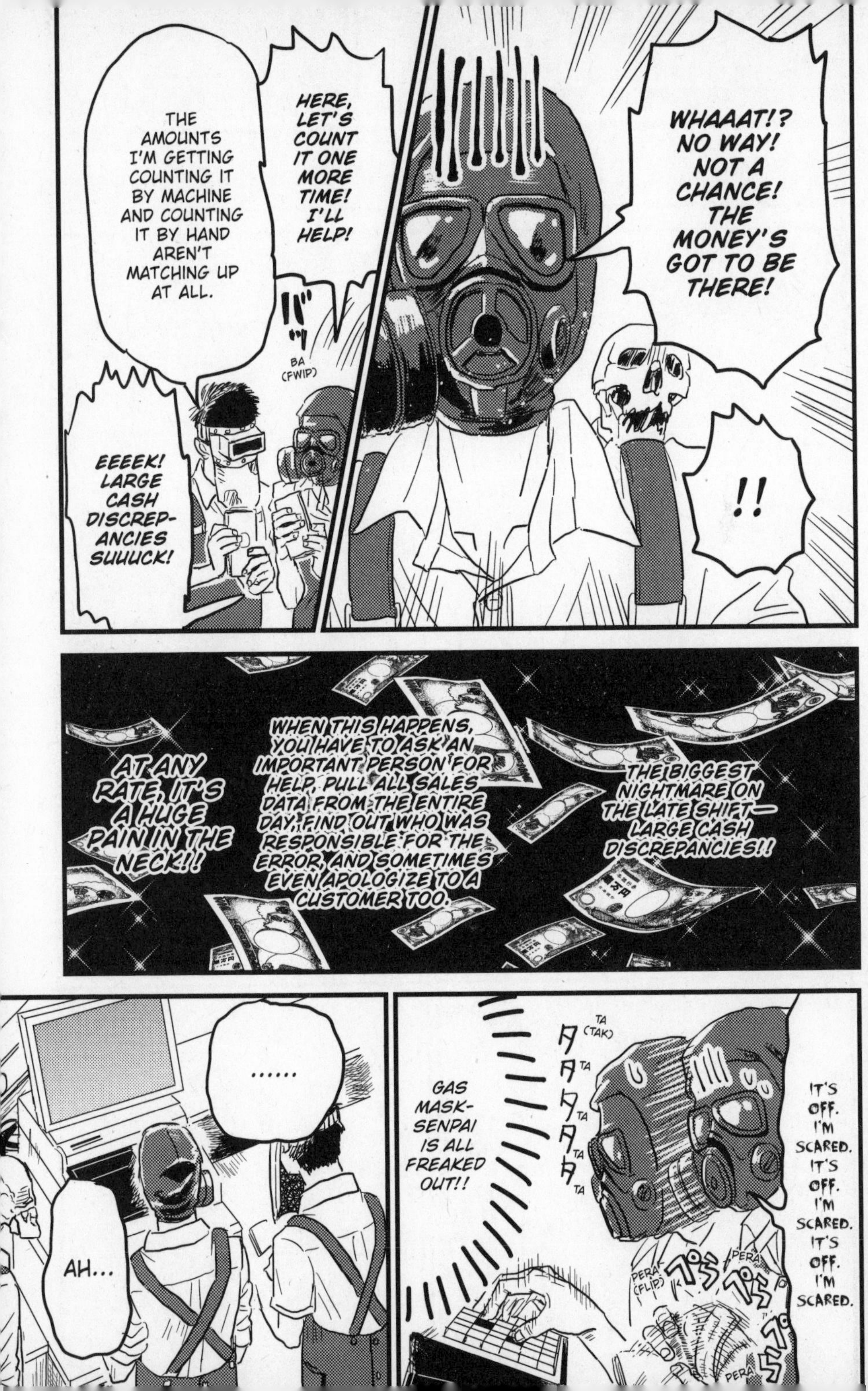
WHAAAT!? NO WAY! NOT A CHANCE! THE MONEY'S GOT TO BE THERE!
!!
HERE, LET'S COUNT IT ONE MORE TIME! I'LL HELP!
BA (FWIP)
THE AMOUNTS I'M GETTING COUNTING IT BY MACHINE AND COUNTING IT BY HAND AREN'T MATCHING UP AT ALL.
EEEEK! LARGE CASH DISCREPANCIES SUUUCK!
THE BIGGEST NIGHTMARE ON THE LATE SHIFT—LARGE CASH DISCREPANCIES!!
WHEN THIS HAPPENS, YOU HAVE TO ASK AN IMPORTANT PERSON FOR HELP, PULL ALL SALES DATA FROM THE ENTIRE DAY, FIND OUT WHO WAS RESPONSIBLE FOR THE ERROR, AND SOMETIMES EVEN APOLOGIZE TO A CUSTOMER TOO.
AT ANY RATE, IT'S A HUGE PAIN IN THE NECK!!
IT'S OFF. I'M SCARED. IT'S OFF. I'M SCARED. IT'S OFF. I'M SCARED.
TA (TAK) TA TA TA TA TA
GAS MASK-SENPAI IS ALL FREAKED OUT!!
PERA (FLIP) PERA PERA
......
AH...

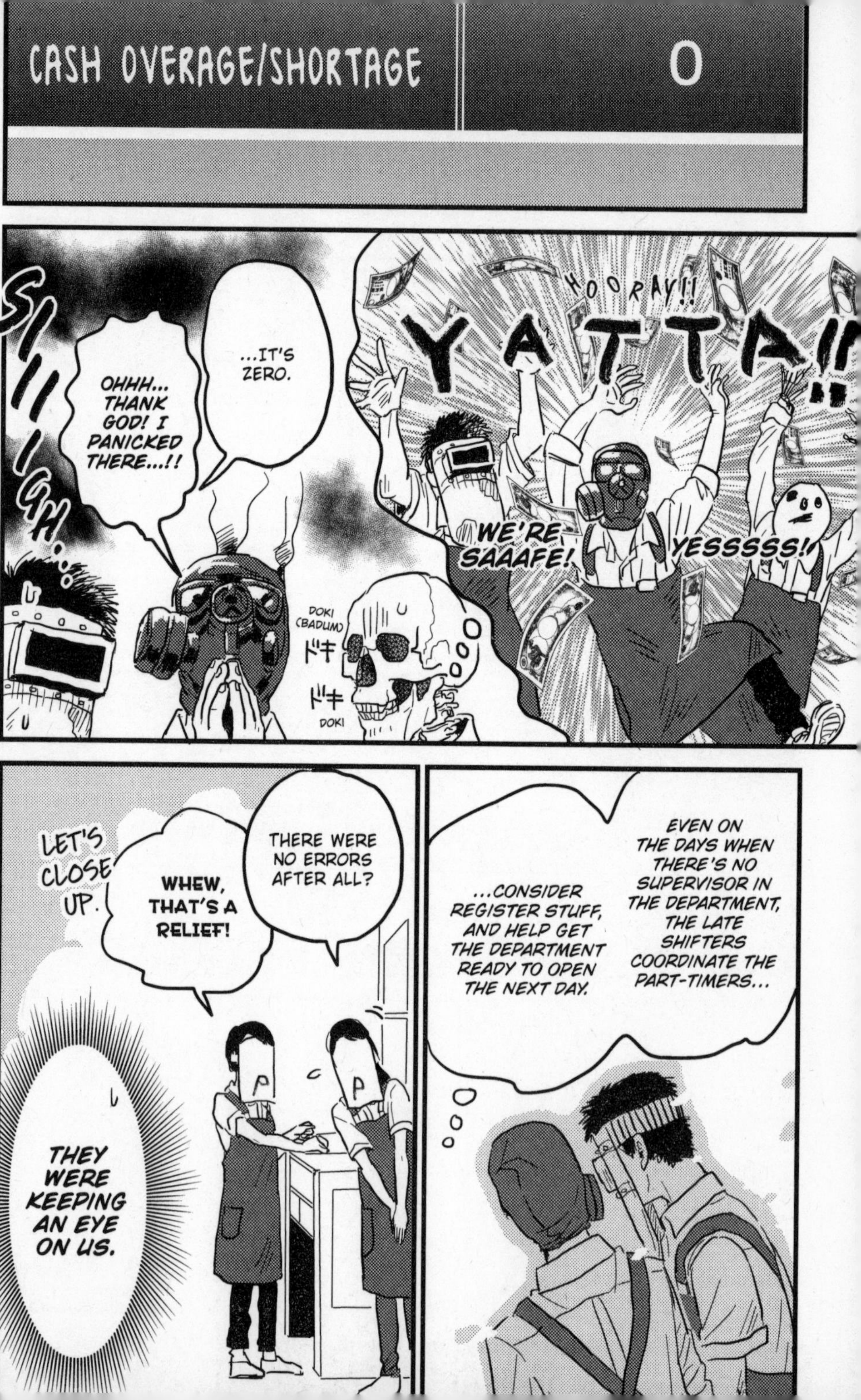
CASH OVERAGE/SHORTAGE
0
...IT'S ZERO.
HOORAY!!
YATTA!!
WE'RE SAAAFE!
YESSSSS!
OHHH... THANK GOD! I PANICKED THERE...!!
DOKI (BADUM) ドキ
ドキ DOKI
SIIIIGH...
EVEN ON THE DAYS WHEN THERE'S NO SUPERVISOR IN THE DEPARTMENT, THE LATE SHIFTERS COORDINATE THE PART-TIMERS...
...CONSIDER REGISTER STUFF, AND HELP GET THE DEPARTMENT READY TO OPEN THE NEXT DAY.
THERE WERE NO ERRORS AFTER ALL?
WHEW, THAT'S A RELIEF!
LET'S CLOSE UP.
THEY WERE KEEPING AN EYE ON US.

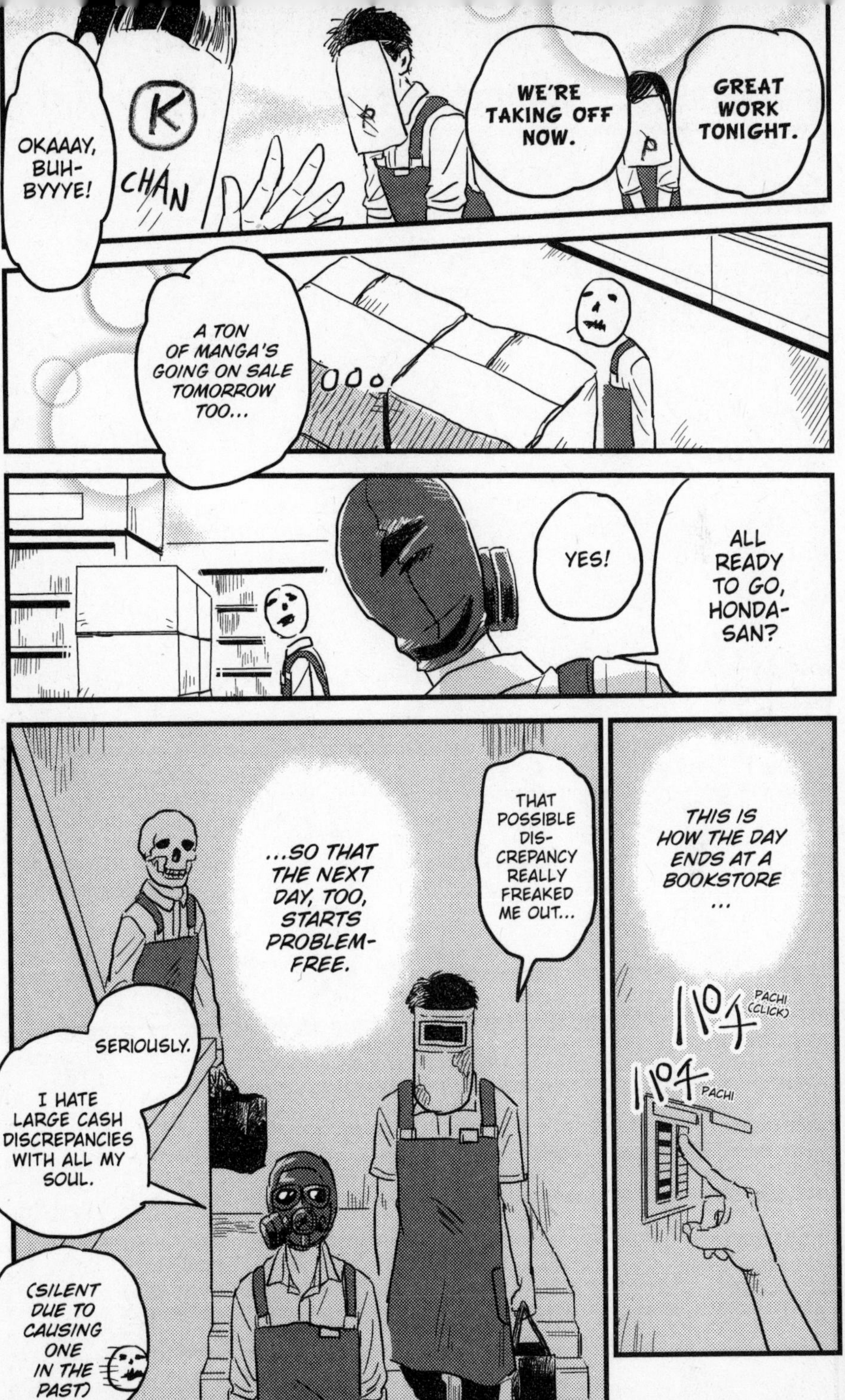
GREAT WORK TONIGHT.
WE'RE TAKING OFF NOW.
OKAAAY, BUH-BYYYE!
K CHAN
A TON OF MANGA'S GOING ON SALE TOMORROW TOO...
ooo
ALL READY TO GO, HONDA-SAN?
YES!
THIS IS HOW THE DAY ENDS AT A BOOKSTORE ...
PACHI (CLICK)
PACHI
...SO THAT THE NEXT DAY, TOO, STARTS PROBLEM-FREE.
THAT POSSIBLE DIS-CREPANCY REALLY FREAKED ME OUT...
SERIOUSLY.
I HATE LARGE CASH DISCREPANCIES WITH ALL MY SOUL.
(SILENT DUE TO CAUSING ONE IN THE PAST)

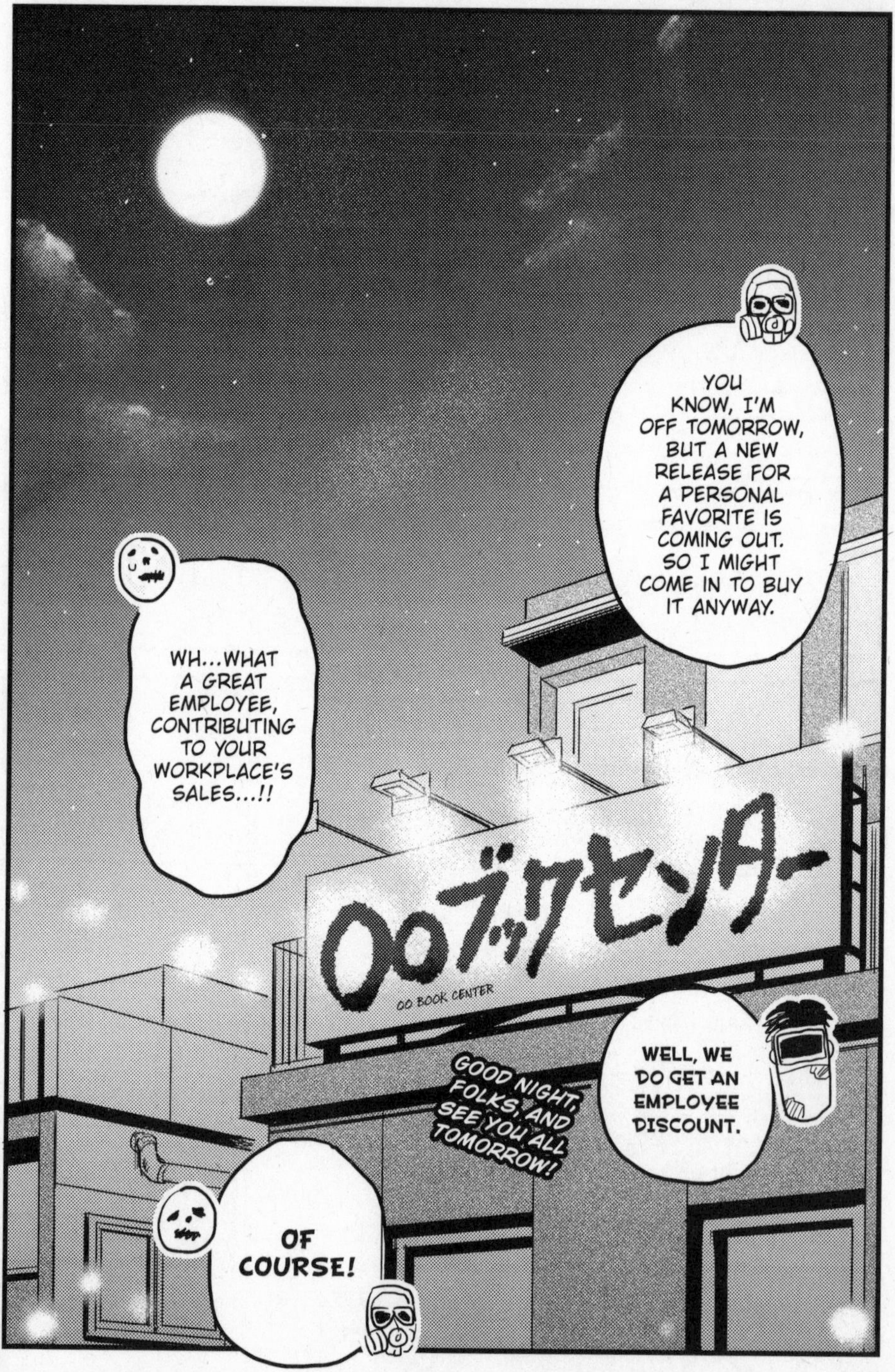
YOU KNOW, I'M OFF TOMORROW, BUT A NEW RELEASE FOR A PERSONAL FAVORITE IS COMING OUT. SO I MIGHT COME IN TO BUY IT ANYWAY.
WH...WHAT A GREAT EMPLOYEE, CONTRIBUTING TO YOUR WORKPLACE'S SALES...!!
○○ブックセンター
OO BOOK CENTER
WELL, WE DO GET AN EMPLOYEE DISCOUNT.
GOOD NIGHT, FOLKS, AND SEE YOU ALL TOMORROW!
OF COURSE!

Continued in Volume 4

Skull-face
Bookseller
Honda-san

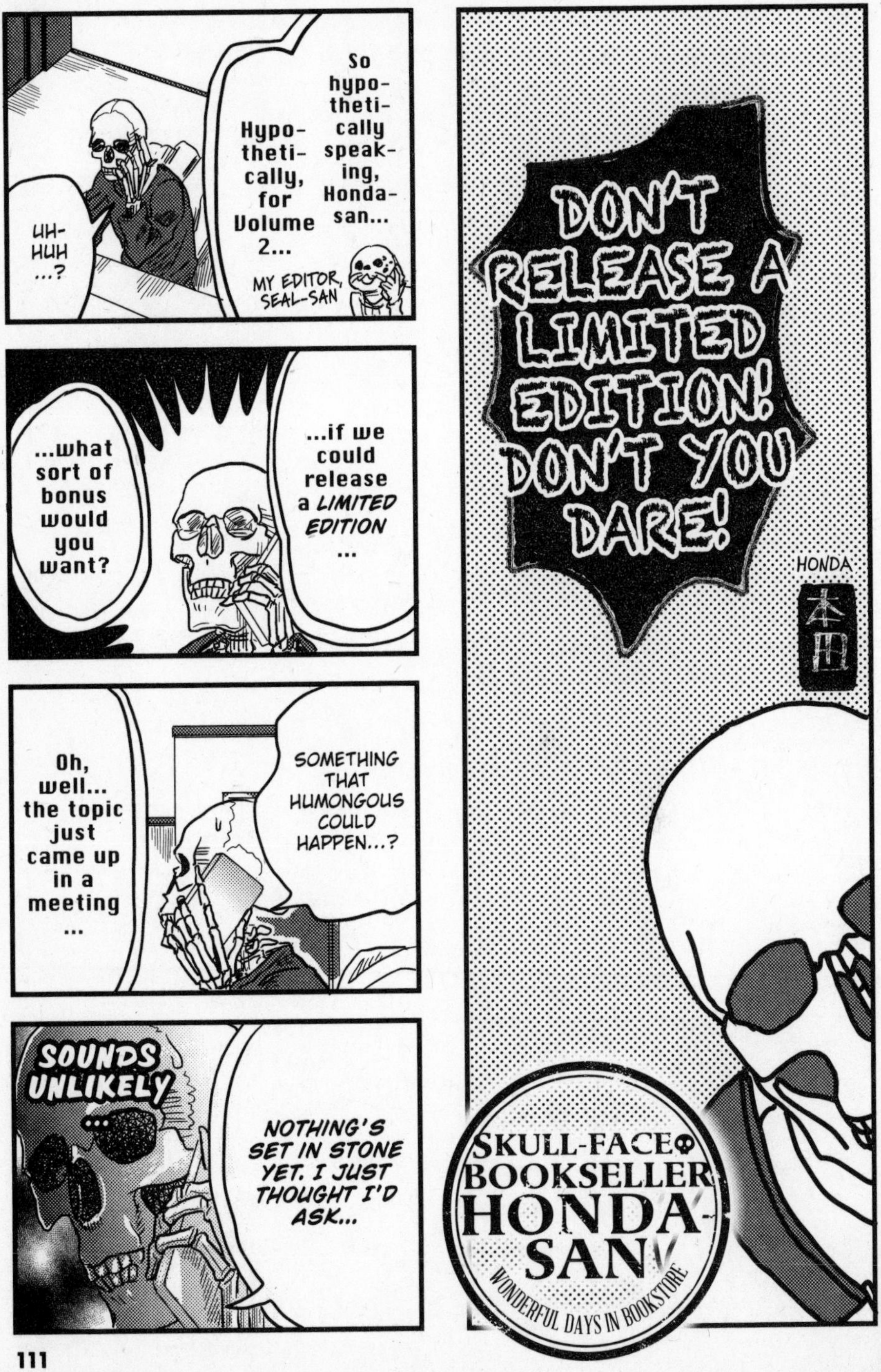
DON'T RELEASE A LIMITED EDITION! DON'T YOU DARE!
HONDA
本田
SKULL-FACE BOOKSELLER HONDA-SAN
WONDERFUL DAYS IN BOOKSTORE
So hypothetically speaking, Honda-san...
Hypothetically, for Volume 2...
MY EDITOR, SEAL-SAN
UH-HUH ...?
...if we could release a LIMITED EDITION ...
...what sort of bonus would you want?
SOMETHING THAT HUMONGOUS COULD HAPPEN...?
Oh, well... the topic just came up in a meeting ...
NOTHING'S SET IN STONE YET. I JUST THOUGHT I'D ASK...
SOUNDS UNLIKELY
...

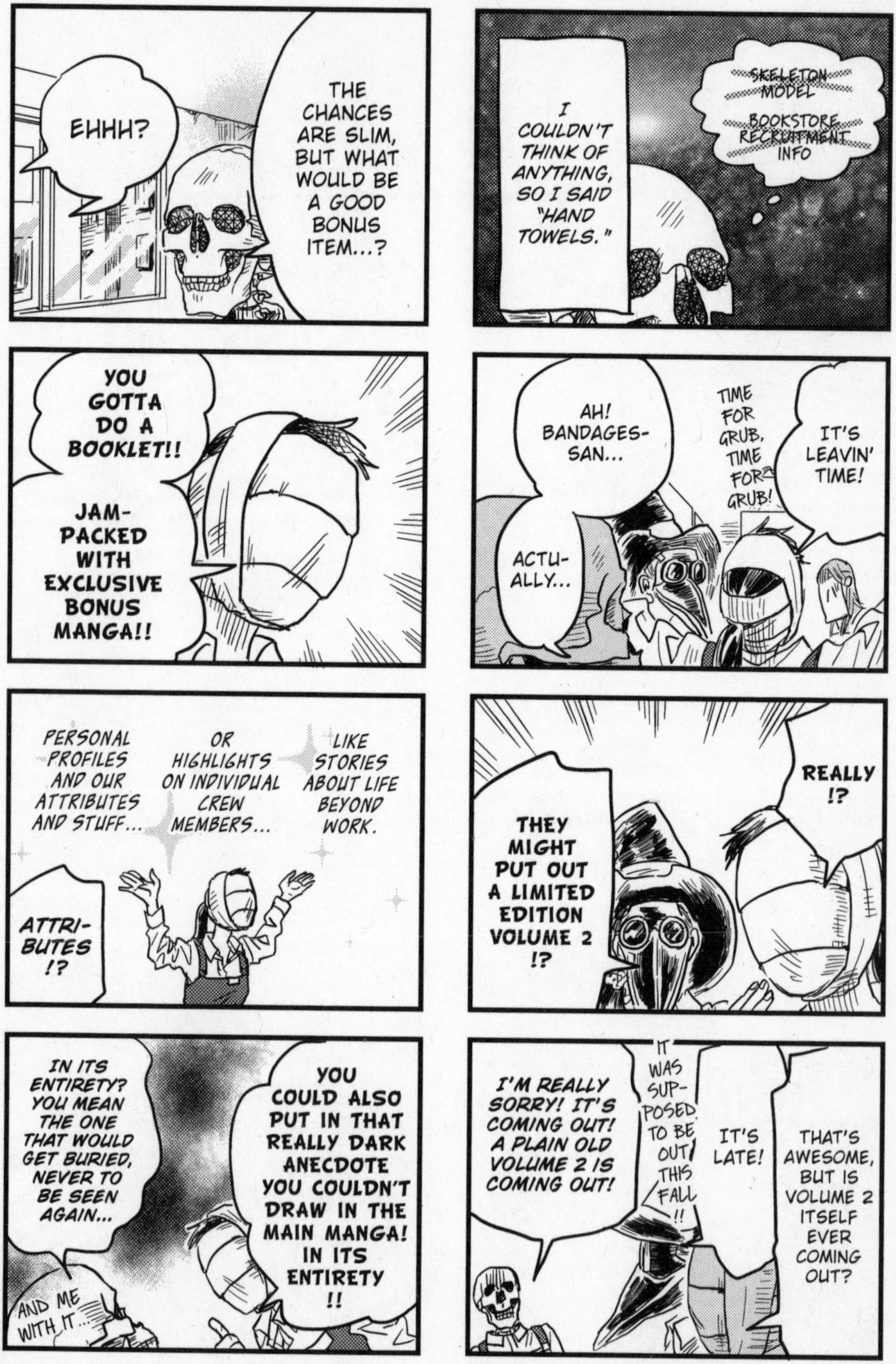
SKELETON MODEL
BOOKSTORE RECRUITMENT INFO
I COULDN'T THINK OF ANYTHING, SO I SAID "HAND TOWELS."
IT'S LEAVIN' TIME!
TIME FOR GRUB, TIME FOR GRUB!
AH! BANDAGES-SAN...
ACTUALLY...
REALLY!?
THEY MIGHT PUT OUT A LIMITED EDITION VOLUME 2!?
THAT'S AWESOME, BUT IS VOLUME 2 ITSELF EVER COMING OUT?
IT'S LATE!
IT WAS SUPPOSED TO BE OUT THIS FALL!!
I'M REALLY SORRY! IT'S COMING OUT! A PLAIN OLD VOLUME 2 IS COMING OUT!
THE CHANCES ARE SLIM, BUT WHAT WOULD BE A GOOD BONUS ITEM...?
EHHH?
YOU GOTTA DO A BOOKLET!!
JAM-PACKED WITH EXCLUSIVE BONUS MANGA!!
LIKE STORIES ABOUT LIFE BEYOND WORK.
OR HIGHLIGHTS ON INDIVIDUAL CREW MEMBERS...
PERSONAL PROFILES AND OUR ATTRIBUTES AND STUFF...
ATTRIBUTES!?
YOU COULD ALSO PUT IN THAT REALLY DARK ANECDOTE YOU COULDN'T DRAW IN THE MAIN MANGA! IN ITS ENTIRETY!!
IN ITS ENTIRETY? YOU MEAN THE ONE THAT WOULD GET BURIED, NEVER TO BE SEEN AGAIN...
AND ME WITH IT...
CONVERSATION FROM AROUND OCTOBER 2016

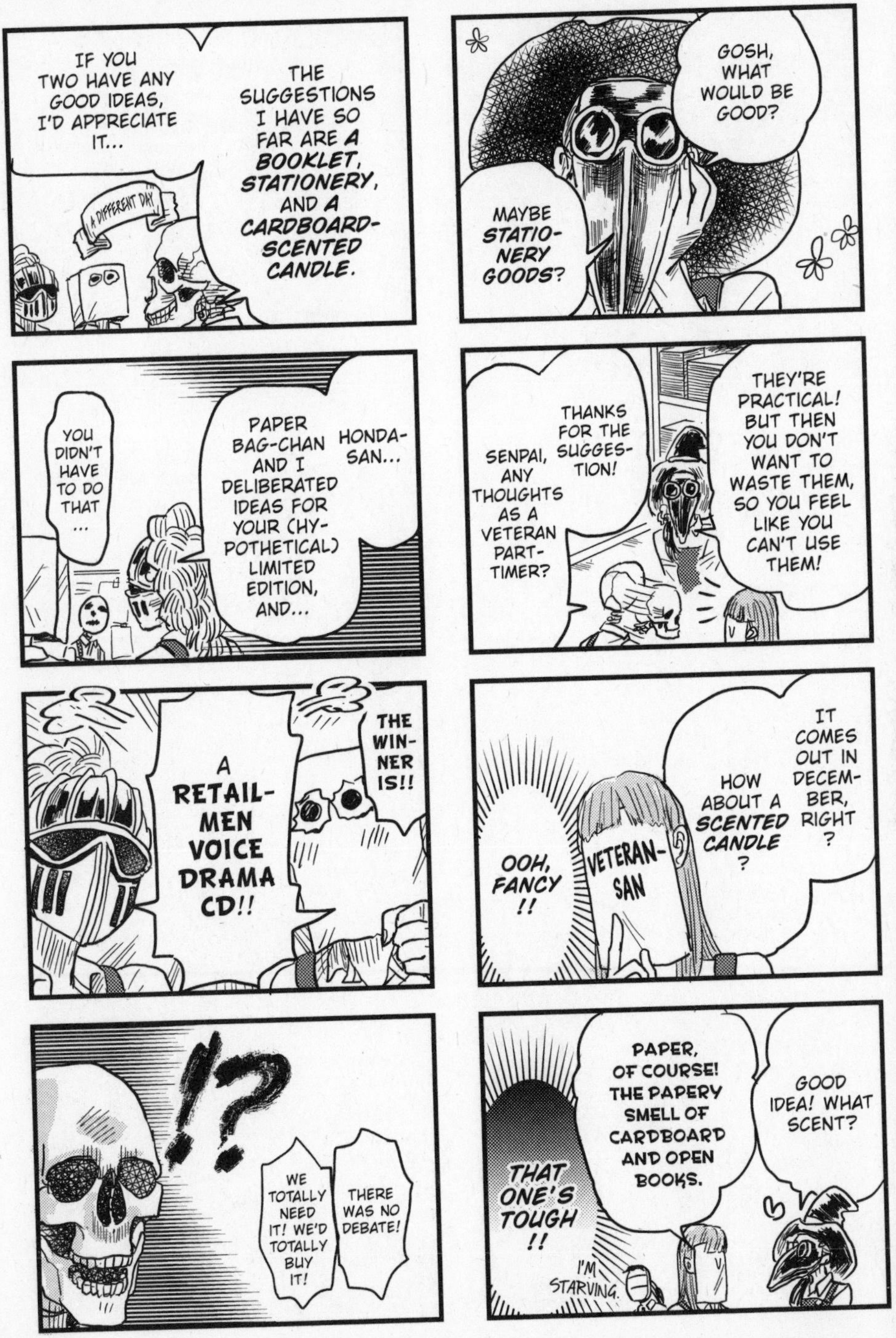
GOSH, WHAT WOULD BE GOOD?
MAYBE STATIONERY GOODS?
THEY'RE PRACTICAL! BUT THEN YOU DON'T WANT TO WASTE THEM, SO YOU FEEL LIKE YOU CAN'T USE THEM!
THANKS FOR THE SUGGESTION!
SENPAI, ANY THOUGHTS AS A VETERAN PART-TIMER?
IT COMES OUT IN DECEMBER, RIGHT?
HOW ABOUT A SCENTED CANDLE?
VETERAN-SAN
OOH, FANCY!!
GOOD IDEA! WHAT SCENT?
PAPER, OF COURSE! THE PAPERY SMELL OF CARDBOARD AND OPEN BOOKS.
THAT ONE'S TOUGH!!
I'M STARVING.
THE SUGGESTIONS I HAVE SO FAR ARE A BOOKLET, STATIONERY, AND A CARDBOARD-SCENTED CANDLE.
IF YOU TWO HAVE ANY GOOD IDEAS, I'D APPRECIATE IT...
A DIFFERENT DAY
HONDA-SAN...
PAPER BAG-CHAN AND I DELIBERATED IDEAS FOR YOUR (HYPOTHETICAL) LIMITED EDITION, AND...
YOU DIDN'T HAVE TO DO THAT...
THE WINNER IS!!
A RETAIL-MEN VOICE DRAMA CD!!
THERE WAS NO DEBATE!
WE TOTALLY NEED IT! WE'D TOTALLY BUY IT!
!?

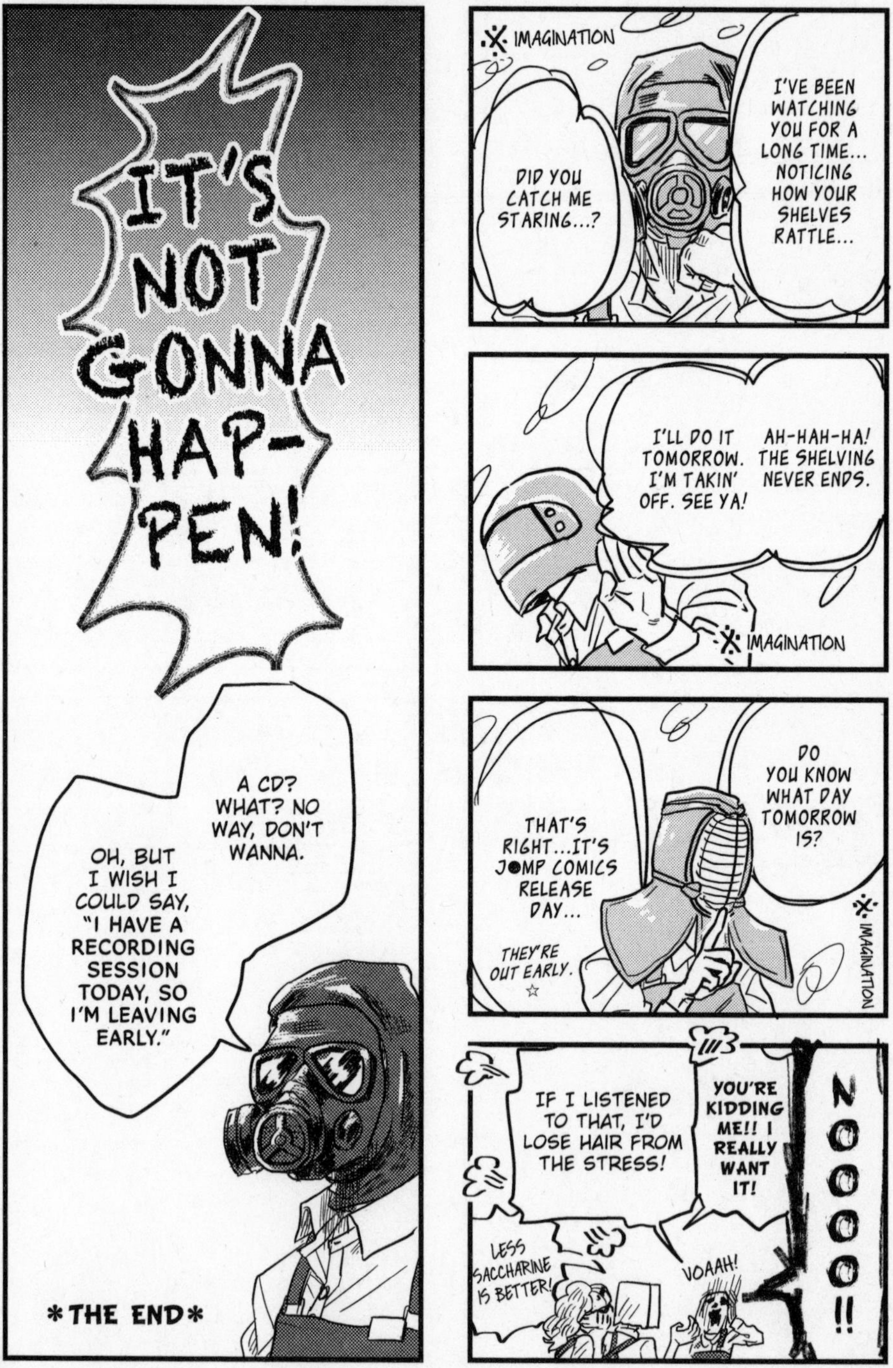
※ IMAGINATION
I'VE BEEN WATCHING YOU FOR A LONG TIME... NOTICING HOW YOUR SHELVES RATTLE...
DID YOU CATCH ME STARING...?
AH-HAH-HA! THE SHELVING NEVER ENDS.
I'LL DO IT TOMORROW. I'M TAKIN' OFF. SEE YA!
※ IMAGINATION
DO YOU KNOW WHAT DAY TOMORROW IS?
THAT'S RIGHT...IT'S J●MP COMICS RELEASE DAY...
THEY'RE OUT EARLY. ☆
※ IMAGINATION
NOOOOO!!
YOU'RE KIDDING ME!! I REALLY WANT IT!
IF I LISTENED TO THAT, I'D LOSE HAIR FROM THE STRESS!
VOAAH!
LESS SACCHARINE IS BETTER!
IT'S NOT GONNA HAP-PEN!
A CD? WHAT? NO WAY, DON'T WANNA.
OH, BUT I WISH I COULD SAY, "I HAVE A RECORDING SESSION TODAY, SO I'M LEAVING EARLY."
THE END

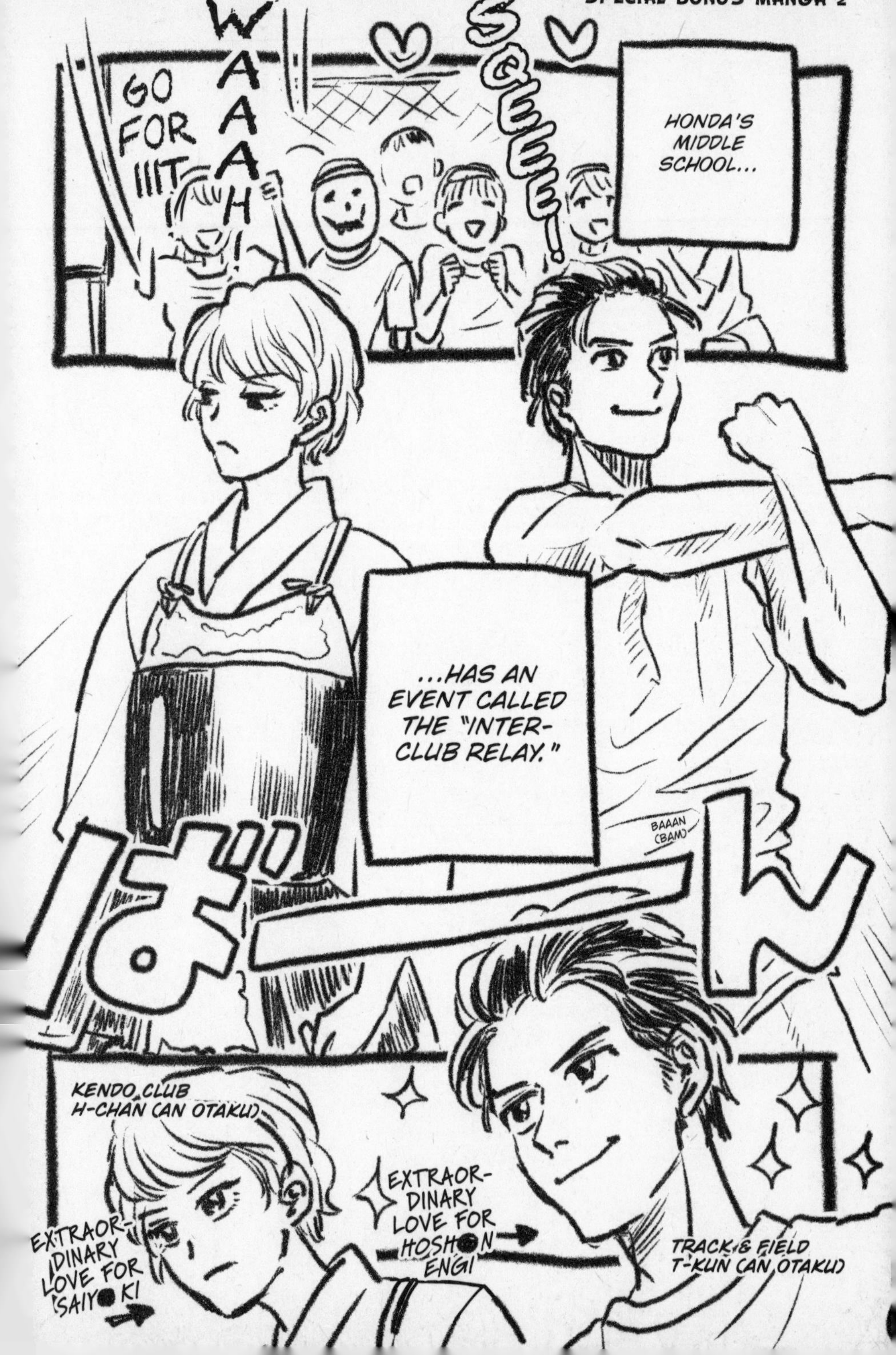
HONDA'S MIDDLE SCHOOL...
SQEEE!
WAAAH!
GO FOR IIIT
...HAS AN EVENT CALLED THE "INTER-CLUB RELAY."
BAAAN (BAM)
ばーん
TRACK & FIELD T-KUN (AN OTAKU)
EXTRAOR-DINARY LOVE FOR HOSH●N ENGI
KENDO CLUB H-CHAN (AN OTAKU)
EXTRAOR-DINARY LOVE FOR SAIY●KI

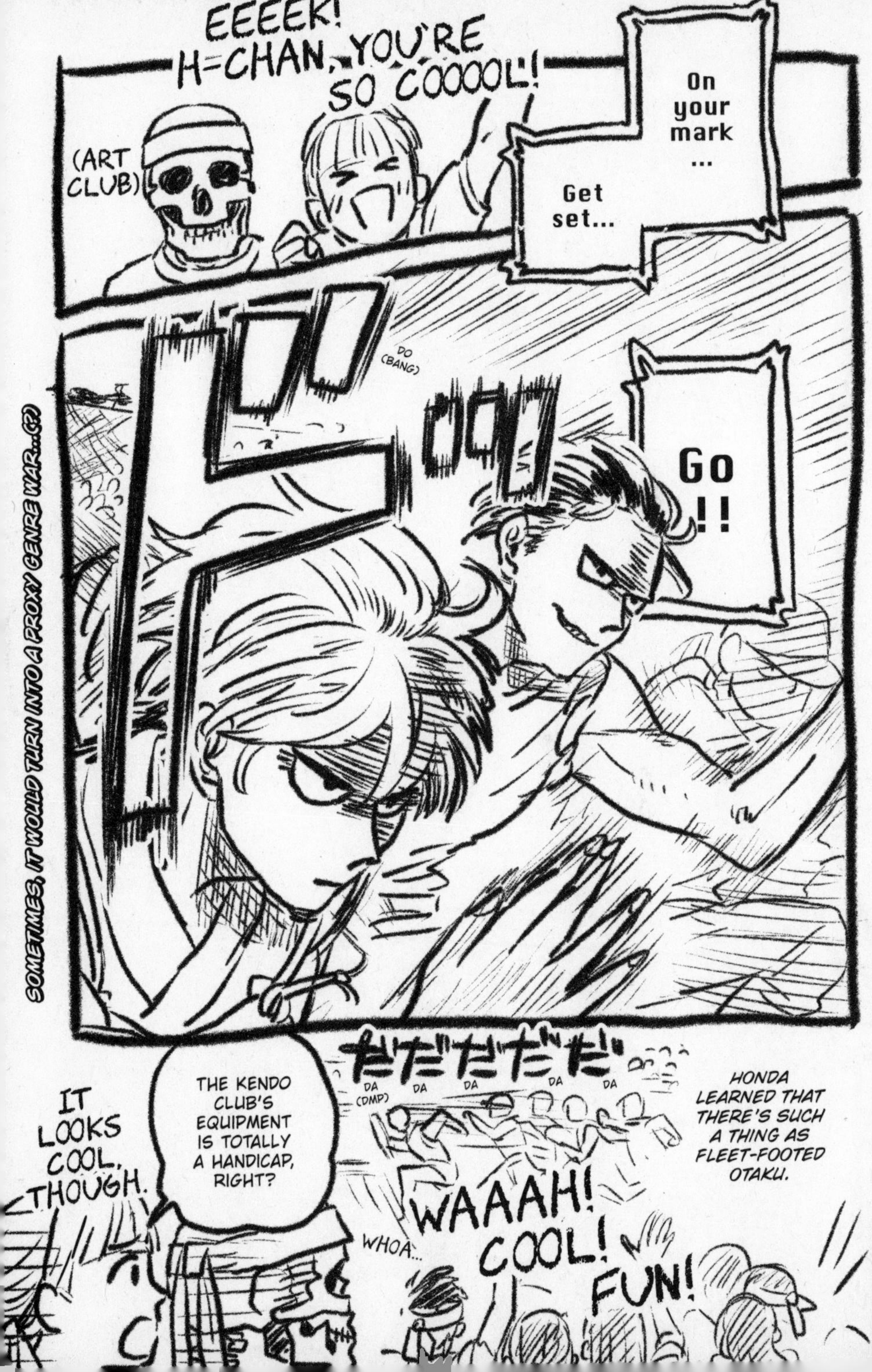

On your mark...
Get set...
EEEEK! H-CHAN, YOU'RE SO COOOOOL!
(ART CLUB)
DO (BANG)
Go!!
HONDA LEARNED THAT THERE'S SUCH A THING AS FLEET-FOOTED OTAKU.
DA (DMP) DA DA DA DA
WAAAH! COOL! FUN!
WHOA...
THE KENDO CLUB'S EQUIPMENT IS TOTALLY A HANDICAP, RIGHT?
IT LOOKS COOL, THOUGH.

SOMETIMES, IT WOULD TURN INTO A PROXY GENRE WAR...(?)

Skull-face Bookseller Honda-san

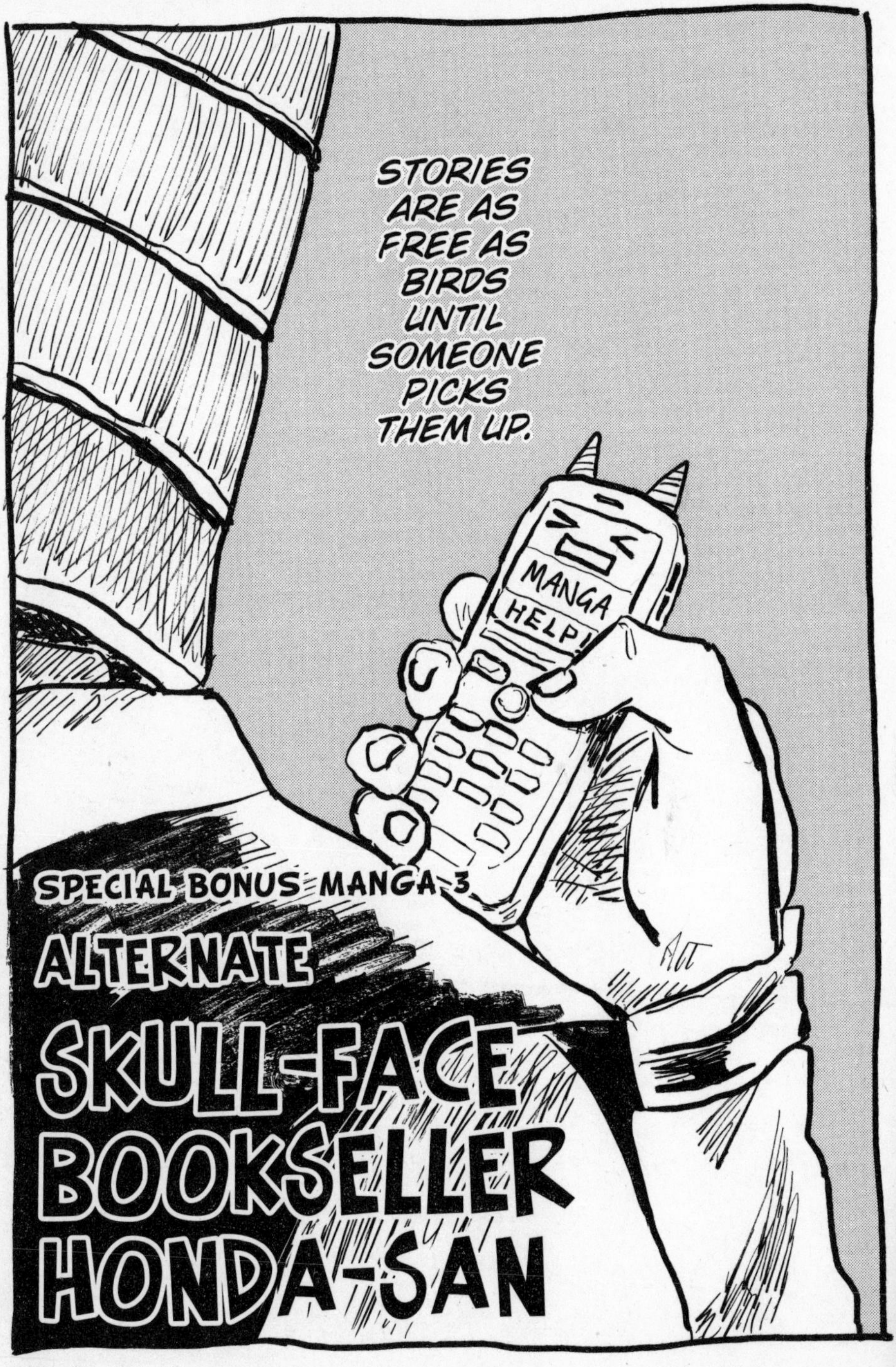
STORIES ARE AS FREE AS BIRDS UNTIL SOMEONE PICKS THEM UP.
MANGA HELP
SPECIAL BONUS MANGA 3
ALTERNATE
SKULL-FACE BOOKSELLER HONDA-SAN

MANY PEOPLE HAVE TOLD ME THEY EXPECTED MY MANGA TO BE ABOUT A SKELETON RUNNING A BOOKSTORE IN A FANTASY WORLD. THIS STORY IS AN IDEA I DEVELOPED AS A RESULT.

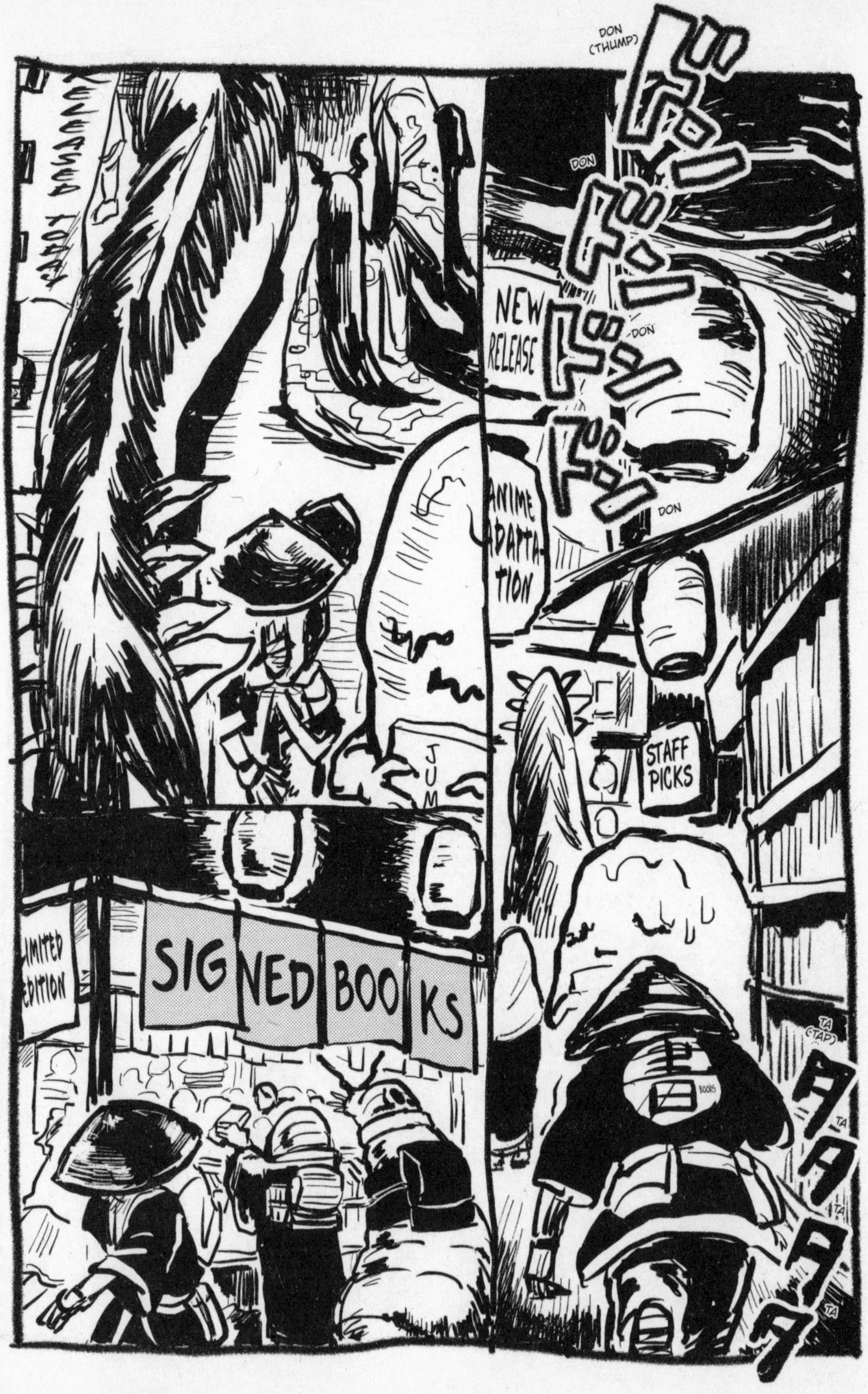
DON (THUMP)
DON
NEW RELEASE
DON
ANIME ADAPTATION
DON
STAFF PICKS
BOOKS
TA (TAP)
TA
TA
SIGNED BOOKS

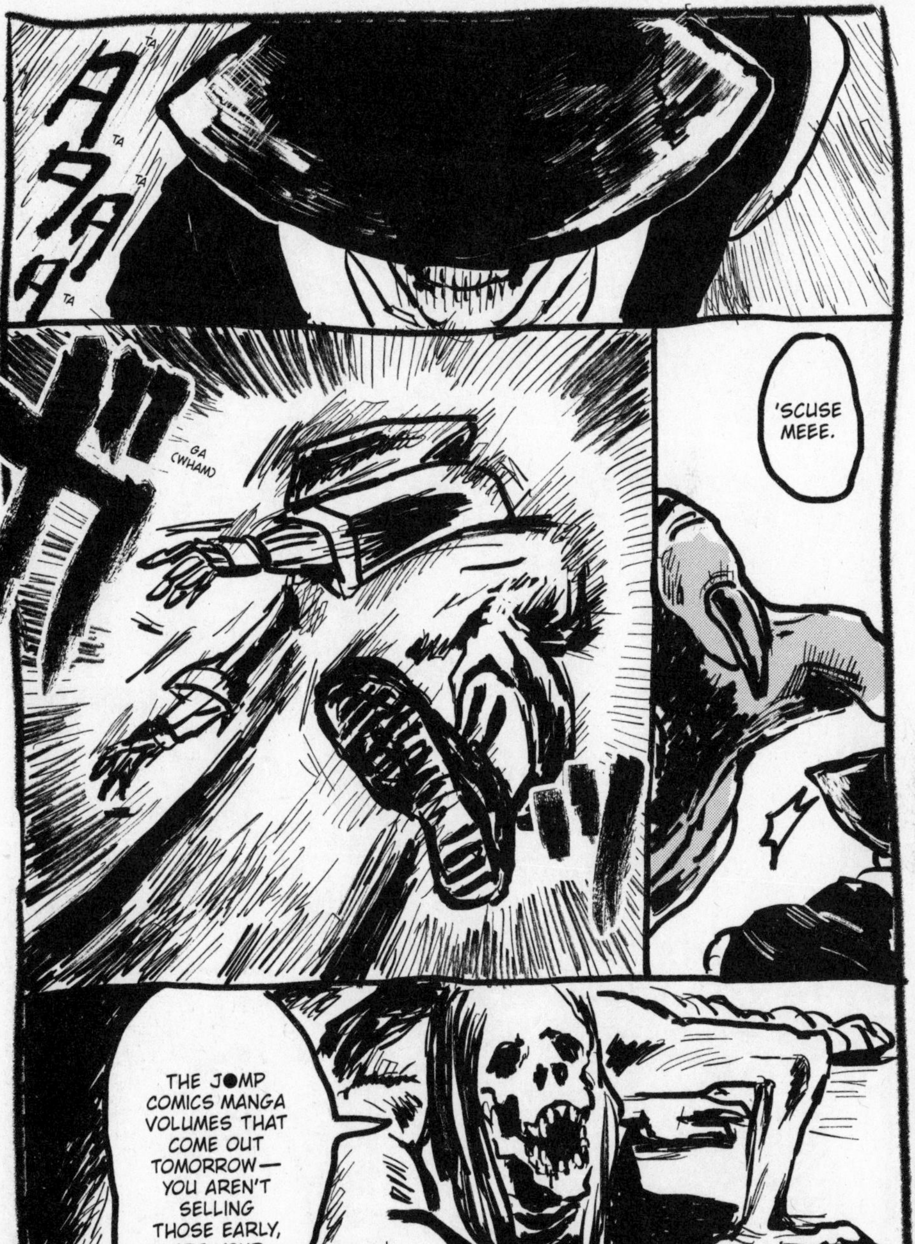
タタタタ
TA TA TA TA
'SCUSE MEEE.
ガッ
GA (WHAM)
THE JOMP COMICS MANGA VOLUMES THAT COME OUT TOMORROW—YOU AREN'T SELLING THOSE EARLY, ARE YOU?

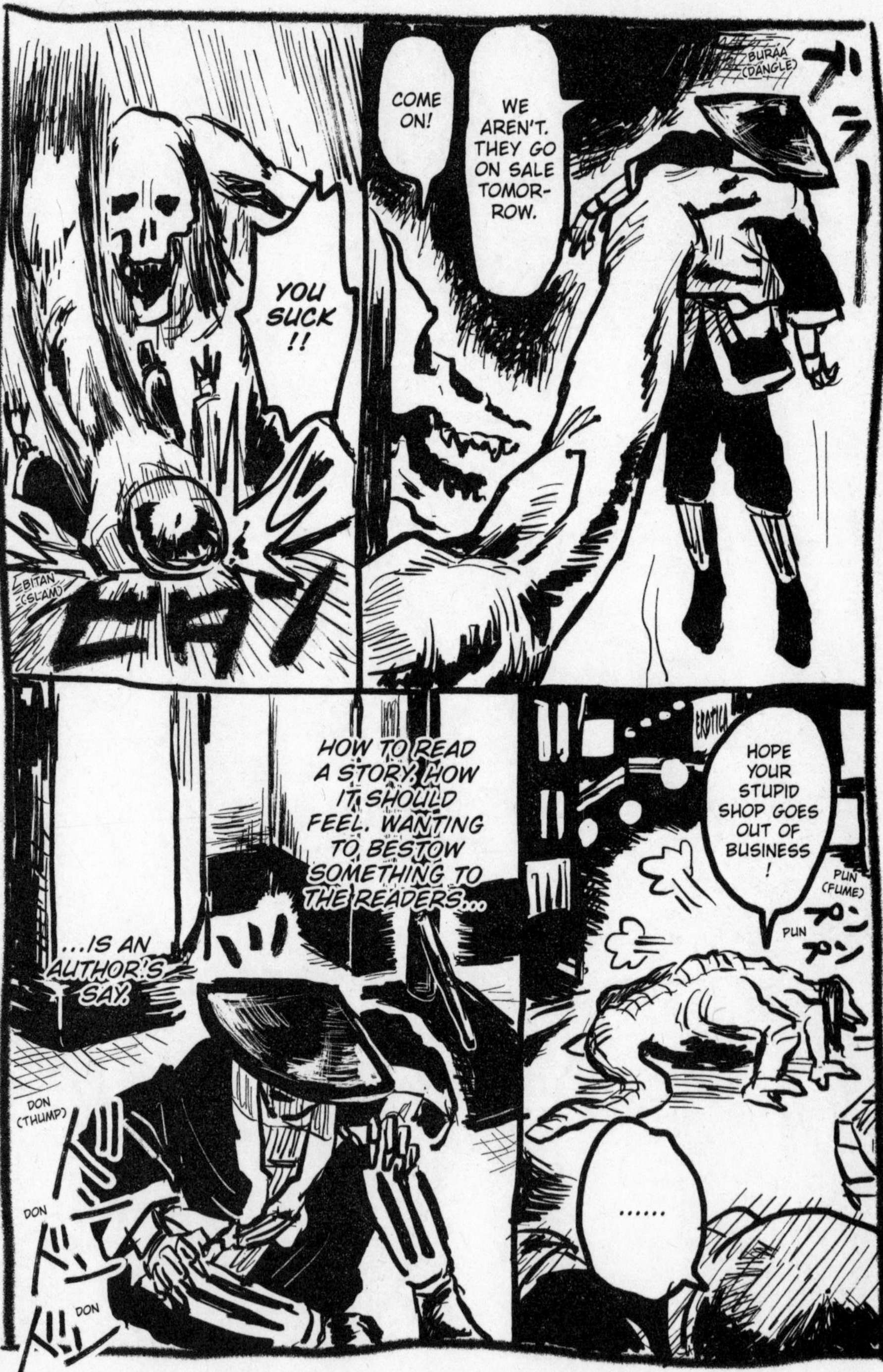
BURAA (DANGLE)
WE AREN'T. THEY GO ON SALE TOMORROW.
COME ON!
YOU SUCK !!
BITAN (SLAM)
EROTICA
HOPE YOUR STUPID SHOP GOES OUT OF BUSINESS !
PUN (FUME)
PUN
......
HOW TO READ A STORY. HOW IT SHOULD FEEL. WANTING TO BESTOW SOMETHING TO THE READERS...
...IS AN AUTHOR'S SAY.
DON (THUMP)
DON
DON

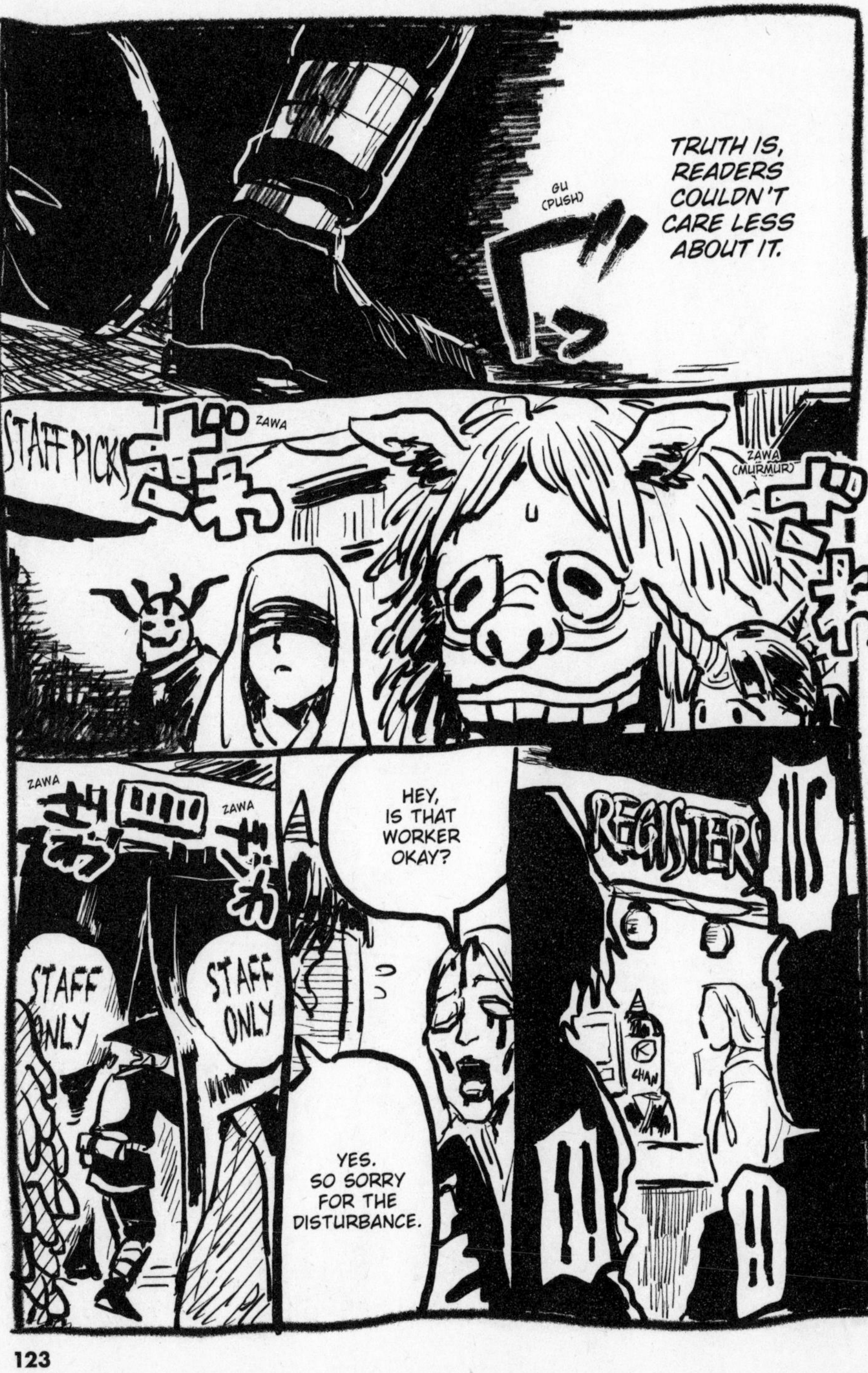
TRUTH IS, READERS COULDN'T CARE LESS ABOUT IT.
GU (PUSH)
ZAWA (MURMUR)
STAFF PICKS
ZAWA
REGISTERS
K CHAN
HEY, IS THAT WORKER OKAY?
YES. SO SORRY FOR THE DISTURBANCE.
ZAWA
ZAWA
STAFF ONLY
STAFF ONLY

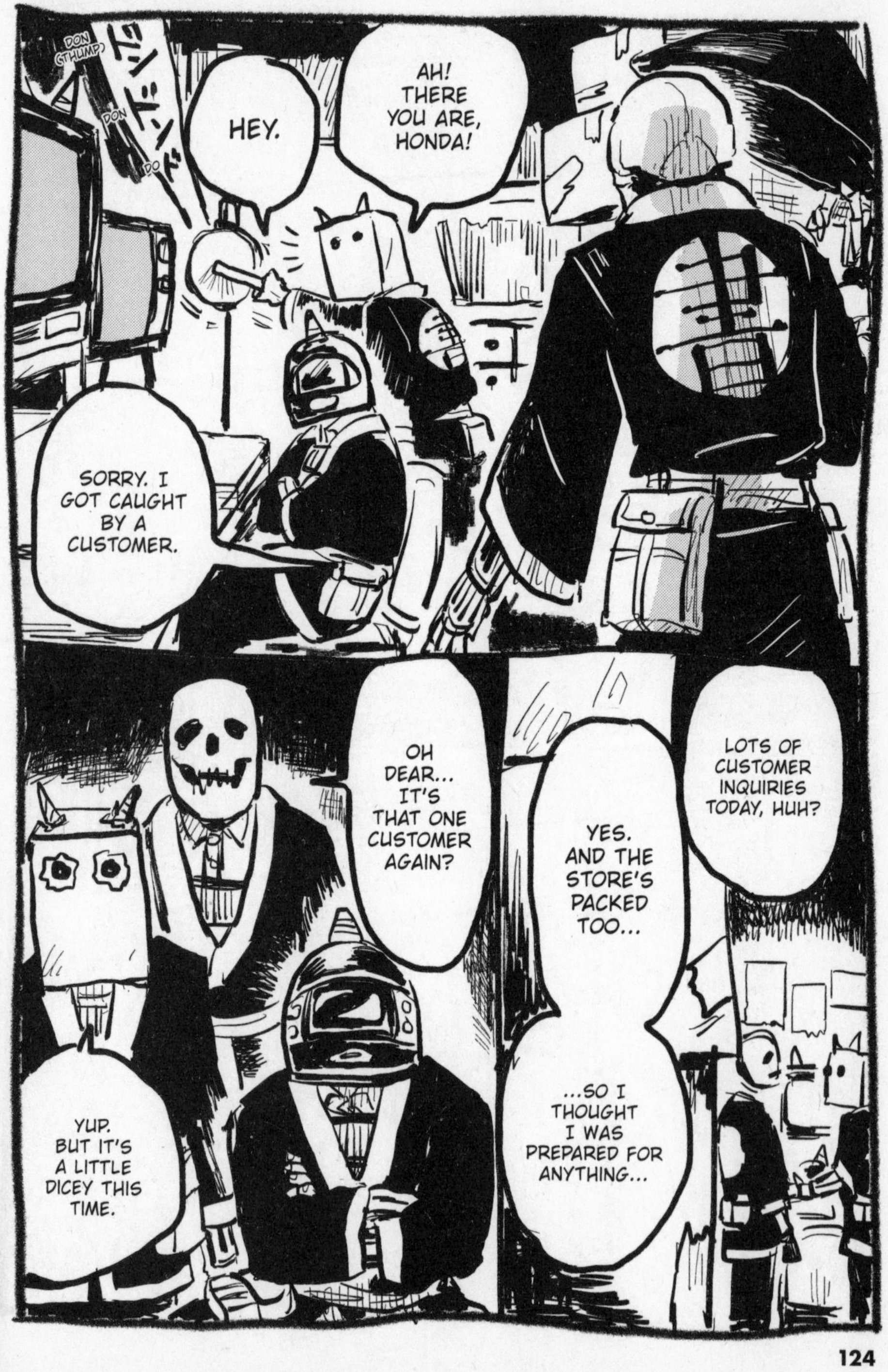
AH! THERE YOU ARE, HONDA!
HEY.
DON (THUMP)
DON
DO
SORRY. I GOT CAUGHT BY A CUSTOMER.
LOTS OF CUSTOMER INQUIRIES TODAY, HUH?
YES. AND THE STORE'S PACKED TOO...
...SO I THOUGHT I WAS PREPARED FOR ANYTHING...
OH DEAR... IT'S THAT ONE CUSTOMER AGAIN?
YUP. BUT IT'S A LITTLE DICEY THIS TIME.

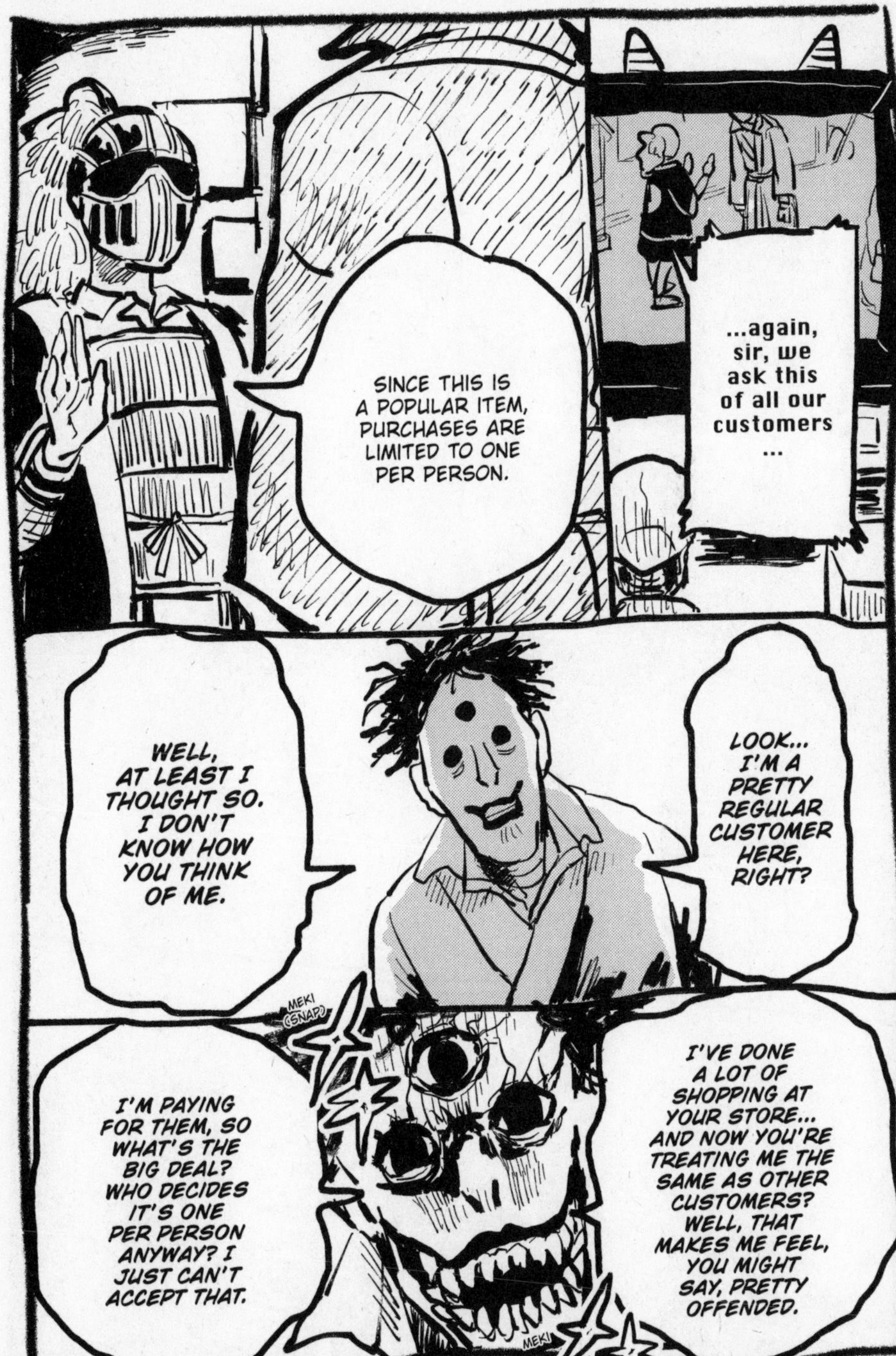
...again, sir, we ask this of all our customers ...
SINCE THIS IS A POPULAR ITEM, PURCHASES ARE LIMITED TO ONE PER PERSON.
LOOK... I'M A PRETTY REGULAR CUSTOMER HERE, RIGHT?
WELL, AT LEAST I THOUGHT SO. I DON'T KNOW HOW YOU THINK OF ME.
MEKI (SNAP)
I'VE DONE A LOT OF SHOPPING AT YOUR STORE... AND NOW YOU'RE TREATING ME THE SAME AS OTHER CUSTOMERS? WELL, THAT MAKES ME FEEL, YOU MIGHT SAY, PRETTY OFFENDED.
I'M PAYING FOR THEM, SO WHAT'S THE BIG DEAL? WHO DECIDES IT'S ONE PER PERSON ANYWAY? I JUST CAN'T ACCEPT THAT.
MEKI

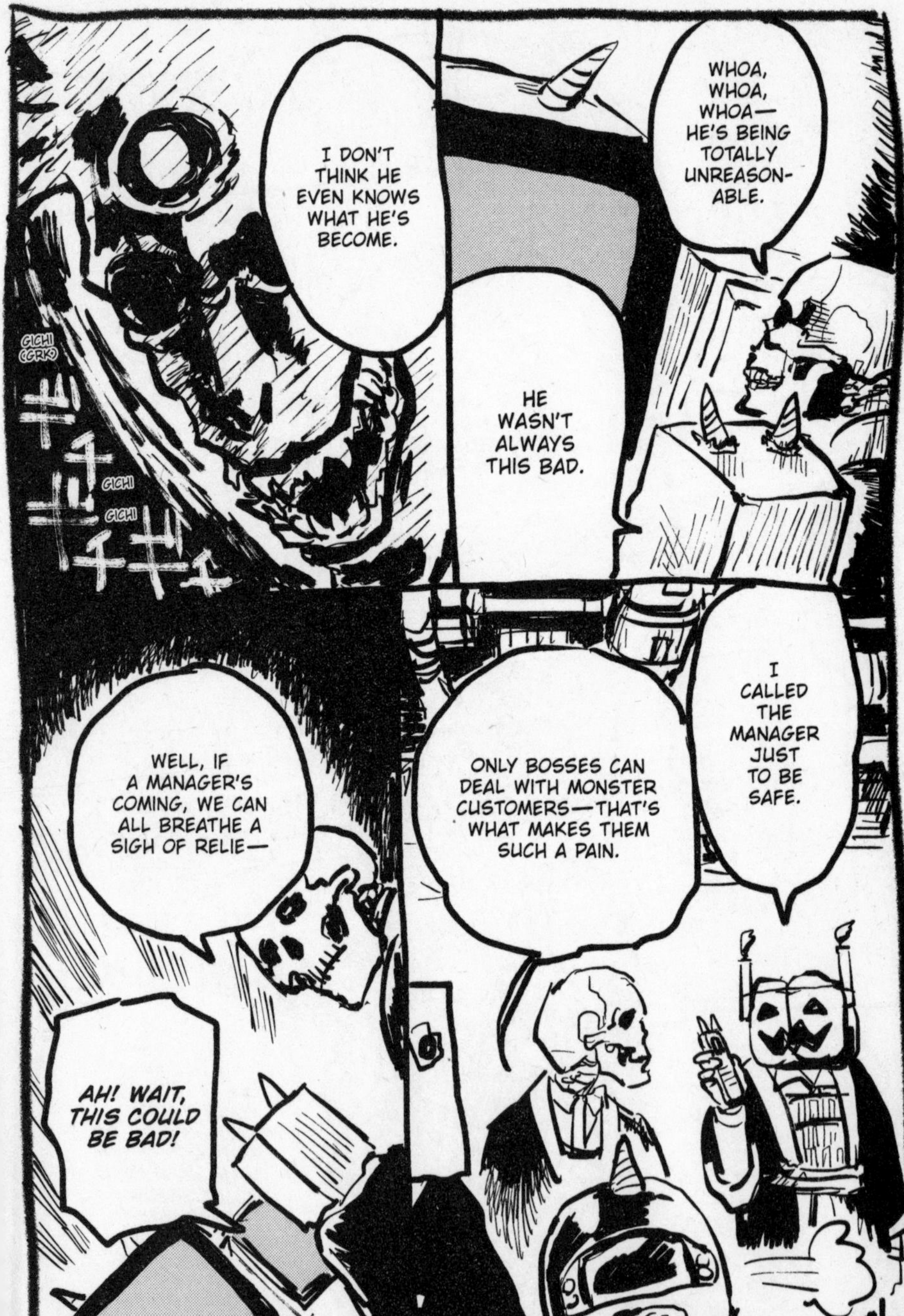
WHOA, WHOA, WHOA— HE'S BEING TOTALLY UNREASON-ABLE.
HE WASN'T ALWAYS THIS BAD.
I DON'T THINK HE EVEN KNOWS WHAT HE'S BECOME.
GICHI (GRK)
GICHI
GICHI
I CALLED THE MANAGER JUST TO BE SAFE.
ONLY BOSSES CAN DEAL WITH MONSTER CUSTOMERS—THAT'S WHAT MAKES THEM SUCH A PAIN.
WELL, IF A MANAGER'S COMING, WE CAN ALL BREATHE A SIGH OF RELIE—
AH! WAIT, THIS COULD BE BAD!

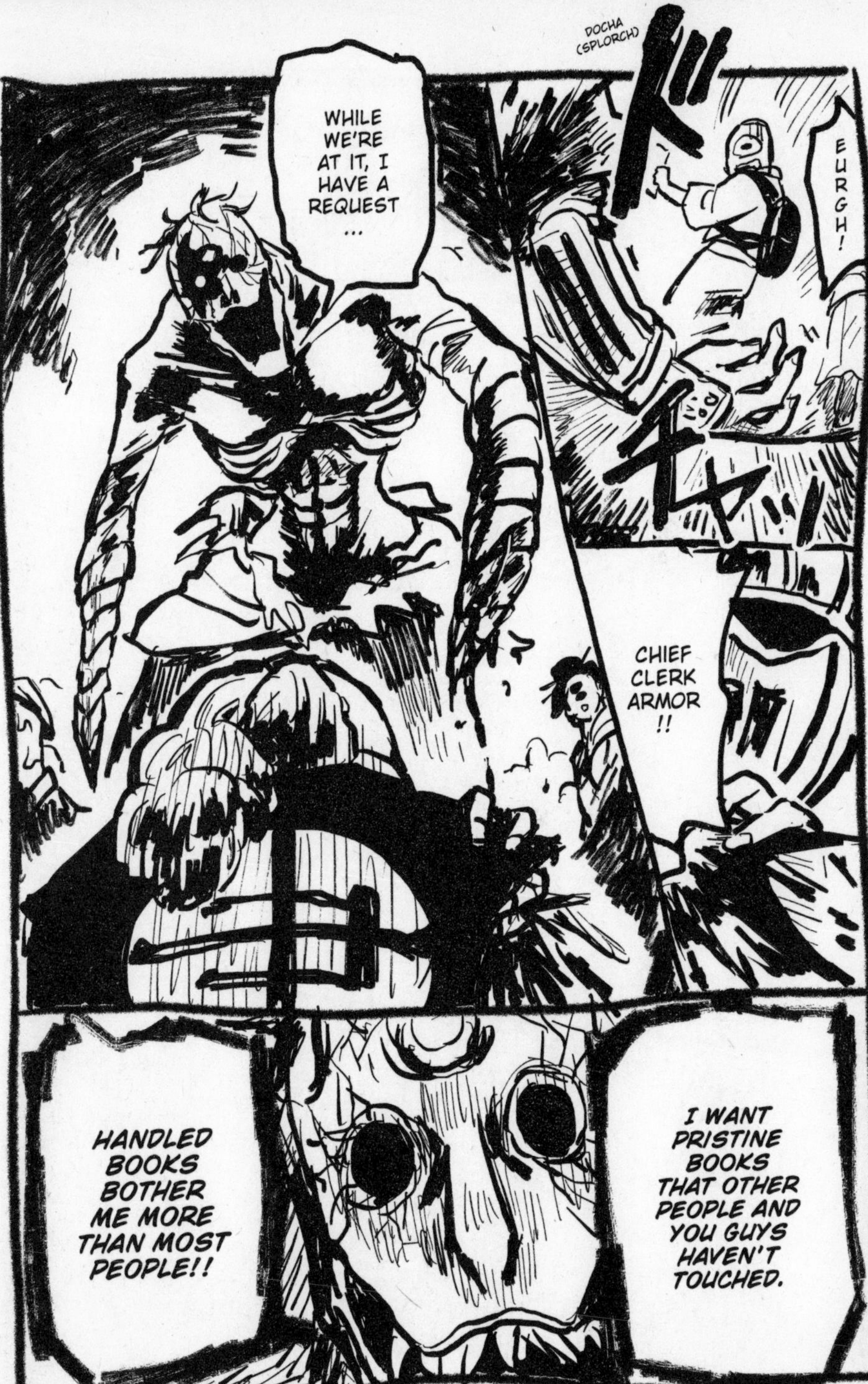

DOCHA (SPLORCH)
EURGH!
CHIEF CLERK ARMOR!!
WHILE WE'RE AT IT, I HAVE A REQUEST...
I WANT PRISTINE BOOKS THAT OTHER PEOPLE AND YOU GUYS HAVEN'T TOUCHED.
HANDLED BOOKS BOTHER ME MORE THAN MOST PEOPLE!!

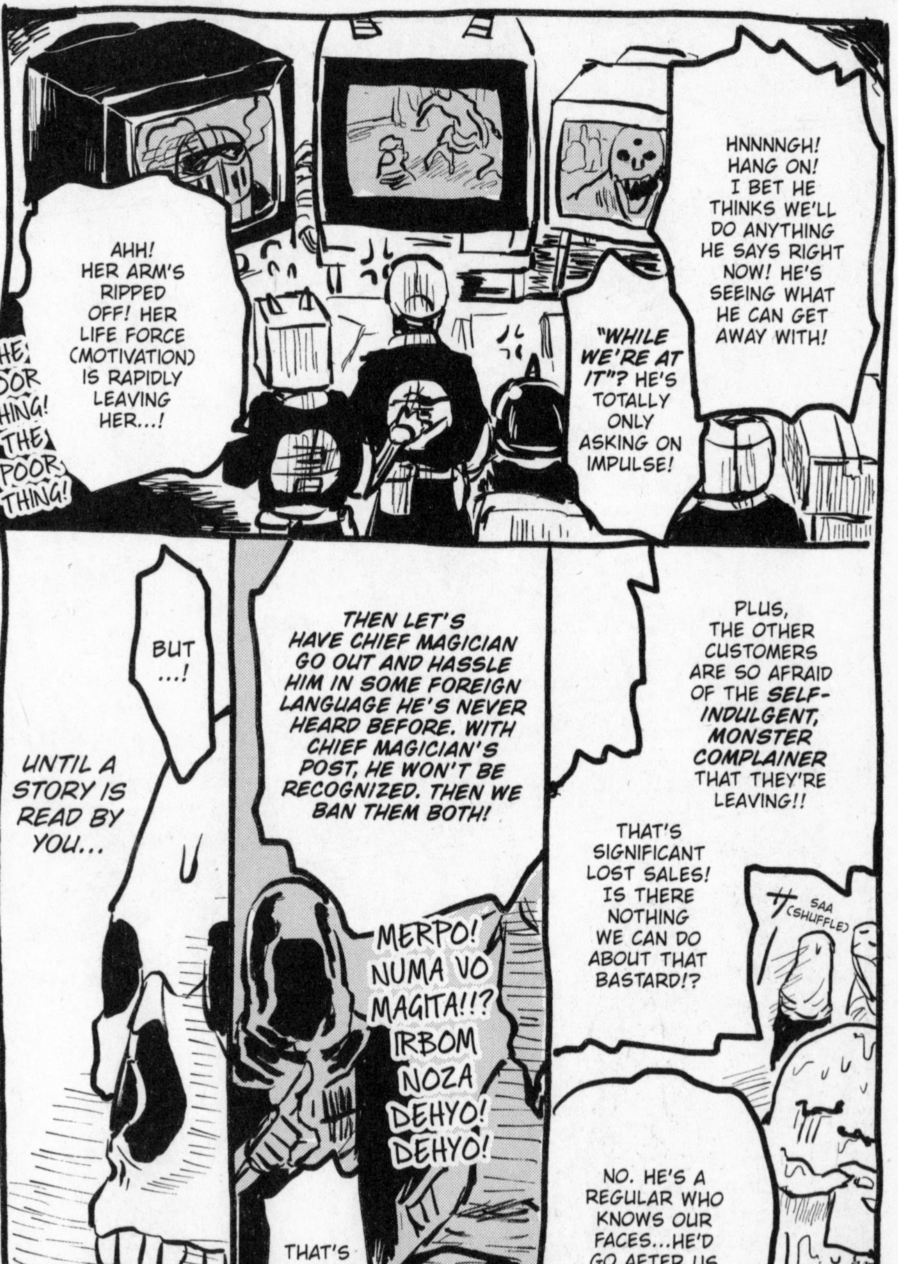
HNNNNGH! HANG ON! I BET HE THINKS WE'LL DO ANYTHING HE SAYS RIGHT NOW! HE'S SEEING WHAT HE CAN GET AWAY WITH!
"WHILE WE'RE AT IT"? HE'S TOTALLY ONLY ASKING ON IMPULSE!
AHH! HER ARM'S RIPPED OFF! HER LIFE FORCE (MOTIVATION) IS RAPIDLY LEAVING HER...!
THE POOR THING! THE POOR THING!
PLUS, THE OTHER CUSTOMERS ARE SO AFRAID OF THE SELF-INDULGENT, MONSTER COMPLAINER THAT THEY'RE LEAVING!!
THAT'S SIGNIFICANT LOST SALES! IS THERE NOTHING WE CAN DO ABOUT THAT BASTARD!?
SAA (SHUFFLE)
NO. HE'S A REGULAR WHO KNOWS OUR FACES...HE'D GO AFTER US LEGALLY.
THEN LET'S HAVE CHIEF MAGICIAN GO OUT AND HASSLE HIM IN SOME FOREIGN LANGUAGE HE'S NEVER HEARD BEFORE. WITH CHIEF MAGICIAN'S POST, HE WON'T BE RECOGNIZED. THEN WE BAN THEM BOTH!
MERPO! NUMA VO MAGITA!!? IRBOM NOZA DEHYO! DEHYO!
THAT'S A HARD ASK!!
BUT ...!
UNTIL A STORY IS READ BY YOU...

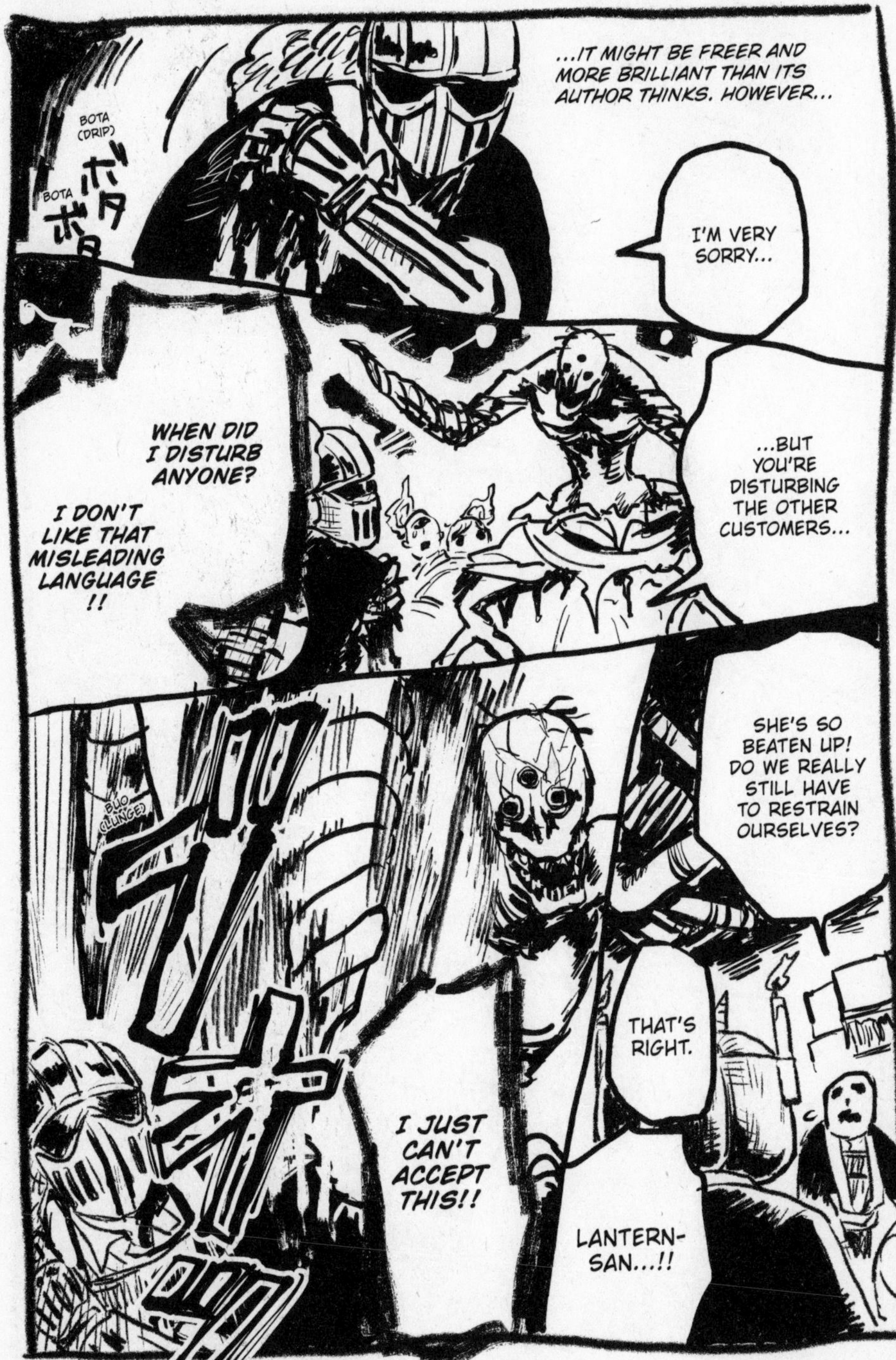
...IT MIGHT BE FREER AND MORE BRILLIANT THAN ITS AUTHOR THINKS. HOWEVER...
I'M VERY SORRY...
BOTA (DRIP) BOTA
ボタボタ
...BUT YOU'RE DISTURBING THE OTHER CUSTOMERS...
WHEN DID I DISTURB ANYONE?
I DON'T LIKE THAT MISLEADING LANGUAGE !!
SHE'S SO BEATEN UP! DO WE REALLY STILL HAVE TO RESTRAIN OURSELVES?
THAT'S RIGHT.
LANTERN-SAN...!!
I JUST CAN'T ACCEPT THIS!!
BUO (LUNGE)

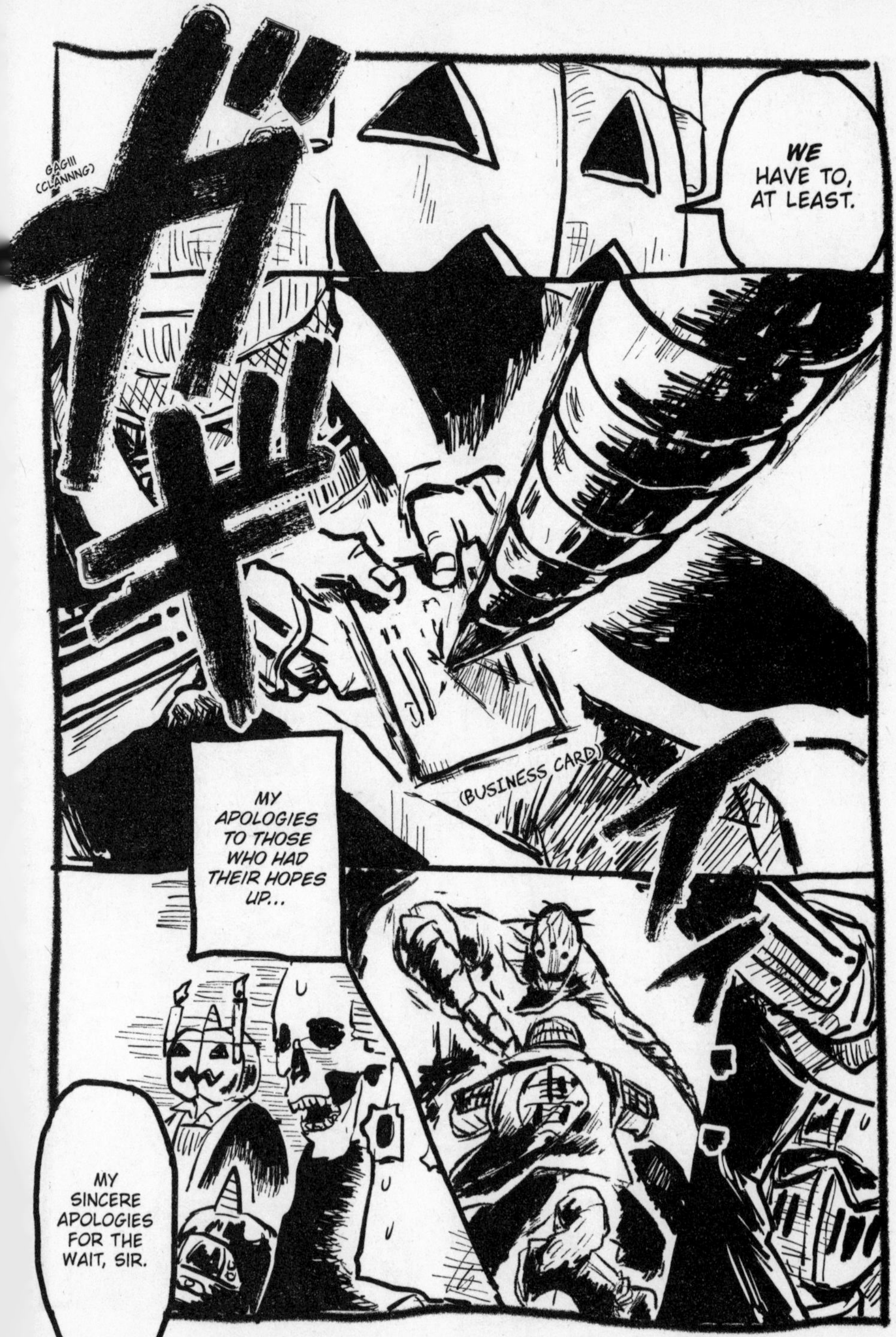
WE HAVE TO, AT LEAST.
GAGIII (CLANNNG)
(BUSINESS CARD)
MY APOLOGIES TO THOSE WHO HAD THEIR HOPES UP...
MY SINCERE APOLOGIES FOR THE WAIT, SIR.

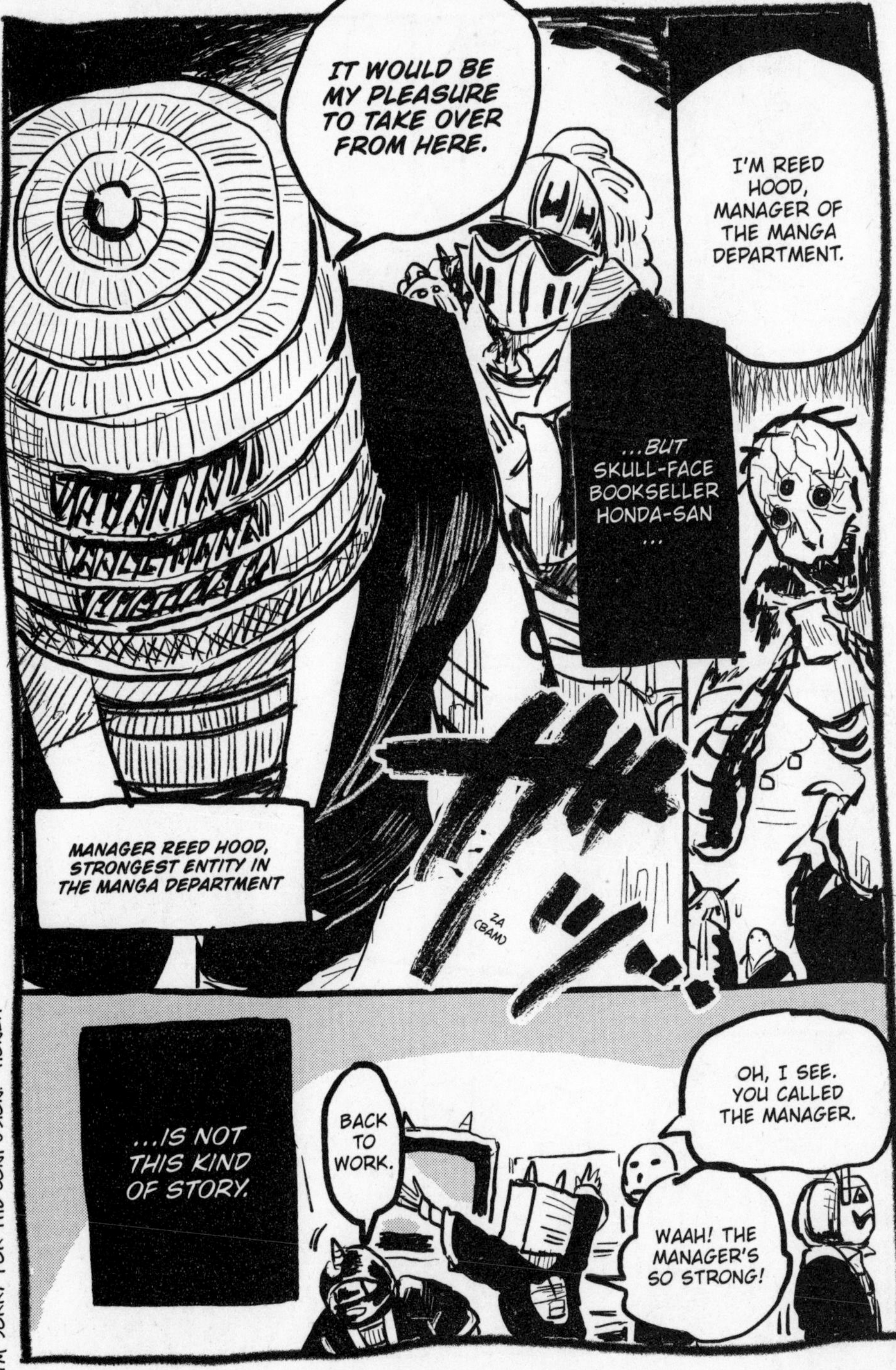
I'M REED HOOD, MANAGER OF THE MANGA DEPARTMENT.
...BUT SKULL-FACE BOOKSELLER HONDA-SAN ...
IT WOULD BE MY PLEASURE TO TAKE OVER FROM HERE.
MANAGER REED HOOD, STRONGEST ENTITY IN THE MANGA DEPARTMENT
ZA (BAM)
OH, I SEE. YOU CALLED THE MANAGER.
WAAH! THE MANAGER'S SO STRONG!
BACK TO WORK.
...IS NOT THIS KIND OF STORY.

I'M SORRY FOR THE CONFUSION. –HONDA

THE END

AFTERWORD

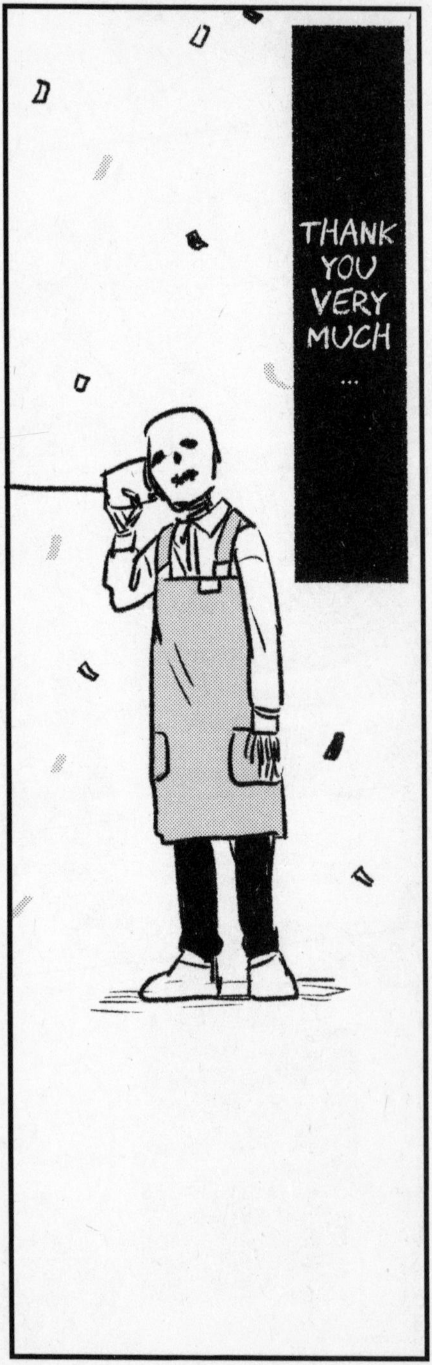
THANK YOU VERY MUCH ...

CHECKING GALLEYS

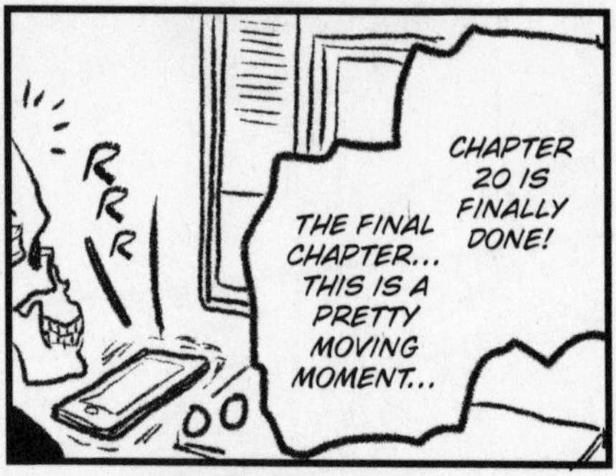
CHAPTER 20 IS FINALLY DONE!
THE FINAL CHAPTER... THIS IS A PRETTY MOVING MOMENT...
RRR

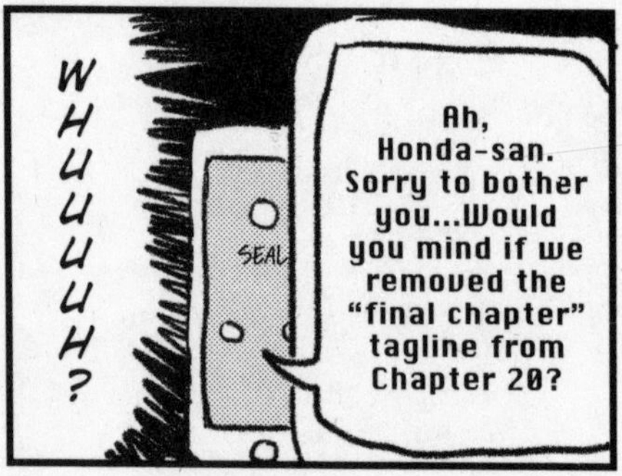
Ah, Honda-san. Sorry to bother you...Would you mind if we removed the "final chapter" tagline from Chapter 20?
SEAL
WHUUUUUH?

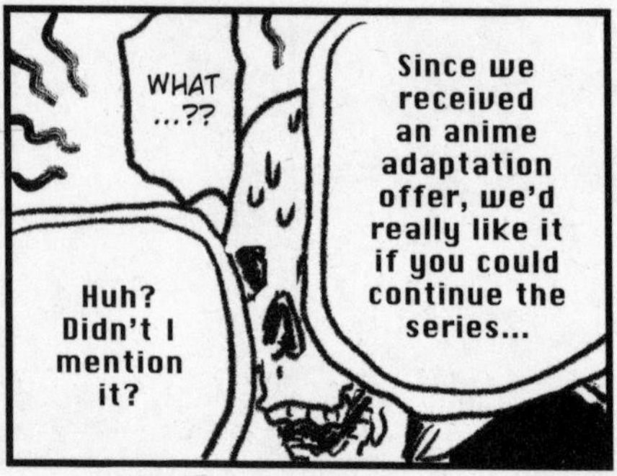
Since we received an anime adaptation offer, we'd really like it if you could continue the series...
WHAT ...??
Huh? Didn't I mention it?

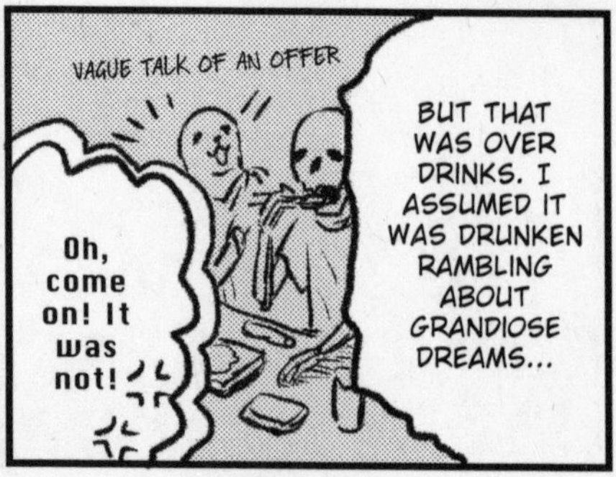
BUT THAT WAS OVER DRINKS. I ASSUMED IT WAS DRUNKEN RAMBLING ABOUT GRANDIOSE DREAMS...
VAGUE TALK OF AN OFFER
Oh, come on! It was not!

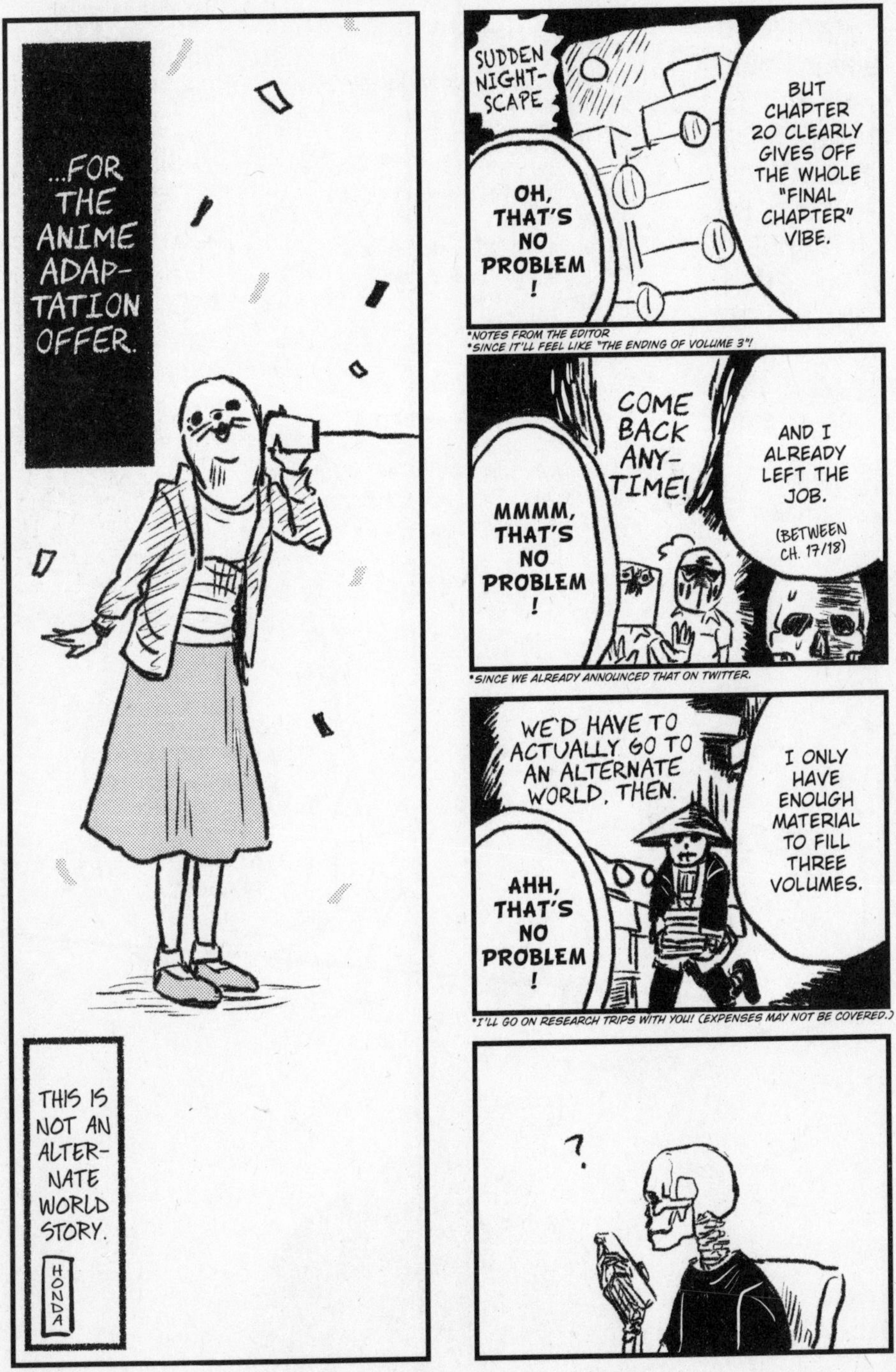
BUT CHAPTER 20 CLEARLY GIVES OFF THE WHOLE "FINAL CHAPTER" VIBE.
SUDDEN NIGHT-SCAPE
OH, THAT'S NO PROBLEM!
*NOTES FROM THE EDITOR
*SINCE IT'LL FEEL LIKE "THE ENDING OF VOLUME 3"!
AND I ALREADY LEFT THE JOB.
(BETWEEN CH. 17/18)
COME BACK ANY-TIME!
MMMM, THAT'S NO PROBLEM!
*SINCE WE ALREADY ANNOUNCED THAT ON TWITTER.
I ONLY HAVE ENOUGH MATERIAL TO FILL THREE VOLUMES.
WE'D HAVE TO ACTUALLY GO TO AN ALTERNATE WORLD, THEN.
AHH, THAT'S NO PROBLEM!
*I'LL GO ON RESEARCH TRIPS WITH YOU! (EXPENSES MAY NOT BE COVERED.)
?
...FOR THE ANIME ADAPTATION OFFER.
THIS IS NOT AN ALTERNATE WORLD STORY.
HONDA

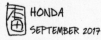

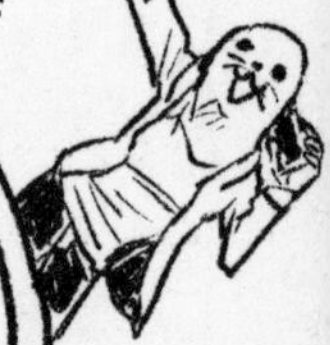

ULTIMATELY, WE ENDED UP IN MYSTERIOUS TERRITORY: WHILE THE SERIES WILL CONTINUE, THE COLLECTED VOLUMES ARE ~~COMPLETE.~~ ON PAUSE WHO KNOWS WHERE THIS THING WILL GO?

FOR THAT MATTER, WHERE WILL MY NEXT MANUSCRIPTS FOR IT GO? I WOULD BE GRATEFUL IF YOU STUCK AROUND TO FIND OUT. THANK YOU SO MUCH.

HONDA
SEPTEMBER 2017

SPECIAL THANKS

All the funny people in my bookstore
Chief Magician
Wholesaler N-san

Mr. G, who replies to e-mails quickly
A. Numa-sensei
My family, my little sister's bosses
The people who sent me letters
My friends

My editor Seal-san
Editor-in-chief Koala
Every bookstore in the country
All the readers
All the people who cheer me on each chapter
All the people who've visited our store
All the people who create good books

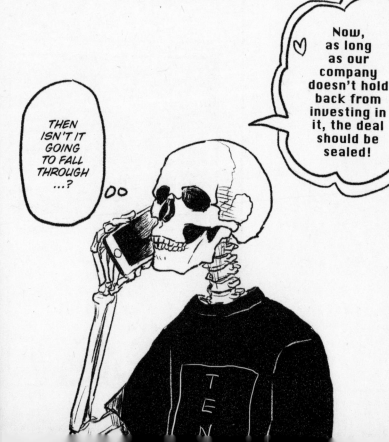

Now, as long as our company doesn't hold back from investing in it, the deal should be sealed!
THEN ISN'T IT GOING TO FALL THROUGH ...?

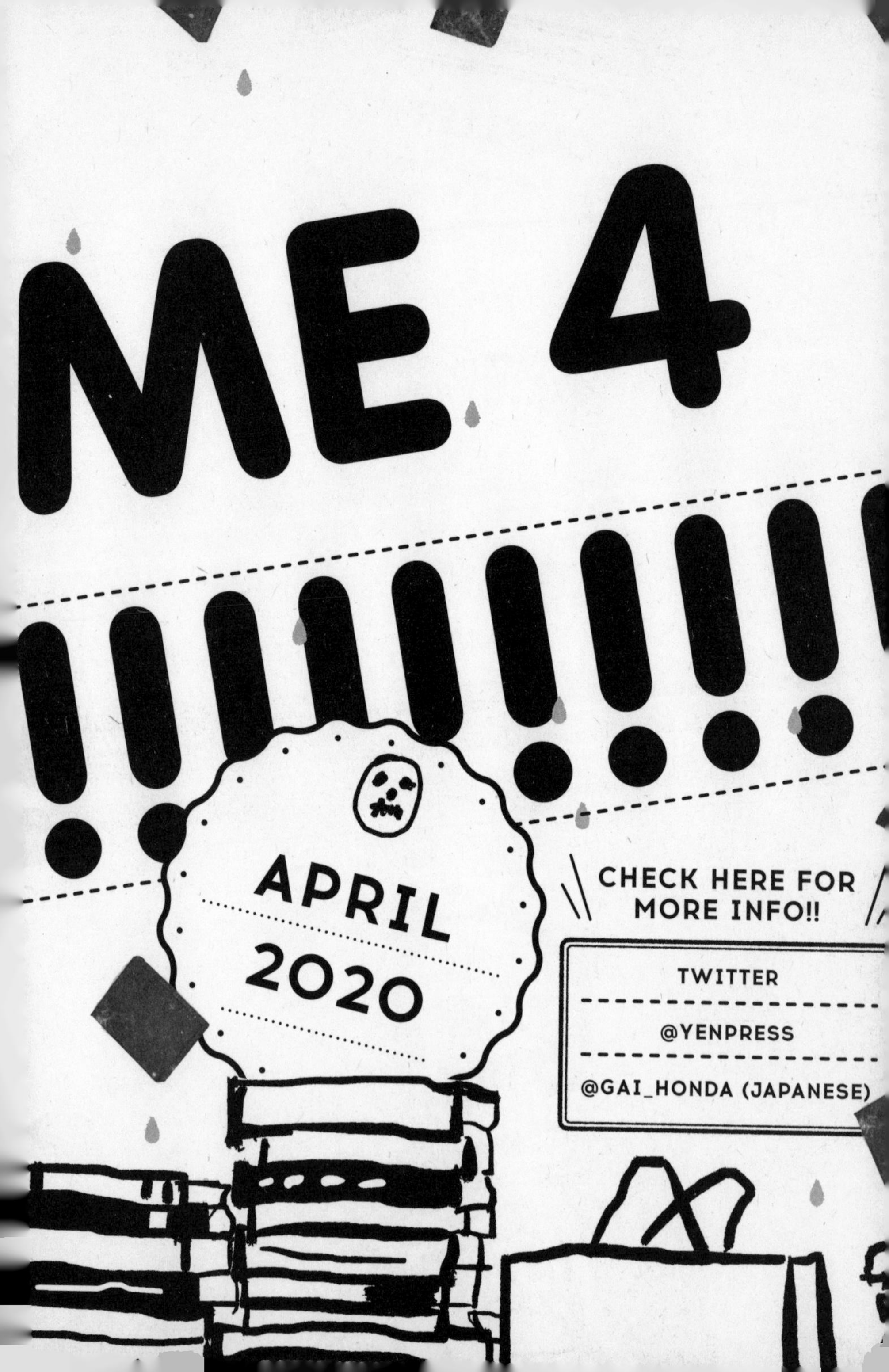
ME 4
!!!!!!!!!
APRIL
2020
CHECK HERE FOR
MORE INFO!!
TWITTER
@YENPRESS
@GAI_HONDA (JAPANESE)

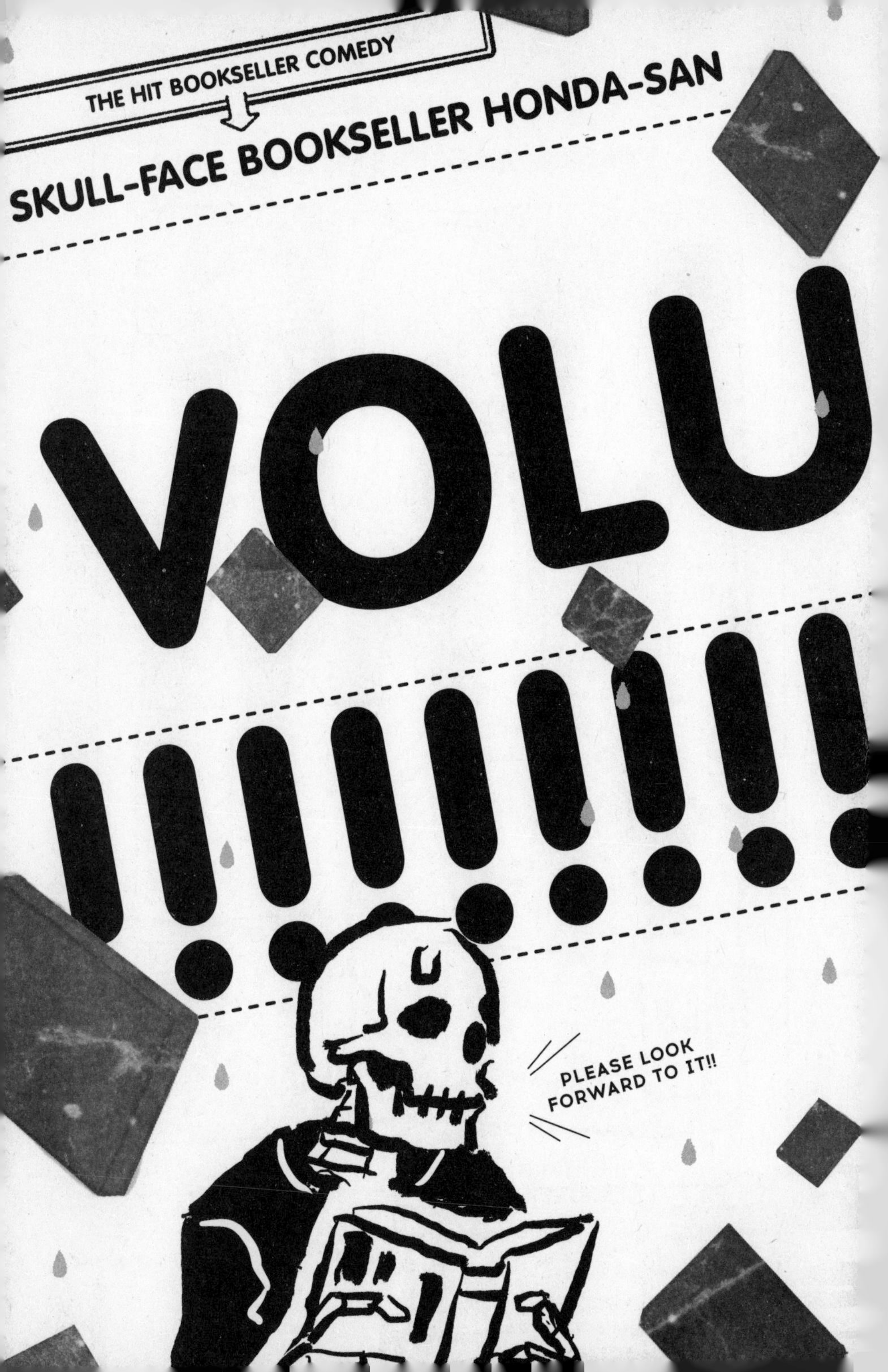
THE HIT BOOKSELLER COMEDY
SKULL-FACE BOOKSELLER HONDA-SAN
VOLU
!!!!!!!!!
PLEASE LOOK FORWARD TO IT!!

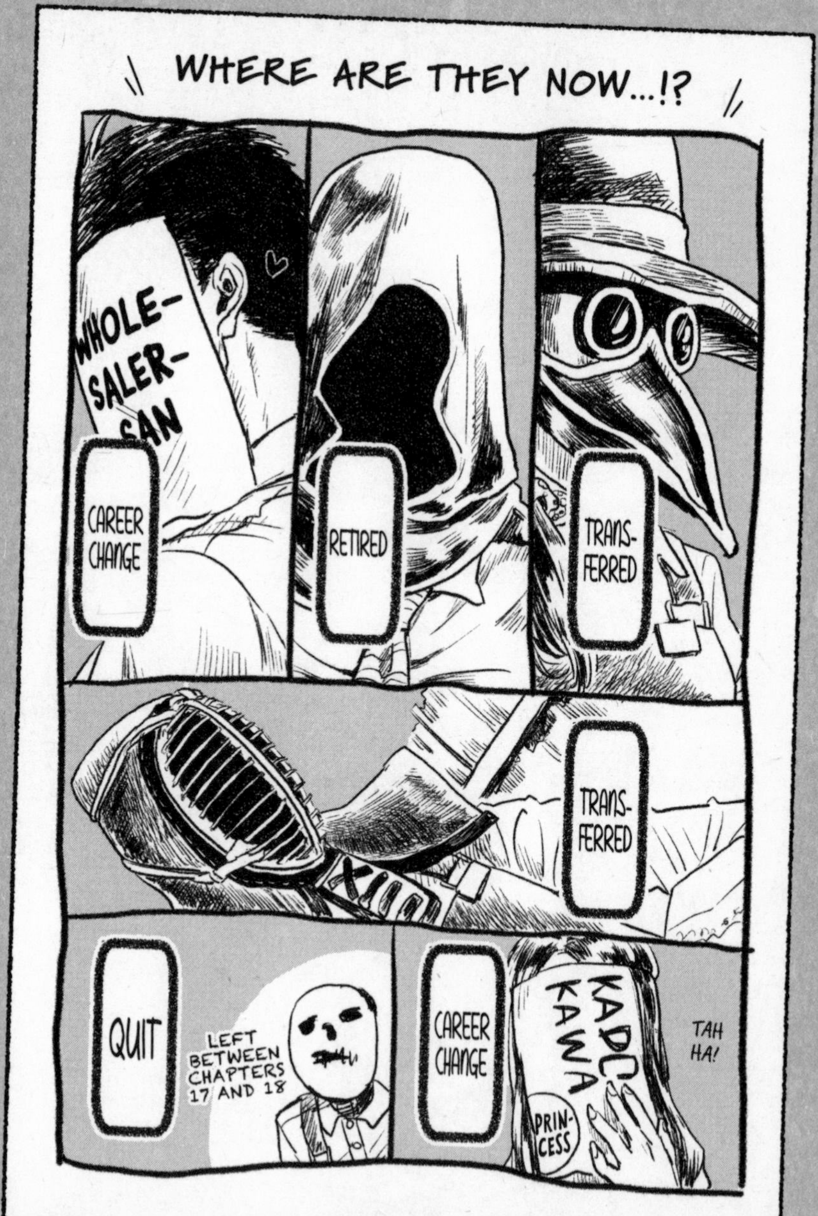
WHERE ARE THEY NOW...!?
TRANS-FERRED
RETIRED
WHOLE-SALER-SAN
CAREER CHANGE
TRANS-FERRED
TAH HA!
KADO KAWA
PRIN-CESS
CAREER CHANGE
LEFT BETWEEN CHAPTERS 17 AND 18
QUIT

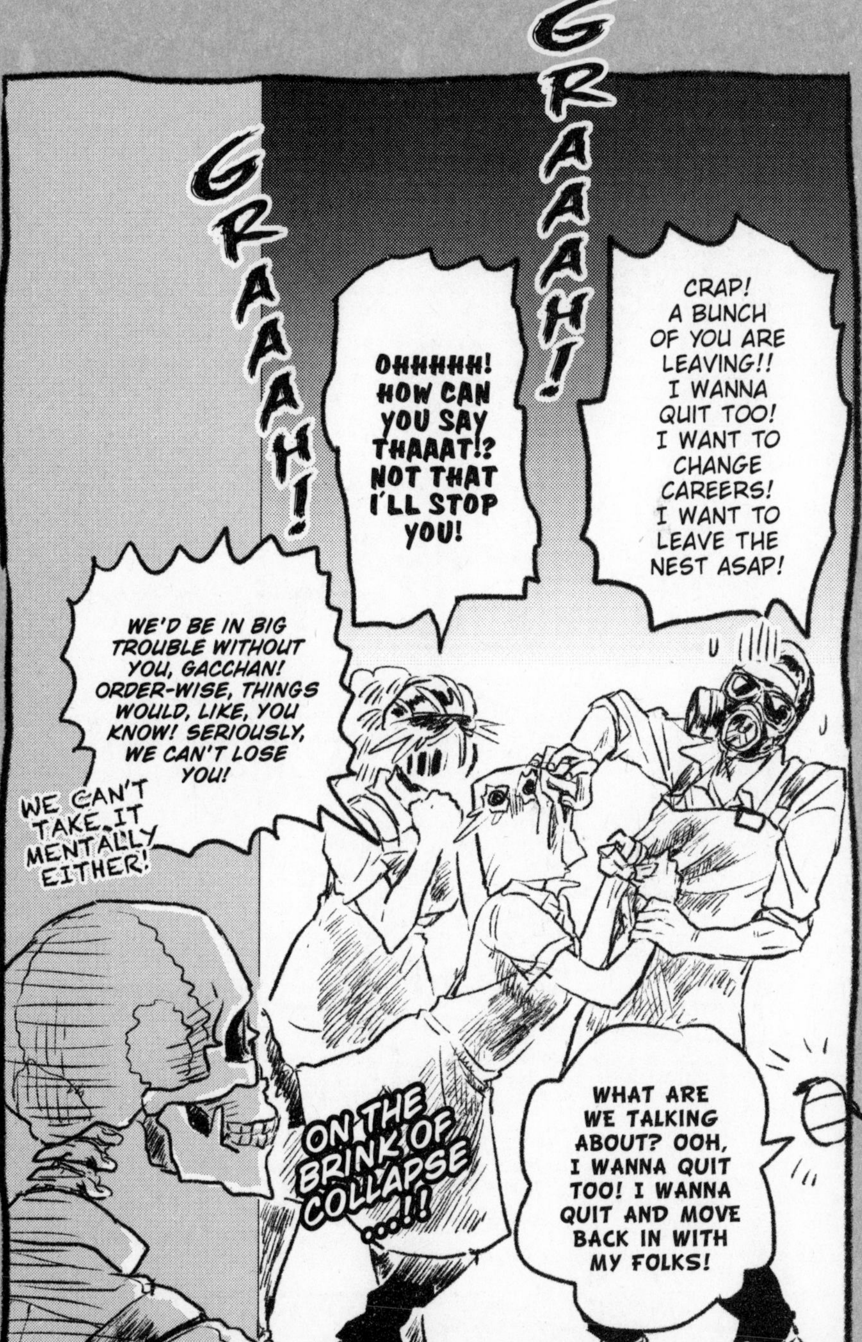
GRAAAAH!
CRAP! A BUNCH OF YOU ARE LEAVING!! I WANNA QUIT TOO! I WANT TO CHANGE CAREERS! I WANT TO LEAVE THE NEST ASAP!
GRAAAAH!
OHHHHHH! HOW CAN YOU SAY THAAAT!? NOT THAT I'LL STOP YOU!
WE'D BE IN BIG TROUBLE WITHOUT YOU, GACCHAN! ORDER-WISE, THINGS WOULD, LIKE, YOU KNOW! SERIOUSLY, WE CAN'T LOSE YOU!
WE CAN'T TAKE IT MENTALLY EITHER!
WHAT ARE WE TALKING ABOUT? OOH, I WANNA QUIT TOO! I WANNA QUIT AND MOVE BACK IN WITH MY FOLKS!
ON THE BRINK OF COLLAPSE...!!

COMMON HONORIFICS

no honorific: Indicates familiarity or closeness; if used without permission or reason, it can constitute an insult.

-san: The Japanese equivalent of Mr./Mrs./Miss. If a situation calls for politeness, this is the fail-safe honorific.

-shi: Similar to -san but especially formal, it's often used when referring to people in newspapers. In this manga, it is often translated to "Mr."

-kun: Used most often when referring to boys, this indicates affection or familiarity. Occasionally used by older men among their peers, but it may also be used by anyone referring to a person of lower standing. -kyun is a cutesy version of this.

-chan: An affectionate honorific indicating familiarity used mostly in reference to girls; also used in reference to cute persons or animals of either gender.

-sensei: A respectful term for teachers, artists, or high-level professionals.

-dono: Originally meaning roughly "master" or "milord," in modern times, it's more a sign of respect. It can sound anachronistic if used in informal settings.

-sama: Conveys great respect; may also indicate that the social status of the speaker is lower than that of the addressee.

(o)nee: Japanese equivalent to "older sis."

(o)nii: Japanese equivalent to "older bro."

PAGE 4
Yokohama Station SF (Yokohama Station Fable) is a 2016 dystopian future novel by Yuba Isukari.

PAGE 8
The censored person next to the books is Japanese comedian Masuda Okada. **"It's out!"** and **"Woooo!!"** are two of his famous catchphrases.

PAGE 12
The text under Paper Bag has been stylized like the blurbs printed at the beginning and end of manga chapters in manga magazines to remind readers of what's happening in the story and get them excited for the next chapter.

PAGE 13
Young Magazine and **Morning** are both manga magazines published by Kodansha.

Slam Dunk is a best-selling basketball and coming-of-age manga series by Takehiko Inoue, originally serialized from 1990 to 1996. There are multiple editions of the series, which vary in size.

The **A5 size** is 5.8 inches by 8.3 inches; **B6** is smaller at 4.9 inches by 6.9 inches. **Pocket paperback size** is then smaller than that at 4 inches by 7.1 inches.

PAGE 14
The **DQ** (Dragon Quest) franchise began as a 1986 fantasy role-playing game on the Nintendo and expanded into other media, including manga and light novels. Dragon Quest is huge in Japan.

PAGE 16
Manga artists will sometimes draw **artboards** (shikishi) for display in bookstores to promote their work, as prizes for contests, etc.

PAGE 17
Honda's costume and the **"There's nothing here!"** line while protecting the stock that won't move are a reference to a scene in Hayao Miyazaki's film Nausicaä of the Valley of the Wind—a flashback in which a young Nausicaa tries to hide a baby ohmu from harm.

PAGE 21
It's common for brand-new books in Japanese bookstores to be covered with **shrink-wrap** to protect their condition (so despite the book's suggestive utterances, it's not necessarily an age-restricted book).

PAGE 29
Ribon and **Nakayoshi** are rival shoujo manga magazines that were first published in 1955 and 1954 respectively.

PAGE 30
The **Ebola book** in question is Richard Preston's The Hot Zone, originally released in Japan in 1994 with a translation by Hiroshi Takami.

PAGE 34
The **book set aside for Honda** is the Yokohama Station SF novel from Chapter 15.

PAGE 37
The chapter title, **"The Bookselling Talent,"** and Full Face's pose are both references to Japanese professional wrestler Hiroshi Tanahashi, whose nickname is the Once-in-a-Century Talent.

PAGE 39
In Japanese, Gas Mask thinks his coworkers are **talking about sex** because Armor keeps saying ochingin (wages), which sounds similar to ochinchin (a word for "penis").

PAGE 42
Kakushigoto (Secret) is Kouji Kumeta's comedy drama manga about a manga artist trying to keep his job a secret from his daughter.

PAGE 56
The book cover in the corner is **Boku no Rinne** (Made in Heaven), Volume 1 by Ako Shimaki, a romantic comedy involving memories of past lives, and not exactly appropriate for children.

PAGE 61
PreCure is a beloved magical girl anime franchise aimed at young girls. The PreCure-like manga in the BL section was 2015's Majo Oji by Tatsuyoshi, starring a grown man who fights erotic battles dressed like a magical girl. Definitely not for kids.

PAGE 63
CoroCoro Comic is a manga magazine aimed at elementary-school aged boys.

PAGE 69
Naruto is Masashi Kishimoto's 1997–2014 megahit ninja manga.

PAGE 70
The Naruto fan is wearing a Dragon Ball shirt.

PAGE 79
The characters depicted include the bacteria from Masayuki Ishikawa's educational comedy Moyashimon, the titular Chacha from Min Ayahana's magical shoujo manga Akazukin Chacha, Doraemon from Fujiko F. Fujio's sci-fi comedy Doraemon, the titular character from Mineo Maya's Patalliro!, Popuko from Bkub Okawa's Pop Team Epic, Alphonse Elric from Hiromu Arakawa's Fullmetal Alchemist, and Pinoko from Osamu Tezuka's medical suspense Black Jack.

PAGE 80
The censored shelves are some of Shueisha's bestselling shounen manga: Hirohiko Araki's **JoJo's Bizarre Adventure**, Tite Kubo's **Bleach**, and Masashi Kishimoto's **Naruto**. The characters looking on are from Kohei Horikoshi's My Hero Academia and Koyoharu Gotouge's Demon Slayer: Kimetsu no Yaiba.

Natsucomi is Shueisha's summer comics fair, and this also happens to be a nickname for Summer Comiket, the big summer exhibition for doujinshi.

Space Brothers is Chuya Koyama's astronaut drama, published by Kodansha.

"What if Hime finds out!?" is a reference to Kouji Kumeta's Kakushigoto (also published by Kodansha), in which manga artist Kakushi Gotou fears his daughter, Hime, will hate him if she finds out that he draws pervy manga.

The humanoid creature looks like it's from Tsutomu Nihei's future cyberpunk manga BLAME!

PAGE 81
The characters depicted are from Shohei Manabe's psychological drama Ushijima the Loan Shark and Ayumi Ishii's historical drama Nobunaga Concerto.

Soutaiseiriron is a Japanese rock band whose name translates to **"Theory of Relativity."** They have a song named "Shogakukan" on the album synchroniciteen. The ladybug is the mascot of Shogakukan's Ladybug Comics imprint for kids.

Conan refers to Gosho Aoyama's bestselling mystery series Detective Conan (a.k.a. Case Closed).

TRANSLATION NOTES 2

PAGE 82
Representing **Akita Shoten** are Keisuke Itagaki's martial arts manga *Baki the Grappler* and Itaru Bonnoki's supernatural comedy *The Vampire Dies in No Time* (the splash in the corner is the vampire turning to dust); representing **Shonen Gahosha** are Kouta Hirano's action adventure *Drifters* and Masakazu Ichiguro's comedy *And Yet the Town Moves*; representing **Tokuma Shoten** is Yushi Kawata's *Fist of the North Star* spinoff gag manga, *Fist of the North Star: Strawberry Flavor*; representing **Shinchosha** is Reika Kajimoto's supernatural horror manga *Akuma wo Awaremu Uta (A Song of Sorrow for the Devil)*; and the representatives for **Hakusensha** include Aki Katsu's sex education comedy *Futari Ecchi* and Kentaro Miura's gory action manga *Berserk*.

PAGE 83
The censored manga publishers are: MAG, Houbunsha, Square Enix, Takeshobo, Futabasha, Leed Publishing, Ohta Books, and Nihon Bungeisha.

Representing **Kadokawa**, Koala is impaled by the Lance of Longinus as Lilith was from Hideaki Anno's *Neon Genesis Evangelion*, while Char from *Mobile Suit Gundam*, Yotsuba from Kiyohiko Azuma's *Yotsuba&!*, and Locke from Yuki Hijiri's *Locke the Superman* look on. Gene refers to *Comic Gene*, a manga magazine published by Kadokawa, as well as other publications under the Gene umbrella (including *Skull-face Bookseller Honda-san*).

PAGE 84
Shounen is manga marketed toward boys. **Seinen** is manga marketed toward older teen boys and adult men. **Shoujo** is manga marketed toward girls. **Josei** is manga marketed toward older teen girls and adult women. As Honda comments, though, some manga are difficult to categorize this way.

PAGE 86
The **foreign comics** covers depicted include Juan Díaz Canales's and Juanjo Guarnido's *Blacksad* and MARVEL's *Spider-Man/Deadpool*. Also shown is an **oversized artbook** for Fuyumi Ono's Japanese fantasy novel series *Twelve Kingdoms*.

PAGE 89
All of the **mass-market comics** shown here are old classics of manga, including Riyoko Ikeda's pre–French Revolution romance *The Rose of Versailles*, Shotaro Ishinomori's science fiction superhero series *Cyborg 009*, and Mitsuteru Yokoyama's manga adaptation of the classic Chinese novel *Romance of the Three Kingdoms*.

PAGE 113
Voice drama CDs often feature audio skits that tell a story (like an audio/radio drama); in some cases, as seems to be the suggestion this time, they are "conversations" the speaking character is having with the listener (whether romantic, comforting, or something else).

PAGE 114
Jump Comics is the line of collected volumes of the titles that are published in *Weekly Shounen Jump*.

PAGE 116
Hoshin Engi is Ryu Fujisaki's 1996–2000 action-adventure shounen manga inspired by a Chinese literary classic (*The Creation of the Gods*). ***Saiyuki*** is Kazuya Minekura's 1997–2002 bromance action-adventure manga, also loosely based on a classic Chinese novel (*Journey to the West*). Both series were popular enough to receive anime.

ENJOY EVERYTHING.

YOU SHOULD COME PLAY WITH YOTSUBA TOO!

Join Yotsuba as she delights in the things many of us take for granted in this Eisner-nominated series.

VOLUMES 1-14 AVAILABLE NOW!

Visit our website at www.yenpress.com.

Hello! This is YOTSUBA!

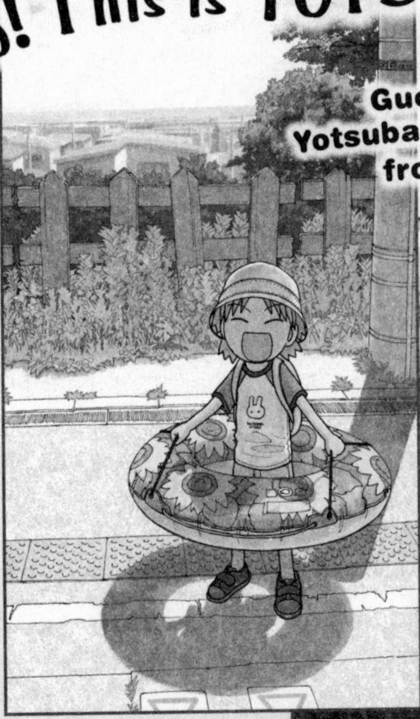

Guess what? Guess what?
Yotsuba and Daddy just moved here
from waaaay over there!

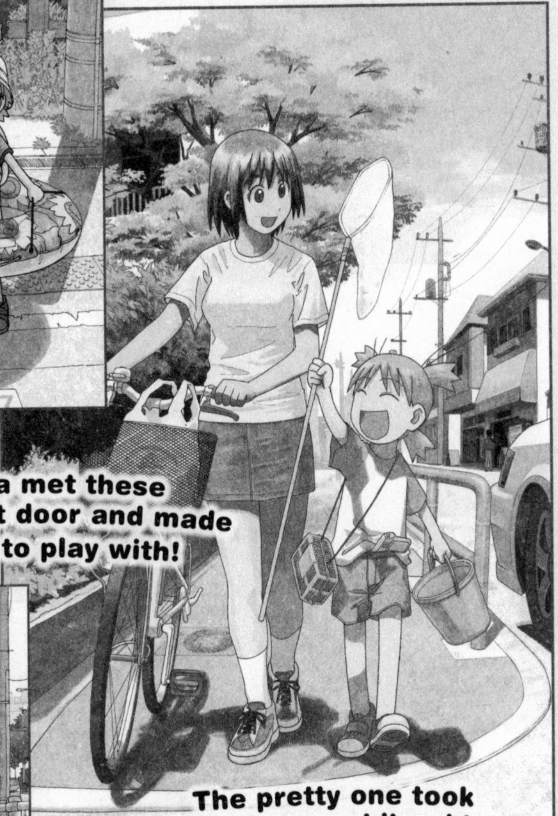

And Yotsuba met these
nice people next door and made
new friends to play with!

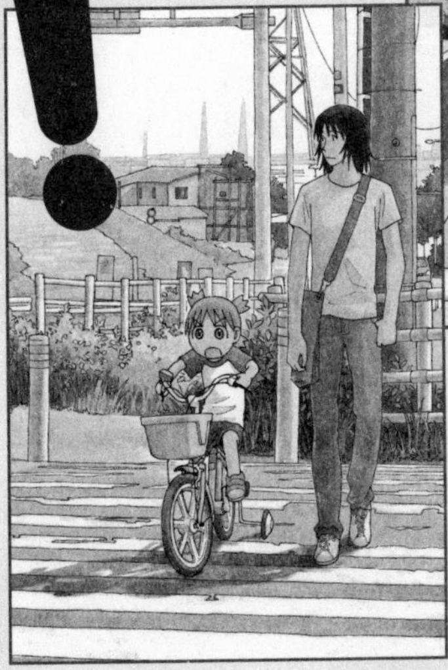

The pretty one took
Yotsuba on a bike ride!
(Whoooa! There was a big hill!)

And Ena's a good drawer!
(Almost as good as Yotsuba!)

And their mom always
gives Yotsuba ice cream!
(Yummy!)

And...
And...
OHHHHH!

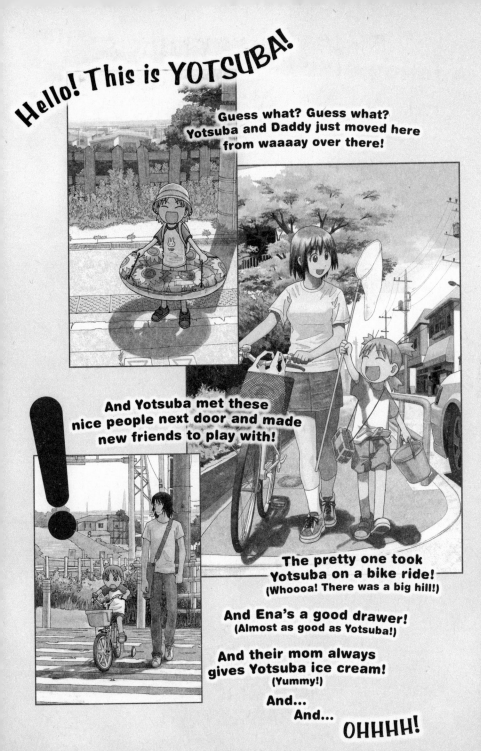

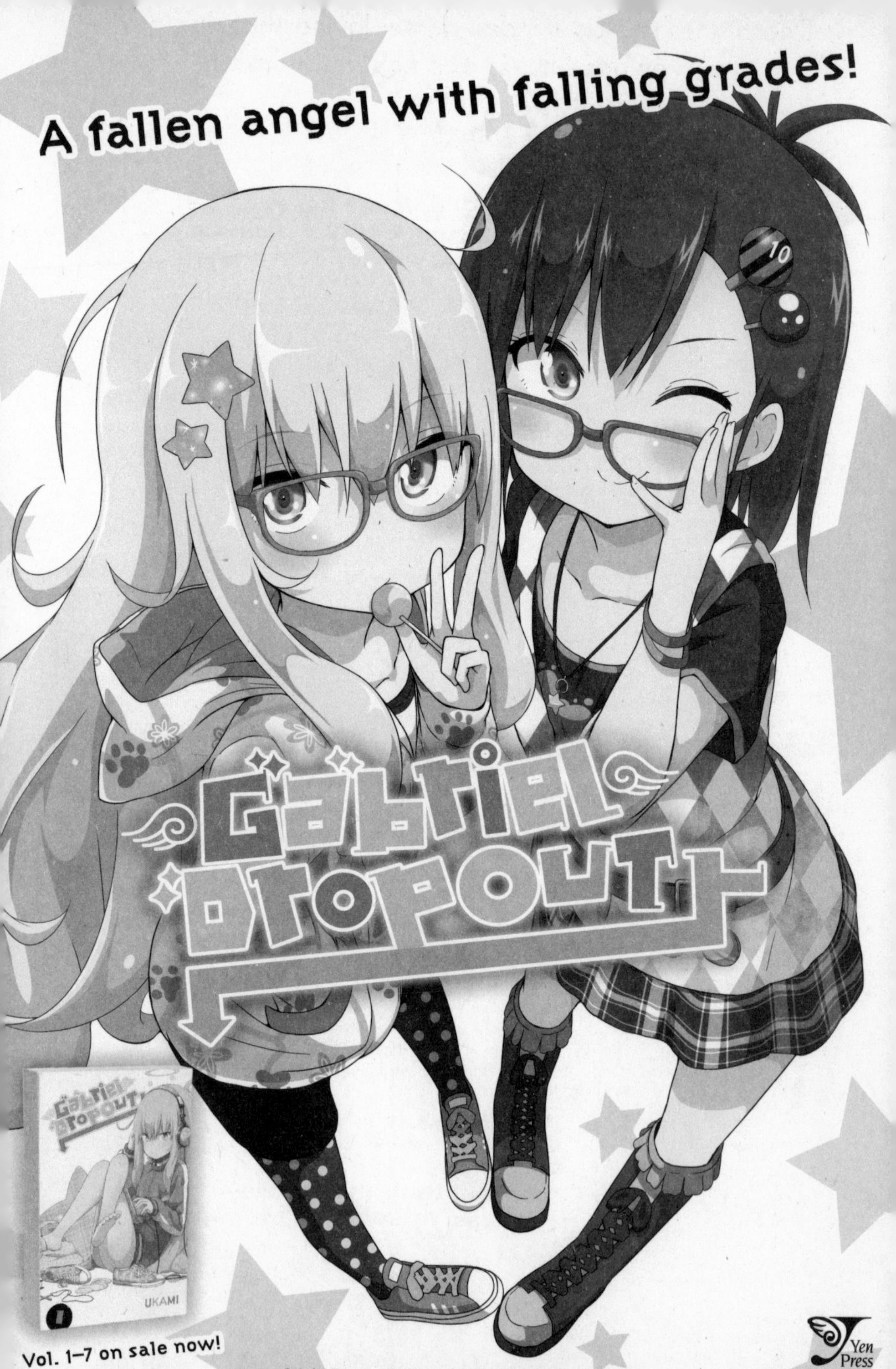
A fallen angel with falling grades!
Gabriel Dropout
Gabriel Dropout
UKAMI
Vol. 1–7 on sale now!
Yen Press

Translation: **AMANDA HALEY**
Lettering: **BIANCA PISTILLO**

GAIKOTSU SHOTENIN HONDA SAN Vol. 3
© Honda 2017
First published in Japan in 2017 by KADOKAWA CORPORATION, Tokyo. English translation rights arranged with KADOKAWA CORPORATION, Tokyo through TUTTLE-MORI AGENCY, Inc.

English translation © 2020 by Yen Press, LLC

Yen Press
150 West 30th Street, 19th Floor
New York, NY 10001

Visit us at yenpress.com
facebook.com/yenpress
twitter.com/yenpress
yenpress.tumblr.com
instagram.com/yenpress

First Yen Press Edition: January 2020

Yen Press is an imprint of Yen Press, LLC.
The Yen Press name and logo are trademarks of Yen Press, LLC.

Library of Congress Control Number: 2019938443

ISBNs: 978-1-9753-3143-6 (paperback)
       978-1-9753-3144-3 (ebook)

10 9 8 7 6 5 4 3 2 1

WOR

Printed in the United States of America